INDIAN MEDICAL SCIENCE SERIES—No. 2

HINDU

Anatomy, Physiology, Therapeutics, History of Medicine and Practice of Physic

K.R.L. GUPTA

Sri Satguru Publications
A Division of
Indian Books Centre
Delhi, India

Distributed by :
INDIAN BOOKS CENTRE
Exporters of Indological Books,
40/5, Shakti Nagar,
Delhi-110007.
INDIA

Published by :
© SRI SATGURU PUBLICATIONS
Indological & Oriental Publishers,
40/5, Shakti Nagar,
Delhi-110007.
INDIA

Second Edition; Delhi 1986
Third Edition; Delhi 1994, 2006

ISBN 81-7030-100-2

Printed at Chawla Offset Printers. Delhi 110 052

PREFACE

—:o:—

What makes books appear? The real authors of books are not those isolated individual persons who cast them up or cause them to be published. It is the request of the public express or implied which brings them into existence. I have never known any book which has been printed without consulting the necessity of the public. A desire has been always expressed by those interested in the dissemination of Hindu medical theories, to compile a work embracing the essential portions of the principal medical books of the Hindus. Certainly it is very desirable to have in possession all the best books of this kind. But it generally falls beyond the resources of many. Moreover it involves an immense loss of time to arrive at few truths after going through an enormous mass of rubbish. A compilation of that sort is therefore a necessity and can never be unwelcome. In order that it may be intelligible to our brethern in the other presidencies as well as to European medical men, I have caused an English translation to be made thereof. I have spared no pains to make the work really useful. For this purpose, I have put in many things which my personal experience has been able to gather and which I honestly believe to be serviceable to those for whom they are intended. If the present work meets with the approbation of the public as all of my previous publications have, I shall not consider my labour spent in vain. In conclusion, I cannot forego this opportunity of thanking the people who have always encouraged my productions and to whom I owe a heavy debt of gratitude.

KAVIRAJ RUSSICK LAL GUPTA.

Contents

Hindu Anatomy

Therapeutics

Origin and History of Medicine

Practice of Physic

HINDU ANATOMY, PHYSIOLOGY THERAPEUTICS

AND

HISTORY OF MEDICINES.

ELEMENTS OF THE BODY

At an early period the Hindu Philosophers reduced the material world to five elementary principles, and primary qualities; by the agency of which, they explained the appearance, composition, and condition of the world, and the structure and functions of the Body. The five elementary principles were earth, water. air, fire and ether.

The peculiar qualities of each of the elements are as follow :—

The earth has smell (*gandha*); the water, taste (*rasa*); tne air, touch (*sparsa*); the fire, colour (*rúpa*); and the pure ether, sound (*sabda*). Besides these they have likewise the following qualities :—

Earth, which is the heaviest element, is possessed of the qualities of smell, sound, tangibility, visibility, and taste. It enters largely into the formation of the body, and of all solid and heavy substances.

Water possesses sound, tangibility, visibility, and taste; bestows the sense of coolness, fluidity, weight, and smoothness on bodies; and has much the quality of happiness (*Satwaguna*), and of inertness (*tamaguna*), and is transparent producing light and weight. It forms the different fluids of the body.

Air is possessed of sonorousness, tangibility, and lightness; and from having the quality of action (*rajaguua*) in excess, it has the moving powers, and qualities of bodies.

Fire possesses sound, tangibility, and visibility, and gives taste. The medical property of fire is to afford heat, digestion, colour, light, and beauty to the body. It produces the passions, bodily strength and valour of the individual; and from possessing much of the quality of goodness (*satwa*), and passion (*rajaguna*), it gives it lightness, and movement.

In viewing the wonderful operations of nature, the Hindu Philosophers seem to have been soon arrested by the beautiful and varied adaptation of design to the end, by the order, harm ny, and mutual dependance which pervades the whole of nature. This seems to have led them to the conclusion, that inert matter was insufficient of itself to produce such effects, and that there was a fifth element for performing the operations of the body, like the great soul which regulates those of the world. This induced them to add, at an early period, another or spiritual element to those of inert matter, which they called pure ether (*ákása*); which was supposed to be separated from the others, and possessed the property of sound, and form. It predominates in the organ of hearing, and fills up the porosities of living bodies, and their hollow cavities, as those of the bones, &c.; and is full of the quality of goodness (*Satwaguna*). This element is altogether undistinguishable by our senses, and is only made known to us through the evidence of our understanding.

These elements are all nourishing to the body, and are contained in different proportions in every sort of food; so that after digestion, each element, by an inherent property, joins with that which already forms a part of the fabric of the body, in the following manner; skin, vessels, bone, hair, and flesh, are made up principally of the element of earth; alvine evacuations (*mala*), urine, semen, blood, and phlegm, of water; hunger, thirst, and insensibility, are produced by fire; movement, conscience, termination of a work, retaining happiness, by air; and desire, revenge, stupidity, fear, shame, is produced by an excess of pure ether. There being both an active or warm, and a passive, or cold principle, which are increased and strengthened by the rays of the sun and moon.

The body or microcosm, is also divided into different parts, which correspond with those of the globe. It has its mountains, its cold and hot situations, with the various oceans. Each of the fluids are also influenced by one of the seven planets which regulate their condition.

The same reasoning, which was supposed applicable to the external world, was used for the explanation of the constitution, and fabric of the animal system. Hence, all living bodies, among which vegetable bodies are placed, are supposed to be composed of the five elements, with the element producing action or life superadded. Living bodies are produced from vapour, vegetation, incubation, and parturition; as insects, plants, birds, fishes, reptiles, and animals. Of the latter, man is the chief, and in proportion to the complicated structure of his body so is his liability to disease.

The essential or elementary parts, when mixed, form vital bodies, which are divided into two classes, one of which is stationary, the other moveable (*jangama*). This class is produced from the womb (*jarâyuja*), as animals (*pasu*), and man (*manusha*). 2nd, from eggs (*andaja*), as birds, snakes (*sadoso*), &c.; 3rd, from the warmth of the earth, as worms, ants, mosquetoes, fleas, &c.; and 4th, (*udjbidgo*) such as break their habitation, and thus gain their liberty, as frogs, &c.

The second or stationary class consists of four varieties :—

1st. *Vanaśpati* or trees in which the fruit is without flowers.

2nd. *Vriksha* trees with flowers and fruits.

3rd. *Verada*, creepers.

4th. *Asudie*, annuals.

The same elements and qualities, by their combination and actions constitute the human body; which is governed by an independent principle, or soul, which acts through the medium of the members; and is an emanation from the great soul of the world; into which after certain purifications, it is again absorbed. As long as the soul remains in connexion with the body, the diseases with which it is afflicted may be removed; and it is proper that during all this time, remedies should be employed for the purpose.

The following is the Hindu theory of the formation of the body :—

——:o:——

CHAPTER II.

Generation.

It is stated in medical works, that as the mould receives the seed which is to form the future plant, so the menses of the female receives the semen of the male, which germinates in it. Hence in treating of generation, the secretion of the menses is first considered.

When the menses appear monthly, the female is moist, plump, has desire; and is happy, with her hair flying about. Her eyes are languishing; her sides, arms, breasts, thighs, and hips are in a state of excitement. The menses continue for seventeen days, during which the woman may be impregnated, and not at any other season. During the flow of the menses the mouth of the uterus, which is like the mouth of a *rahoo* fish, is open like the water lily, (*Padma*) exposed to the rays of the sun; and after this season, the mouth of the uterus again contracts, and closes like the petals of the lily, when the benign influence of the sun is absent.

The menses are of a red colour, like the blood of a hare, or of lacdye. It should not stain cloth, when it falls upon it; and should be without smell. The menses are derived from the two vessels of the uterus, which discharge their contents by the influence of the vital air, into the uterus and vagina. The menses remain till the 50th year, when the woman is of a weak constitution; but it continues longer, when the individual is strong.

During the discharge of the menses, much attention is required to be observed regarding the conduct of the woman, as the state of the parents at the time of conception will affect the offspring in a very powerful manner. During the first three days of the discharge, the woman should remain pure, she must sit and sleep in a purified situation, upon the sacred grass (*kush*); she must eat out of a new earthen vessel, or from a leaf, she must not sleep during the day while the menses flow, or her offspring will be very sluggish: should she shut her eyes at the time of conception, the child will be blind; should she shed tears, the child's eyes will be sore; should she cut her nails during the flow of the menses, the child will be deformed; should she anoint or bathe herself during these three days, the infant will be afflicted with leprosy; should she laugh or speak loud, the infant will be unhappy and deaf; and should she fatigue herself, the offspring will be employed in low occupations.

The father should neither be very old, nor very young. If the father is not twenty-five, and the woman beyond sixteen, the offspring will die in the uterus, if it be born alive it will live but a short time, or if the infant lives the senses and other parts will be incomplete. Therefore a very young man, or a very old woman should be avoided. They should be in good health, the genital organs free from disease, and the female should neither be hungry, nor have eaten recently before connexion. The semen should be received into the menses as a seed dropped into a good mould, and like it germinate, producing conception. As milk taken into the stomach nourishes the child, so the semen requires to be animated with the menses to form the germ.

Should conception take place on the first or second day of the menses, the offspring will die soon after birth. If conceived on the third day, the child will be weak, diseased, and deformed, and will die at an early age.

If the husband is not at home on the fourth day of the menses, the wife is first to regard the sun after bathing, as the best object; in order that her offspring may resemble that luminary in his qualities of bestowing strength and beauty, and should the first object she sees, after bathing on the 4th day, be a deformed individual, her offspring will also be so. The female is next to perform the necessary ceremonies to ensure offspring with the assistance of the Brahmans; she is to eat in the afternoon of the fourth day, bathe, rub her body with scented oil, put on clean clothes, and ornaments, and at night visit her husband. But should there be a great discharge of the menses on this day, she must not visit her husband; as the semen will be washed away as by a swollen river, and will thus prevent conception. Such cases are to be treated as other cases of Menorrhagia.

When the female conceives on the 4th, 6th, 8th, 10th and 12th days of the menses they are the fortunate days. It is when conception occurs, towards the last of these days, that the offspring will live long and have few diseases. If conception occurs after the 12th day, it is unfavourable to the offspring. When conception occurs on the unequal days of the menses, a female child will be born; while on the equal a male will be produced.

Numerous forms of irregularities, and diseases of the menses prevent conception, the principal of which are derangements of the humours, in which cases the air, bile, and phlegm stop the flow of the menses, by closing the passages by which this evacuation flows.

When the menses are irregular, or are stopped, the woman should live on fish, a kind of pulse called *kulotha*, linseed (tel), masculi, butter, curdled milk, acids, and sura (a kind of wine).

Durga asked Siva the nature of the body, Siva answered; know, O Durga! That the body is formed by a mixture of the energy of the male and female, in this way: During a fortunate connexion the heat produced gives the semen the quality of the water, and the air conveys it to the urethra of the male, from which it passes into the vagina. When it enters the uterus it mixes with the heating qualities of the *sun*, which the menses possesses and forms the embryo. It is when the mixture takes place, and has become solid, by their respective qualities of cold and heat to which the soul is added. Should the germ have more of the qualities of the semen, a male child will be formed, and of the menses a female child; and should the qualities of both be equal the child will be a hermaphrodite.

Signs of conception. The indications of conception, during the day it has taken place are; the woman feeling fatigued languid, and thirsty, a weakness of the two thighs, a retention of the semen and blood in the uterus, and a throbbing in the vagina.

The signs of Pregnancy, are the skin round the nipples becoming of a dark colour, and the hair upon the body becoming more distinct and prominent. The person feels weak, the eyelids heavy, and the eyelashes closed; much saliva is secreted; sickness and vomiting occur; and even pleasant smellings things are disliked, and produce sickness. In this condition the woman must not approach her husband; she must avoid fasting, vomiting, or strong purgatives; grief or fear; stretching or severe coughing; dragging heavy weights; riding on horse back; sleeping during the day; or sitting up at night. She must not be bled, nor strain in passing her dejections.

During pregnancy, if the woman is not gratified with what she wishes to eat, and the air is deranged, the child will be crooked and cripple, or will be small in size, dumb, or cannot speak distinctly; will be blind, or have his eyes defective, or will be an unbeliever in the sacred shastras. In other such cases these defects are produced by acts of previous wickedness of his own, or of his parents in a former state of existence.

Whatever is wanted by the pregnant woman should therefore be supplied, when a perfect child will be born. If the woman desires to see a Rajah, the child will be great and rich; should the mother wish to adorn herself, the child will be well formed and vain; should the mother wish to see a holy man, the child will be holy, and just, and if she longs to see ferocious animals the offspring will be of that description. In like manner the desire for particular sorts of food indicates the disposition of the infant, and the form of his body. when the mother wishes to eat buffalo's flesh the child will have blood-shot eyes, much hair, and he will be warlike; and when hog's flesh, he will be sluggish, and sleepy.

If any injury be done to the mother, or she suffers in any way, the child in like manner suffers. The menses, after conception, goes in part to form the placenta, and as the blood flows every month, it coagulates to form the embryo; an upper layer being added every month to the embryo, and another portion to the breasts, of the mother by which the mammæ are increased in size.

The period of delivery extends from nine to twelve months, and after this time when the female is not delivered, the abdominal swelling must be considered as the effect of disease.

——:o:——

CHAPTER III.

Growth and Functions of the Body.

There is no peculiar organ for the semen, but it is supposed to be contained in every part of the body, as butter is in the milk, or sugar in the sugar-cane. There is a duct on the right side of the mouth of the urinary bladder, where it is collected, and passes through the urethra in the time of coition.

The menses of the woman disappears when she conceives, and it circulates towards the mammæ where it is collected and produces milk.

The germ thus formed contains a small proportion of the five elements; each of which assists in promoting the developement of the other elements, and of the body in general. Jiva or the soul is last engendered, and like fire produced by a burning glass, the mixture of the menses and semen produce heat. When the air separates the particles of the semen it produces twins, triplets, &c. When one of the constituent parts of the embryo is unhealthy, the conception will be so; and, if both the menses and semen are impure, as when the parents are affected with leprosy, the offspring will also be afflicted with this disease.

The germ in the uterus is like a shrub, the vessels of which are connected with the uterus, by which the blood of the mother is circulated in it, and nourished. The germ is near the fire of the mother at the navel, is inflated by the air (*bayu*) and fire, which the embryo contains, by which it is expanded into its different parts, forming the vessels, circulating the juices, and from which its members are formed; like the potter giving figure to the piece of clay upon his wheel.

In the first month, the mixture of the semen and menses forms a small mass like a pea (*kalai*); seven days after conception it has the form of a bubble, or inflated bag. On the tenth it is red, and on the fifteenth it resembles a small round piece of flesh. This shortly enlarges in the same imperceptible way as the moon enlarges in size (*Jyotistatwa*). At one month it has small fibres proceeding from it, and is animated with life (*prana*). The point of the vertebral column, is to the body, what *Mount Sumeru* is to the world, and in that point the gods of the body reside (Bramha, Vishnu, &c.)

Should the germ become of a circular form (*pinda*), it denotes a male; an oblong form (*Pashie*) a female; and an irregular form (*Arbuda*) a hermaphrodite. In the third month five eminences appear, which when developed become the hands, feet and head. The other smaller parts of the body are then but imperfectly formed.

In the fourth month the members are more distinctly developed; and the heart of the fetus being perfectly formed, life receives its active powers, and has a desire for the assistance of sense and activity. Life then acts as in its former state of existence.

In the fifth month, the powers of the mind are increased; and life performs its usual actions. The nose, mouth, eyes, throat, and abdomen may now be distinguished; and at six months all the members are formed, and the understanding is added.

At the seventh month, the body is completely formed, and the members can act separately, and possess life, mind, and understanding. The essence of the strength of the system (*ozah*) is imperfectly formed, even at the 8th month; and on this account, should the infant be born during this month, it will die. During the 8th month the joints are formed, the parts move on each other, the fetus requires food, and, by the heat of the mother strength is added. At nine months the mind and memory are active, it moves about, and it receives nourishment from the mother. According to some, by means of a vessel which passes from the mother's breasts to the mouth of the embryo; by others it is stated that the vessels of the umbeliacal cord have a communication with the vessels of the mother, and convey blood to the fetus, by which it is increased in size. In the 9th month, the woman is to remove to the house (*sutiká griha*) prepared for her delivery.

At the tenth month the fetus acquires knowledge, and prays to God, and sees the seven heavens, the earth, and the inferior regions. By the air of the pelvis (*apana bayu*) the fetus is then expelled; as an arrow is shot from a bow, and the child falls insensible to the ground. All his former knowledge is immediately forgotten, and on losing so many pleasing illusions, he cries (Jotis).

During the time the fetus is in the uterus it does not discharge its evacuations because they are in small quantities, and the air which discharges them is not present in the intestines *pakasia*). The fetus does not cry in the uterus, as the mouth is closed by the fetal membranes, the wind-pipe is filled with phlegm, and there is no passage for air. The respiration, sleep, and turning of the fetus are performed by the mother, as she sleeps, &c.

By nature, the situation and form of the different parts of the body are developed. So that the hair is formed on one part, and is absent at another part of the body. If the quality of happiness (*satwaguna*) be in excess, the child knows the state it held in its former condition; and does good or bad actions accordingly, and acquires its former qualities.

The hard substances of the fetus, as hairs, bones, nails, teeth, vessels, ligaments, &c., are produced from the semen, and resemble the same parts in the father; and the soft parts as flesh, blood, fat, marrow, heart, navel, liver, spleen, intestines, are formed principally from the blood of the mother, and resemble her.

The growth and strength of the body, the different colours and the duration of life, are produced from the (*rasa*) according to the qualities of the food of different kinds generally taken by the parents. The senses, knowledge of the arts, and life (jiva), happiness, misery, are produced from the parent's good or bad actions in a former state of existence.

The fetus in utero is bent on itself with his head upwards, and mouth towards the spine of the mother. His hands and feet are bent, and during parturition the air turns the body and brings the head downwards, and he knows his former history. The uterus a dark and disagreeable place, which the Brahmans alledge is a kind of purgatory. If the mother eats proper food, the child receives its nourishment from the umbelical cord which is connected with the mother, and by means of the cord the blood is conveyed to the fetus which thereby grows.

The sex of the infant is known by the right mammæ containing milk first, the right eye being larger than the left, the woman wishing food of the masculine kind, and dreaming of the water lilies of different species, and her mouth, and the colour of her lips of an agreeable colour. The opposite indications are the proof of an infant being of the male sex. Twins are known by a depression along the centre of the abdomen; and when the two sides of the abdomen are depressed, and the lower end is a little prominent, with a depression in the middle, a hermaphrodite is known to be contained in the uterus.

The small vessels in the embryo produce first its growth, before the members are produced. The mixture of the semen and blood or embryo increase, and life enters it; the air separates the different members, the fire prepares the elements, the water moistens, the earth stiffens, and the sky (ákása), increases the fetus. When the embryo has hands, feet, mouth, nose, ears, buttocks, &c., then it is called the human body, and is composed of six principal parts; four extremities, the trunk, head, abdomen, back, umbilicus, forehead, chin, nose, neck, bladder, are the single parts of the body. The pairs are the ears, eyes, nostrils, eyebrows, temples, shoulders, cheeks, axillas mammæ, testicles, sides, buttocks, knees, arms, thighs &c. The body has nine orifices, like a house with nine doors. They are the urethra, anus, mouth, nostrils, eyes, and ears. The vagina forms the tenth in the female. There are ten fingers and ten toes. The other parts of the body are the skin, Kolah, (tissues) fluids (dhátu); dejections, (mala); and humours (dossoh); with the liver, spleen, lungs, pancreas, heart, stomach, urinary and gall bladders; the intestines, kidnies, vessels, ligaments, tendons, membranes, *median* connections of the body, bones, joints, muscles, vital parts, the veins, arteries, nerves, and capillary vessels, esophagus, wind-pipe, &c.

Saunaka says that the head is first formed, because; it is the principal part of all the organs of sense. *Kritabirya* says that the heart is first formed, because it is the seat of the mind and knowledge. Others that the umbiliacus is first formed, because from that centre the other members grow. †Some say the trunk, and others that the hands and feet are first formed, as they are the root of the active members. *Dhanwantari* says that all these opinions are incorrect, and that all the members are formed at the same time but are, extremely small, as the first sprig of the bamboo contains the leaves, &c., of the future plant; and as a constituent part of the mangoe is only visible in its state of ripeness, and cannot be detected when the tree is green.

With the child is produced, the period of his life, his actions, whether virtuous or vicious; his acquirement of riches, or experience of the senses, and death, will be varied according to the actions he performed in his former state of existence. The acuteness of his senses, the extent of knowledge, the duration of his life, aud happiness or misery, being produced from the soul; so the strength, colour, health, memory, will be derived from the nature of the food used by the parents.

As long as the elements remain in due proportion, the body remains in health, this state is called *prakriti*, and when increased or diminished in its proper proportions it is called *vikriti*.

On these qnalities, and to these alone, the physician attends. From the elements, the eleven senses are produced to perform their peculiar offices, as the sound of the ear, &c., and is confined to it.

The parts of the fetus are formed in the following manner :—

The Liver and spleen are formed from the blood; Lungs from its froth; and the large intestines (cecum) from its impurities. The essential parts of blood and phlegm are concocted by the fire of the body, into which the air (*bayu*) enters, and forms the intestines, anus, and bladder. The tongue is formed from the essential parts of blood, phlegm, and flesh.

Air, with the assistance of a proper degree of heat, separates the soft parts, and forms canals, and passing between the flesh forms the different muscles. When these canals are filled up with marrow they form nerves. This opinion arises from their supposing that the brain and spinal marrow are the marrow of these bones. The air entering among the soft parts forms the different receptacles of the body, as the stomach and kidnies, which are derived from the essential parts of the blood. The *testicles*, and its appandages are formed from the pure part of flesh, blood, phlegm, and fat. The heart is formed by the essential parts of blood and phlegm, to which all the principal arteries are connected, by which life is preserved. It resembles a w.ter lily, with its head turned downwards. When the person is awake it is in activity, and when asleep it is sluggish. It is the seat of the understanding; and if the quality of darkness and ignorance predominates (*tamaguna*) the person sleeps, and when the (*satwaguna*) prevails the person remains awake.

Sleep is a kind of death, derived from *Vishnu*, and the ignorant sleep much, and those who have much *satwaguna* sleep about midnight, and those who have much *rojaguna* sleep occasionally and without any reasonable cause. When the *tamaguna* and phlegm predominate in the heart, a kind of sleep (syncopy) occurs, from which the individual cannot be awaken. In this it resembles death.

Sleep during the day should always be avoided, except during excessive heat, as it is considered a sin, and is unfavourable to health by deranging the humours and producing disease; such as coughing, asthma, catarrh, heaviness of the body, pain of the body, dyspepsy, fever. Want of sleep at night, produces the diseases of air and bile. But children and old people, and those who have indulged in an excess of venery, who have consumption, drink much, or are much fatigued by travelling, or other exercises, or those who are very hungry, or labour under indigestion, may sleep an hour in the day time. If the person does not sleep during the night, he may take half the quantity of sleep during the day. Sleeping during the day deranges air, bile, and phlegm, and many diseases are produced by it; as coughing, difficult breathing, &c. Night watching deranges air, and bile, and produces various diseases; hence sleep should be taken at night. By sleeping at the proper time it will prevent disease, and will retain the heart, as well as strength, colour, and semen in their proper state. It will also prevent too great thinness or fatness, and such a person, with a good constitution, may live a hundred years.

When phlegm is diminished, and air and bile increased, by passions, and any humour of the body lessened by their causes, the sleep is disturbed.

If a person regulates sleep by his will, it will not be favourable. A certain period of sleep daily, is necessary to health. Too much air, bile, or grief, destroys sleep, diminishes the *dhâtu*, and injures the health of the body. In such cases oil with turmeric and other like things applied to the head, and the body will promote sleep. Bathing has a like effect, as also shampooing, eating good rice, flour, peas, cakes, sweet-meats, oleaginous food, milk, with the juice of flesh, especially animals that burrow in the ground, or the flesh of birds, rasins, and sugar eaten at night. The bed, &c., being soft and agreeable, will also promote sleep.

When sleep is protracted it is to be obviated by vomits

(*songsodhana*) and a purge, by spare food, blood letting, and causes producing mental depression. When cough, or fat, or poison have produced it, exercise is to be taken at night. When there is thirst, colic, or hiccough, want of digestion, or diarrhœa, sleeping in the day is proper.

Dreaming. It is the soul which dreams. Whatever was seen or heard when awake, is represented by the mind, during sleep; and is the impression of good or bad actions, when there is much *rajaguna* in the heart.

Drowsiness, is indicated by the senses not remaining in their state of activity; the body is heavy, the person yawns, he is tired, is drowsy, and desires to sleep. It is produced by an excess of air, phlegm, and *tamaguna.*

Yawning. During a long inspiration the mouth is extended, followed by a short expiration, and a flow of tears from the eyes, is called yawning.

Langour is when the person is fatigued without a cause, and the respiration is weak, and imperfect.

Laziness when the person has the capacity, without the inclination to act; and wishes enjoyment without exertion.

Nausea is accompanied with an increased flow of saliva and tears, with pain in the breast, and an effort to reject the food, but it does not reach the mouth.

Fainting. When bile (*pitta*) and *tamaguna* are in excess, it produces this effect.

Swooning is produced by an excess of *rajaguna.* with bile and air.

Digestion. Six varieties of the digested part of food or chyle are distinguishable. When the food is astringent, sour, moist, &c., the chyle will become of the same nature. When digestion is accomplished, the respective elements unite with those which had entered into the formation of the body; the earth unites with the earth, the water with the water, &c., and they, acting on the inherent qualities of each of the five elements, mix and increase those in the body; smell, the property of earth, with that of the body; taste with water, touch with air, and noise with ether (*ákása*). The juice thus separated from its impurities is called chyle (*rasa*), which nourishes, strengthens, and gives colour to the body.

Some suppose that it requires a day and night to form and distribute the digested mass, to the last deposited part the semen and menses; others, suppose six days are required, and some one month before digestion is completed. Some suppose the fluids are formed and circulated as a wheel turning round, and supplying the various essential parts of the body (*dhátu*). If an article of food or medicine increases much§ the semen, and fluids, they may require only a day and night to accomplish this, and such an increase cures some diseases of the body. As the beard does not grow, nor the flower yield its smell at an early stage of their growth; so in the child, the semen, and the menses remain for a certain time undeveloped which is also the case in old age, like over ripe fruit.

The strength, or vital principle of the body (*Oja* or *tej*) is situated in the chest along its centre, and is produced by a mixture of the pure fluid; in the same manner as a bee sucks the juice from different flowers, and produces honey. *Oja* exists as long as the person lives, and it is this which retains the body in its healthy state.

—:o:—

CHAPTER IV.

Structure of the Corporeal part of the Body (Anatomy).

The body consists of Humours, (*Dossoh*) and essential parts, (*dhátu*) with their appendages:—

—:o:—

SECTION I.

Humours.

The air (*váyu**), Bile (*pitta*†), and Phlegm (*kafa*‡), are the three pillars or supports of the system. If deranged they are the cause of disease, and death; and, with the blood, they retain, and eventually destroy the body. Without these three Humours and the blood the individual could not exist. With the essential parts of the body, and the appendages, and impurities, they form the fabric of the body.

As the moon sheds moisture, and abstracts the Sun's rays which dry up and bestow energy upon the earth, and the air moves from place to place, so does phlegm bestow moisture, bile withdraws it by its heat, and air wafts it about in the microcosm, or animal body.

---

* Vayu from *Va*, to go, was first formed.

† Pitta, from *Tapah*, hot; from which the heat of the body is derived.

‡ Kafa, *sleshma*; from sleshma, to embrace.

1st. *Váyu*, spirit, or air, flows through all parts of the body; and performs all its actions. It is of the active quality (*rajaguna*); is invisible, is of a cooling quality, is extremely light, and is always flowing more or less quickly; it conveys the essential parts over the body; performs respiration, and all the actions at the outlets of the body, the circulation of the fluids, and activity of the senses, and of the understanding. It dries up the fluids, is soft, but is affected by heat, and cold; and like the Sun's rays, it prepares and separates the fluids, and dejections. It produces happiness when healthy, and with heat increases the hot state of the system. It is principally found in the small intestines (*puckassia*), thighs, ears, eyes, senses, and all the canals, the testicles, and the anus. It produces the active properties of the body and its organs, and retains the body in its proper state. There are five kinds of *air* according to the situations they occupy.

a. Vital air (*Prána váyu*) which passes through the mouth and nose, and by it diglutition is performed. It is situated in the chest, and is the supporter of *prána*, or life. While this remains in health, so does the individual; it gives movement to the blood, and by it the food and drink are conveyed to the stomach, and strength to the body: when diseased it produces hiccough, and difficulty of breathing, &c.

b. *Apána váyu* is contained in the rectum, urethra, &c.; and is situated under the *puckassia*. It separates the dejections, urine, semen, menses, and expels the fetus. It is also situated in the buttocks. When deranged it produces diseases of the bladder, and the anus, diseases of the semen, and constipation.

c. *Sámana váyu* is situated in the stomach, and small intestines (*amassia*, and *puckassia*); performs the digestion of the food, separates the impurities, produces blood, and fat, and separates the urine, alvine evacuations, &c. When diseased it produces loss of appetite, goolmoh, diarrhœa, &c.

d. *Udana váyu* is situated in the hollow of the neck, above the sternum. In health it produces speech and singing; and other functions of the voice, above the colar bones. When deranged it produces various diseases of the upper part of the neck.

e. *Beana vayu* is found acting in conveying the fluids over the body, and in performing its functions, and those of the juices. It produces the flow of the blood; and performs walking, jumping, opening of the eyes, raising or depressing things, &c. If diseased all the body becomes affected.

Vital air is thus supposed to flow over the body, to produce, and to retain the various vital functions of the body; as joy, respiration, and its various actions: it also mixes with the humours, and regulates the movements of the body.

When the air is diminished weakness is produced, the person speaks little, he is melancholy, and it diminishes the understanding, &c. Vital air, is deranged by carrying heavy weights, by severe exercise, by excess in venery, much study, falls, or walking very fast: by always pressing the body, by injuries, fasting, jumping, or swimming; by not sleeping at night, by riding upon horse-back, elephants, or in carriages; by much walking, or using much sour, pungent, bitter, or dry substances, or light cooling vegetables, flesh or certain kinds of pulse, &c. Air may be deranged by the quantity and quality of the food which is eaten, by certain actions of the body, and by exposure to the cold, and moist air, early in the morning. If all the varieties of *Váyu* are diseased the person dies.

2nd. Bile (*pitta*) is a hot, bitter, oily fluid, having a peculiar smell, like that of raw flesh. It is of a blue colour and sour, when unconcocted; and is hot and pungent like fire or pepper, and of a yellow colour when properly prepared. It produces animal heat; and it possesses the quality of *Satwaguna.* It is situated principally in the stomach (*Amassia*), and small intestines (*puckassia*); but it is also found in the liver, spleen, heart, eye, and skin; where it is mixed with the blood, and other fluids. Its principal situation, however, is between the stomach and small intestines, from which it passes to the different parts of the body in which it is found. There are the following five kinds of Bile.

a. *Pacheka*, or that which assists digestion, and is situated between the stomach and small intestines. It digests the six kinds of food; and separates the chyle, urine, and fæces. As the sun imparts its properties (*tej*) to the moon, so bile imparts its properties to the phlegm, situated in the stomach. The stomach is therefore like a cooking pot containing water and food, which is boiled by the heat of the bile underneath it. In this way digestion is performed, and the blood is rendered more fluid.

When digestion is performed its qualities are like fire, and dries up the thin part of the food, and is called *anala* or fire, and separates the pure part from its dregs. It gives strength to the body, and as a candle enlightens objects around, so bile conveys its properties over all the body.

b. In the liver and spleen the bile gives a red colour to the chyle, and is called *ranjaka*.

c. In the heart it produces sense, memory, pride, and is called *sadaka*.

d. In the eyes it produces sight, and is called *álochoka*.

e. It gives the skin its shining, clear, and healthy colour; absorbs applications to the skin, and is called *brajoka*. Bile when not deranged produces the sense of sight, digestion, and the functions of organs by its heating and concocting properties. It produces appetite, and thirst, and retains the body soft, giving the proper colour to the body; and also joy, pride, memory, &c. Bile varies in different seasons; in July and August it is increased; in September and October it is liable to be diseased; and in March and April it is diminished.

When deranged, the internal fire or heat of the body is diminished, is also its colour, and digestion. In this case the nourishing chyle (*rasa*) is not properly separated in the organ called *Amassia,* and produces the indigestable dejections called *áma* or more properly white slimey discharges. If the slime be mixed with air, bile, and phlegm it deranges the seven *dhátu.*

The increase of the five elements, and their five qualities, of which the body is composed, will be best understood by following the course and changes of the food when eaten. The food by means of *prán váyu* reaches the stomach (*amassia*), where it is softened and mixed with the phlegm in the stomach, and becomes red and sweet. By the air situated in the navel (*samána váyu*), the fire is increased, and it digests the food in the stomach, which becomes frothy and sour, it then passes to the place of bile (*grinni*), which is situated between the stomach and small intestines. When well concocted by the bile situated there, the food becomes pungent, being mixed with the chyle. It then passes to the *pakassia,* or place in which digestion is perfected, and is separated from its impurities. The impure fluid part passes by means of vessels into the bladder; and the solid impurities by means of the *apán váyu,* passes into the *molásia,* or large intestines. The pure part of the digested food is of a milky colour, and is conveyed to the heart by means of the domonnic vessels, where it is mixed with the blood. *Charaka* calls these vessels the chyle carrying vessels (*rasyani*)

Should the fire be too strong it burns the food, and it becomes sour, and generates bile. When the fire dries the food, it produces a hard mass, which is bitter. After digestion the prepared food sometimes becomes sour, by its mixture with substances of this quality. When digestion is not properly performed, the internal fire and strength are diminished; the person becomes weakened, and diseases are produced, particularly the disease which is called *áma.*

When morbidly increased in the body, bile produces a yellowness of the skin, much heat, a desire for cooling articles of food, and a loss of sleep and strength. The person cannot see perfectly, and his eyes. fæces, and urine become yellower than usual.

The hair of a person with such a temperament, becomes quickly grey, he perspires easily, his body is pale, his eyes are easily, inflamed, and he is impatient, perverse, opiniative, vain, and consequential; is amorous, his conversation unguarded, is addicted to falsehood, is tond of abstruse studies, &c. Bile is deranged by anger, grief, fear, covetousness, malice, great fatigue, fasting, by eating roasted articles of food, by excessive venery, by sour, salt, and hot or heavy food, by mustard oil, or cakes; by certain kinds of pulse, as mustard seed; by vegetables, fish, flesh, curdled milk, butter-milk, spirits, and heat of all kinds.

3rd. The Phlegm (*Kafa*), is the impurity of the chyle, and it is conveyed by the *prana váyu* along the domonic vessels, and mixes with the rest of the phlegm in the body. It is cooling, moist, sweet, and when imperfectly prepared it is salt, and mixes substances together, &c. It is white, heavy, oleaginous, and glistening, and possesses the quality of *tamaguna* in excess. It is principally found in the stomach, in the breast, in the heart, at the root of the neck, in the head, in the eyes, in the throat, and tongue; and is found in the joints, in vessels, and all moist parts. There are five kinds described :—

a. In the stomach (*amasia*) it softens the food, and lubricates them together, and is called *Kledoka.*

b. *Abalambana,* is situated in the shoulder-joint, and neck, and it strengthens these parts, and also the breast.

c. In the tongue and throat, it produces the various tastes, and is called, *Rasana.*

d. In the head, it keeps the brain, the eyes, and other senses moist. It retains their respective qualities, and is called *Strehena.*

e. It keeps the joints moist and ready to perform their actions, and is called *slesona.*

If not deranged it retains the body in its proper state, produces its glistening appearance, and moist state. It strengthens the joints, produces the heaviness and strength of the body, and enters into the formation of semen. The temperament it produces is indicated by a greenish colour, and the person is fortunate, is of a fine colour, and is fond of sweet things. He is grateful, patient, and is without covetousness. He is strong with a white eye, his hair is black, and he dreams of water.

When morbidly diminished it produces impurities; the body dries, the internal heat is increased, digestion is diminished, the joints move with difficulty, the person is incommoded with thirst, weakness, and watching. In this state it leaves its natural situations, and passes to other parts of the body. It is deranged by sleeping during the day, taking no exercise, using much sweet, salt, sour, or cooling substances; as also oleaginous and heavy articles of food, as milk, and the like; barley, various kinds of rice, the flesh of the buffalo, and those animals which live in water. It is also deranged by eating always the same food, or eating too often, or cooling things of all kinds. This humour is also deranged by the seasons; in November and December it is increased, in March and April it is liable to be deranged, and in May and June it is diminished. When much increased it produce indigestion, loss of appetite, languor, lassitude, and vomiting.

It is supposed that the phlegm is contained in the parts above the navel, bile in the trunk above the pelvis, and air in and below the pelvis. In the morning phlegm predominates when the body feels cool; in the middle of the day, bile predominates, when people feel hot; and in the evening air is the strongest; at night the same order is observed. When these divisions meet, phlegm and air are the strongest. In like manner the age of man is divided into three periods; to the 15th year phlegm is strongest; to the 50th, or manhood, bile is the strongest; and after that, or in old age, air predominates. In like manner where these periods meet, phlegm and air are strongest.

The same changes are observed in the seasons, and in the period of digestion of food, and physicians should be careful of them in the employment of remedies. On this account hot things should be given in the morning or to the young; cooling things in the middle of the day, or to adults; and tonic and pungent food in the evening, or in old age.

The seven *dhátu* and the impurities remain at rest and incapable of action until acted on by air (*bayu*), and are wafted by it over all parts of the body, as clouds are wafted about by the wind, and through its influence they perform their respective actions. The air (*bayu*) presides over the ten senses, and is therefore the natural lord of all the actions of the body; it acts quickly and strongly; often deranges bile and phlegm, and produces many diseases. It is always present in the body, gives strength, and retains it in a state of health. It is diffused every where over the body, as well as in the world, of which it is the ruler, performing all the actions in it.

Sometimes the different humours are increased in quantity, either separately, or in combination of two or more together; but bile and phlegm cannot pass from their own receptacles by themselves, without the assistance of air, which is the only active humour, as a high wind striking upon water, throws it about, so vital air acting upon the other humours increase them in quantity, and they are thrown about out of their proper receptacles. Thus, when air, bile, phlegm, and blood are increased, they pass from their own receptacles and mix with the othe humours.

Sometimes they are diffused over the whole body; at other times to only a part which is irritated, and then form disease, like the cloud which accumulates over a part, throws down rain there.

If air is much deranged, it leaves its own receptacle, and passes to another situation, producing noise in an unusual situation. Bile in like manner produces heat, a burning sensation, and dryness; when phlegm is increased, and is changed in its position at the time of its passage, it destroys appetite and digestion, and produces languor and vomiting. In cases where air, bile, phlegm, and blood are deranged, and accumulated in the abdomen; they diminish appetite and strength, produce *gulma* and *bradrodri*, or large abscesses in the abdomen; also costiveness, cholera dysentery, &c.

If deranged, air passes to the receptacle of bile, the medicines for this disease are to be employed for its cure; and bile, if deranged, passes to phlegm. This is to be cured by removing diseased bile. If phlegm passes to the locality of air, this is to be cured in the usual way.

Bramhá, the creator of the world, is full of the *rajaguna*, and resembles air; while bile resembles *Vishnu*, and is like him full of *satwaguna*. In like manner phlegm resembles *Siva*, with his inactive qualities, and is the destroyer of the body.

When these humours accumulate in the bladder they produce diabetes, stone, disuria, and other diseases of the urine. When they accumulate in the penis they produce strictures, swellings, &c. In the anus they produce fistula-in-ano, piles, and the like. In the scrotum and testicles, they produce different forms of Hydrocele. If towards the head they produce the various diseases of the head, eyes, &c. When collected in the blood and flesh, the humours produce leprosy, different kinds of cutaneous diseases, and inflammation. If to the fat they produce different kinds of tumours and swellings, particularly of glandular parts. In the bone they produce inflammation, and other like diseases. In the feet elephantiasis, rheumatism, and the like. When diffused over the whole body, fever and other diseases of the body, as small pox, &c., are the consequence.

If such derangements of the humours remain for some time their effects may appear afterwards, and slowly produce the peculiar symptoms of disease.

——:o:——

SECTION II.

Essential Parts (*Dhátu.*)

The Essential Parts, or the supporters of the body, consist of the hard and soft parts, and fluids of the body.

These are the chyle (*rasa*), blood (*rakta*), flesh (*mánsha*), fat (*meda*), bone (*asthi*), marrow (*majjá*), and semen (*sukra*). These seven essential parts of the body form the fetus, nourish, and sustain life, and retain the system in a healthy state; they give the soft feel, the colour, and the strength of the body, and the action of the senses. When diseased or diminished, the body wastes, and the person dies. Thus will the period of life vary with the kind of food which is used. Good chyle produces good health, and with it bravery, strength, and a fine colour of the body and retentive memory.

a. Chyle (*rasa*) that moves in the body is obtained, and is separated from the four kinds of food which is digested, and is said to be the essence (*sára*) of the food. It has a glutinous, cooling, and liquid appearance; is sweet, and is of a white colour. It is principally situated in the heart, liver, and spleen; and by means of the vessels called damanee, it is conveyed to the different parts of the body by the *samàna bayu*; and nourishes the *dhàtu*, and is changed by the bile (*ranjaka*) into blood (*rakta*) in the liver. This kind of bile is supposed to redden the fluids, when it is called blood. The chyle thus changed mixes with the blood, by means of the *sámana bayu*. If the Bile be either too strong, or not strong enough; or the food is not properly digested, it becomes pungent, leaves a sour taste in the mouth, and like poison produces disease. The chyle then passes along to the heart, to nourish and increase the *dhátu* and parts of the body, as fields are irrigated by canals of water, which moisten, and afford them its qualities. When chyle is much increased it produces nausea, and an increased secretion of saliva. There are two varieties of chyle *áma* (chyme), slightly impure, and *pakwa* or chyle in its pure state which nourishes the body.

There is a difference of opinion as to the uses of the chyle, some supposing that it nourishes the parts directly, others suppose that by means of vital air (*prán bayu*), it is conveyed to the damanee vessels by which it is sent to the blood, and mixes with it in the spleen and liver, where it becomes red, is purified by the bile, and remains there for five days and a half. It then passes to the flesh, and remains there some time, and is purified by the bile (*pitta*), or a kind of internal fire, and is conveyed to the different parts of the body, which it retains at its proper temperature, and nourishes the flesh. In the same way it passes to and remains in the fat, bone, &c., which it nourishes, and purifies with one part; while another impure part (*mala*) is rejected. Perspiration is the impurity of the blood in the fat; as the tartar is the impurity of the teeth; and other secretions have impurities which are in like manner thrown off. The last *dhátu* to which the chyle passes is to the semen, which has no dregs: so that the chyle, like sugar, requires different processes to purify it, and at each stage it throws down impurities.

The chyle retains the person in good spirits, increases the blood, &c., and if not properly prepared, it becomes sour; and deranges the *dhátu*. If diminished there is pain in the breast, the person shakes, has swimming in the head and moistness in the eyes, with thirst. In one month the chyle changes to blood, flesh, fat, bone, and marrow, from which semen, and the menses are produced.

b. Blood (*rakta*). The blood is derived from the digested parts of the chyle, and by being concocted by the bile becomes red, when it is called blood; which combines, and nourishes the other essential parts of the body (*dhátu*).

The blood is thin and limpid, like water, has a peculiar smell, is if a red colour, and light. These qualities are derived from the five elements; as the smell from the earth, the fluidity from the water, redness from the fire, mobility from the air, and lightness from the ether (*ákása*). When blood predominates it produces the redness of the eyes and body, and fullness of the vessels. In a healthy state it keeps the body of a good colour, increases strength, and the flesh or bulk of the body, nourishes the organs, and moves, lives, and retains their being. It preserves vitality (*jiva*) which it distributes over all the body; but in different quantities, being derived from the heart as its fountain.

The blood is known to be in a healthy state, when the nails, eyelids,, palate, tongue, lips, palms of the hands, and soles of the feet are of a reddish colour, and of a shining appearance. It retains the fullness and hardness of the abdomen, gives the yellow tinge to the skin, reduces the heat of the body, and renders it heavy, and listless.

The blood is changed and produces the menses, which differ from the pure fluid, being formed by the internal fire of the body, and flowing continually three whole days during every month; from the 12th to the 50th year of age.

When the blood is diminished in quantity in the body, the skin becomes dry and rough, the vessels feel lax and feeble; it increases the internal heat of the body, and produces fevers, and other diseases; in which sour and cooling food and drink are desired.

Blood is never deranged by itself, as whatever acts unfavourably on it produces first its effect upon the air, phlegm, and bile, and then it acts on the blood. On this account the diseases of the blood are cured, by first curing the derangements of the humours.

c. Flesh (*mánasa, muscles*), is produced by air (*bayu*) thickening the blood, which is digested by heat. This increases the firmness of the body. The air passes through the body, and being accompanied with the proper degree of heat, forms the large canals, and divides the flesh into different muscles; in which the vessels are lodged that contain blood. By means of these, it proceeds as the lily rises from the ground, and is nourished by water, &c., in its progress upwards. When the blood is digested in the flesh, with the internal fire, its essential parts nourish the flesh, and its dregs produce the wax of the ears, &c.

When diminished and dried up in the abdomen, cheeks, and lips, pelvis, thighs, breasts, armpits, nates, and neck; it produces pain, and the principal vessels are diminished in size. When it predominates it increases the size of the buttocks, cheeks, lips, thighs, arms, and calves of the legs, and gives a general heaviness to the body.

d. Fat (*meda*) is generated from the blood in the flesh, and is in large quantities round the eyes, throat, and breast, when properly digested by the action of its internal fire. It produces perspiration, keeps the body shining, and hard; is oily, and heavy; and is the cause of the growth of the body, its obsity, and strength. It is diffused over the body, but its chief seat is in the abdomen.

When the fat is diminished the spleen may be easily felt, the joints seem dried, and moving them gives pain. In such cases animal food is always desired. When fat predominates, the body appears smooth and glistening, the abdomen and sides are increased in size; cough and asthma are produced, and the body has a disagreeable smell. It is supposed that the essential part of the blood and fat produce bone.

e. Bones (*asthi*), and cartilages (*toruna*) as new bone, are usually considered under the same head These give form to the body, and to them all the soft parts are attached. When the bones are all united together, they form the skeleton (*kankála*). Bone, with blood are the parts from which the marrow of long bones, including the brain and spinal marrow, are formed. When digested the excretions (*mala*) of bone form the nails and hair. When the elements of bone are diminished in the system they become painful, the teeth and nails crack, become loose, and the body becomes dry. Where bone predominates, another portion grows over the old bone; and a more than usual number of teeth are formed.

Some authors say there are 300 (Sushruta) others 306 (Charaka), bones in the body. This difference is owing to their counting the cartileges with the bones. The bones are connected together by capsular ligaments. The bones are:—

1st. Extremities.

Number—English Authors.	Up.	Lr.	*Number—Sanskrit Authors.*	Up.	Lr.
Fingers and toes ...	14	14	Bones in the fingers and toes ...	30	30
Metacarpus and metatarsus ...	5	5	Long bones of each hand and foot ...	8	8
Heel bone ...	0	1	Wrist and ankle ...	16	12
Carpus and tarsus ...	8	6	Heel ...	0	2
Fore arm and leg ...	2	2	Fore arm and leg ...	4	4
Patella ...	0	1	Knee ...	0	2
Arm and thigh ...	1	1	Arm and thigh ...	2	2
	30	30		60	60
	60	60	Bones of the extremities*		120
Number of bones of the extremities ...		120			

2nd. Head and Trunk.

Bones of the skull, Temporal bones ...	8	Bones of the skull ...	6
		Temples ...	2
External cartilages of the ear ...	2	Ears cartilages ...	2
Cheek bones ...	2	Cheeks ...	2
Jaw bones ...	2	Jaws, upper and lower ...	2
Palet bone ...	1	Palet ...	1
2 os nasi, and 1 cartilage ...	3	Nose ...	3
Teeth of adult ...	32	Teeth in Adult† ...	32
Throat { 3 Hyoid Cartilages. 1 Arytonoid Cartilage. 1 Os Hyoides. }	4	Throat ...	4
		Neck ...	9
		Bones above the neck	63
		(Akoka) or clavicles ...	2

* Sesamoid bones are not counted.

† Charaka says there are 32 al eolar bones, and 30 teeth.

Neck cartilages of the wind pipe ...	9
Bones above the neck	63
Clavicles ...	2
Vertebræ ...	24
Sacrum ...	4
Scapulæ ...	2
Breast bones ...	4
Cartilages between sternum and clavicle ...	2
Enciformed Cartilage ...	2
Ribs ...	24
Sternal Cartilages ...	24
Cartilages, tubercles, &c. ...	24
Coccyges ...	2
Sacrum ...	1
Annominata ...	2
Bones of the trunk ...	117
Number of bones in the body ...	300

Back	24 Vertebræ. 4 Bones of the sacrum 2 Scapulæ	* 30
Breast	4 Breast bones 2 Cartilages between the sternum and clavicle. 2 Pieces enciformed cartilages	8
Sides 36 in each.	24 Ribs 24 Sternal cartilages 24 Cartilages tubercles and the transverse processes of ver tebræ	72
Pelvis		
Coccyges ...		2
Sacrum ...		1
Annominata ...		2
Bones of the trunk ...		117
Number of bones in the body ...		300

There are five varieties of bones :—

1: Flat bones, *kapalá*; as of the knee, hip, shoulder, cheek, palet, temple, and head.

2. Teeth, *Ruchaka*.

3. Cartilages (*toruna*) nose, ears, neck and eyelids.

4. Round Bones (*bolia*) are those of the hands, feet, back, sides, abdomen, and sacrum.

5. Long bones (*nalaka*) as those of the arms, legs, metacarpal, and metatarsal bones, and the other like bones of the body.

Bones are insensible, immoveable, and as the centre of a tree is the hardest, so the bones are the most durable part of the body; and remain after all the other parts have decayed.

f. *Brain* and *Marrow* (*majjá*). The Brain and Marrow are

* Charaka says 25, with 24 ribs.

situated within the bones and nourish them, and their impurities are the secretions from the eyes. The *Majjá* gives strength, and the shining appearance to the body. When the marrow is increased there is a heaviness of the eye, and of the whole body; and when diseased it diminishes semen, and produces pain in the long bones. The essential parts of marrow and brain mix with the blood, and produce semen.

g. Semen (*Sukra*). Is the last essential part formed, and nothing is produced from it in the body. It retains the body in its proper state of health and strength, is the generative principle, and during its excretion it produces pleasure; when diminished, it causes pain in the penis, and testicles, and the person becomes impotent. When it predominates there is an increased flow, and it produces stone. The female has desire for the sex during the flow of the menses, which acts in them as the semen does in the male.

These seven essential parts of the body (*dhátu*) are contained in seven organs called *kollá*, or their receptacles.

The blood retains all these parts in their proper state of health. Some believe that life is the blood, and others say that life is the *satwa, raja* and *tamagunas*, with the five senses and the soul.

Ozah is the essential part to the seven *dhátu* above enumerated which gives them strength. It is cooling, oily, of a reddish, or slightly yellow colour; is diffusible and transparent, and is the principal supporter of life. It is spread over all the body. If destroyed, the body will soon die. It is deranged by severe wounds, by the diminution of any the seven essential parts; by the passions, anxiety, much labour, and hunger. If it is in a healthy state the body becomes firm, the proper functions of the organs are performed, a good colour is given to the body, the external and internal functions, and the organs of sense are retained in a healthly state. When deranged the person feels languid, with a loss of strength. The body feels heavy, swollen, and drowsy, and its colour changes. If diminished, the person becomes thin, with fainting, delirium, and death.

—:o:—

SECTION III

Excretions (Mala)

Are the impurities of the seven essential parts, the dregs of the chyle is phlegm; of the blood, bile; of the flesh, the secretions of the ear, nose, &c.; of the fat, perspiration; of the bone, he nails, and hair; of the brain and marrow, the secretions from the eyes, &c. The semen has no dregs or impurities, but others say that (Ozah), an oily transparent fluid, which is formed all over the body, is the essential part of life, and is its impurity. This is the strength of the body, and is principally situated in the thorax.

Alvine evacuations are the superfluous part of the nutritious food, which form the feces; when diminished by dysentery, purgatives, or the like, pain is felt in the breast, and sides of the abdomen. When much increased it produces pain in the belly, with a gurgling noise. When in the proper quantity it keeps the body in a proper state; and it supports the air, and internal fire in a healthy condition.

Urine is contained in the bladder, and keeps the parts moist. When diminished, pain is felt in the pelvis, and little urine is discharged. When much increased there is a frequent flow with pain in the pelvis, and swelling in the part.

Perspiration retains the skin in a soft and moist state. If diminished, the pores of the skin are closed, the skin becomes dry, tough, and deranged in its action. For the removal of this state, oil is to be rubbed over the body with warmth and moisture. When the perspiration is increased there is a bad smell of the body with itching.

Milk increases the size of the mammæ and is the food of the infant. When diminished, the mammæ become lessened, and little milk is secreted, and in these cases medicines which increase phlegm are to be used. When much increased the mammæ are enlarged, with a flow of the milk, and pain.

These impurities will be diminished by much purging or vomiting; and also eating those substances in considerable quantities which diminish air, bile, &c., will have this effect. One mola when constipated, diminishes the others. In like manner disagreeable food or melancholy; violent exercise, fasting, excess in venery, &c., have the same effect. There is however no certain quantities as they vary in different individuals, according to their size, &c. The increase or diminution of their fluids is therefore stated by comparison. When healthy, all the secretions and essential parts are supposed to be in a proper state; and it is the duty of the physician to restore them to their just quantity; if increased, they must be diminished; and if diminished increased.

Others state that oily exudations, seminal fluids, blood, dandrif, urine, fæcis, earwax, nail-parings, phlegm, tears, concretions in the eyes and sweat, are the twelve impurities of the human frame." (Menu p. 164. Ch. V. 135.)

——:o:——

SECTION IV.

JOINTS (*Sandhi*)

The joints are of two kinds the moveable (*chala*) and immoveable (*sthira*).

Of the first kind are the joints of the extremities, jaw, and vertebræ. All the others belong to the second, or immoveable class. The moveable joints are :—

The 4 toes, 3 in each	12	
Large toe	2	
The foot, knee and hip, one each ...	3	
	17	
In each leg	17 both	34
Hand in like manner		... 34
Joints of the extremities		... 68
The Loins	3	
Spinal column	24	
Thorax	24	
Breast	8	
Joints of the trunk	—	59
Neck	8	
Throat	3	
Connection of vessels with the heart and organ of thirst (*kloma*)	18	
The roots of the teeth	32	
Pomum Adami	I	
Nose	1	
Eyelids	2	
Jaws	2	
Ears	2	
Temples	2	
Cheeks	2	
Above each eye-brows	2	
Above each temples	2	
Head	5	
Crown of the head	1	
Joints above the neck	—	83
Total ...		210

There are eight forms of joints:—

a. *Kara*, hinge joint as those of the fingers, toes, wrist, ankles, knees, elbows.

b. *Udukhala*, as the ball and socket joint, shoulder, hip, teeth.

c. *Samudga*. Like the instrument for cutting beetlenut; as the shoulder-blade, coxis, pubes, and innominata.

d. *Protara*, as the neck, back.

e. *Tunnoscbanee* (sown as with thread), sutures of the skull, joinings of the illium, ischium, and pubes.

f. *Biosatunda*, the joints of the lower jaw, which resemble a crows beak (coronoid process).

g. *Mundala* (round) as of the orbits, throat (larynx) and thorax; in which the eyes, wind-pipe, bronchæ, and heart are situated.

h. *Sunkhaburta* in the ears, as the os hyoides.

——:o:——

SECTION V.

LIGAMENTS, &c. (*Snáyu.*)*

Ligaments bind together and strengthen the frame work of the bones, like the strips of ratan which are employed to bind the pieces of a boat together, so as to prevent the entrance of water, and to support heavy weights.

These Ligaments are divided into those of the extremities, trunk and head.

In each toe there are 6 ligaments ...	30		
Soles, sides, and joints of the feet ...	30		
Leg	30		
Knee	10		
Thigh	40		
Hip-joint	10		
	——	opposite	
	150	side	150 or 300
The proximid extremities ...	150	Do.	150 or 300
			——
Ligaments of the extremities			600
Ligaments of the trunk.			
In the Loins	60		
Back	80		
Chest	30		
Sides, 30 in each side	60		
	—		230

* This includes nerves which are not considered separately.

Back of the neck ...	... 36	
Head	... 34	
	—	70
Number of Ligaments of the body	...	900

There are four varieties of Ligaments.

a. Protanobutee, long ligaments, as of the legs, feet, and joints.

b. Britto, round ligaments and tendons, as of the penis, &c.

c. Prithu, thick ligaments and tendons; as along the sides, breast, back, and head.

d. Susira, those with holes in them, as in *amasia, pakasia,* and bladder (bustee).

The physician, by knowing exactly the situation of the external and internal ligaments, will be able to remove extraneous bodies which have penetrated far into their substance.

Wounds of these Ligaments (and nerves) are most painful and dangerous.

——:o:——

SECTION VI.

Muscles (Pashee)

Muscles cover, strengthen, and retain in their places, vessels tendons, bones, and joints.

The size of the muscles differ according to their situation and uses. They are :—

Bahala, or broad and large.
Peleba, small.
Unu, narrow.
Sthulah, thick.
Birta, round.
Krussa, short.
Sthera, hard.
Mirdu, soft.
Sluckno, smooth and shining : and,
Korkasha, rough.

They are as follows :—

In the two hands and feet	... 400	
Trunk	... 66	
Above the nape of the neck	... 34	
	—	
1st. In the extremities		500
Each finger and toe 3 or	... 15	
In front of the foot (tarsus)	... 10	

Above the foot (metatarsus) ...	10
Under the ankles ...	10
In the leg	20
Knee	5
Thigh	20
Hip	10
- 100 two feet	200
Two hands the same	200
	400
2nd. In the Trunk	
Anus	3
Penis	1
Frenun of do.	1
Testicles	2
Hips, 5 on each side	10
Above the bladder	2
Abdomen	5
Umbiliacus...	1
Vertebral column	10
Side	6
Breast	10
Upper breast	7
Place of life, and amasia ...	2
Liver, spleen, and rectum, 2 each ...	6
3rd. Muscles above the nape of the neck	66
Nape of the neck	4
Jaws	8
Throat and upper part of the chest ...	2
Pallet	2
Tongue	1
Lips	2
Nose	2
Eyes	2
Cheeks	4
Ears	2
Forehead	4
Head	1
Above the neck and head	34
Total umber of muscles	500

Females have 20 more muscles, viz :—

Five in each mammæ	10
Vagina, 2 external and 2 internal ...	4

Uterus ...	... ...	3
For conveying the semen and blood internally	... ...	3
		20

In these positions the muscles vary according to their actions. The muscles of the penis and testicles of the male are retained internally in the body of the female. Besides which there are spiral muscles like those of a shell; the first circle being the vagina, the second the neck of the uterus, and the third its cavity. In the uterus is contained the fetus with the mouth of that organ turned downwards and shaped like that of a *ruefish.*

—:o:—

SECTION VII.

Vessels.

The vessels are distinguished from each other by the names *será, demanee* and *srota.* The appearance of these vessels is nearly the same; but they differ from each other, by their actions.

The navel is the origin of all the vessels, and the principal seat of the life (pran), as it is situated there in larger quantities than elsewhere. The navel may be said to resemble the root of a waterlily, from which the different vessels proceed to all parts of the body. The navel is thus the root of the vessels of all living animals.* It is surrounded by vessels like the central part of a wheel which receives spokes from the circumference. Among these, forty principal vessels are enumerated.

Será are the vessels which convey blood, air, bile, and phlegm. The branches of these vessels are like those of the leaves of trees, which ascend, descend, and cross. They nourish the body as a garden is irrigated by a small brook. These vessels, as a river, distribute nourishment in their course, and keep the body flexible, and ready for action. Of the forty principal vessels, ten contain air, ten bile, ten phlegm, and ten blood. Each trunk is attached to its own receptacle *dosa.* They are of all sizes, and life is contained in different degrees in different vessels. The midling size contain principally air.

---

* This idea is derived from the appearance of the vessels in their fetal state.

The ten trunks of vessels which convey air are divided into			...	175 branches
do	Bile	do	...	175 „
do	Phlegm	do	...	175 „
do	Blood attached to the spleen and liver		...	175 „
Total				700

Air vessels have 25 branches in each lower extremity	...	...	50	
Do. do. 25 in each upper do.		...	50	
				100

The air vessels of the trunk are as follows :—

In the anus, penis, and buttocks		...	8	
Two sides	...	...	...	4	
Back	...	...	...	6	
Belly	...	...	...	6	
Breast	...	—	—	10	
					34
Neck	...	...	...	14	
Two ears	...	...	—	4	
Tongue	...	—	—	9	
Nose	—	—	—	6	
Eyes	—	—	—	8	
Air vessels in the neck and head					41
Number of air vessels					175

The vessels that convey bile, phlegm and blood are the same in number as those which convey air. But, in the eye, bile has ten, air has two instead of four; and in the ears two. The phlegm and blood have the same number. All vessels, therefore, are supposed to contain air, bile, phlegm, and blood, but in different proportions. When they contain more air, bile, phlegm or blood, they are called air vessels, phlegm vessels, or blood vessels.

The colour of air vessels is red, and air appears in them; those of bile are blue and hot, and those of phlegm are cool, of a whitish colour, thick, and their contents seem to remain at rest.

If *air* circulates properly in its own vessels, the person will act properly, and the functions of the body will be performed in such a manner that the individual will enjoy health; his understanding will be good, and he will possess all the other good qualities of air. If deranged, various kinds of the disease of air, will be produced.

If *Bile* is in a proper condition, the person will have a healthy appearance, his appetite good, the internal fire will be strong and healthy, and he will possess other good qualities. But if deranged, the diseases of bile will be produced.

If *Phlegm* acts properly the skin will be smooth, the joints healthy, and the strength will be good, and he will have the other good qualities of phlegm. If deranged, it produces the peculiar class of diseases of phlegm.

Blood. This fluid produces and nourishes all the other essential parts of the body. If the blood is in a healthy state, the persons colour remains good, the surface is sensible, and it produces the other good qualities of blood, and when deranged it developes the various diseases of blood.

When the air vessels are alone deranged, disease is not produced, but when deranged, with an increased quantity of bile, and phlegm, disease is the consequence. By the state of the eight principal vessels the physician knows if the patient will die or live. There are two vessels in the hands, two in the feet, two in the throat, two in the temples, and two in the nose, which are thus to be examined. In the foot the vessel is behind the maleolus internus, and is in length two fingers breadth ; in the hand it is three breadths of the fingers, in the neck two breadths of the finger, and in the nose two, at which the pulse is felt. The two vessels of the hand are however the principal ; and if their contents flow naturally the person will live and do well. In these situations are the vessels containing the indications of life, and a sensible physician will examine them all, and if air flows naturally it will be favourable. If in any of these the semen is deranged in the vessel, and air flows naturally, the person will live, this air produces the pulse. * When the pulse is to be judged of, three fingers are to be put upon the vessel at the wrist ; the first, next the hand, represents or indicates air or Brumha, the second bile, or Vishnu ; and the third phlegm, (Mahesur or Siva).

Should air be deranged in the vessels, sometimes it will be cured by pressing, shampooing, or opening the vessel ; or by perspiration or friction. These remedies must always be employed.

When air, bile, and phlegm are deranged, and increased in quantity, they do not remain in the same vessels, but pass into different channels, as into those of one of the other fluid.

---

* Physicians feel the pulse at the wrist, ankles, temples ; and sometimes at the nose, or neck.

The vessels carrying principally blood, are very red; but are neither very hot nor cold Some of these vessels may be opened, others cannot be opened with impunity. Should they be wounded, the person will die, or the part will be rendered imperfect in its actions.

There are four vessels which should not be opened in each extremity :—

1. Íjála dára		1
2. Urbee	deep seated	3
1. Lohetaka		
		—
		4

There are in the trunk 136 vessels, of which 32 should no be opened; 4 are in the buttocks; 3 in each side of the spina column; in the belly 4; and in the breast 14. Above the clavicles 5o are not to be opened. In the neck 16; in the jaw two on each side; 4 below the tongue, 4 near the nose, 1 in the soft palate, one on each side of the eyes, and one in each ear, one in each side of the forehead, two in the temples, two above it, one between the eyebrows; and six in the upper part of the head.

It is stated in some books that there are innumerable vessels consisting of those of a large and very small size, which are like decayed leaves in which the interstices of the leaves have been removed. They are said to form 3½ cotees * of vessels, or 300 lacks of all sizes and figures. These all arise from the navel.

Damanee vessels †.

These include vessels and nerves; by which the different functions of the body are performed.

There are 24 of these vessels, which for the most part proceed from the navel. There are 10 that proceed upwards, ten downwards, and two laterally. The upper ten perform the functions of hearing, touching, seeing, tasting, and smelling. They also perform breathing, gaping, sneezing, coughing, laughing, speaking, and crying; when these vessels approach the heart, the ten are divided into three each, forming thirty branches. Two of these are divided into twelve, of which two convey air, two bile, two phlegm, two blood, and two chyle. Eight others perform hearing, seeing, tasting, smelling, two being allowed for each func-

* One cotée is equal to one hundred lacks.

† A tubular vessel of the body, as a vein, nerve, &c. Other shastres say that they proceed from the turtle situated in the navel with four legs; ten vessels from the proximid extremity, ten from the lower, two from the mouth, and two from the anus (Tantra).

tion. By two speech is performed, two make a noise, two produce sleep, two waking, two convey tears, two the milk of the female, and two in the male convey semen. These constitute the upper vessels.

The actions of the ten lower vessels, situated under the navel, are to carry the air of the abdomen, for acting on the urine, dejections, semen, menses, and the like. They separate all these parts from each other; and by them the chyle is separated, and the body nourished, and retained in health.

These ten vessels become thirty in the stomach (*amasia*) and intestines (*pakasia*); two of which convey air, two bile, two phlegm, two blood, two chyle, two the solid, and two the fluid food, two for the urinary organs, and two for producing the semen, and two for conveying it externally, two for the menses, and by two the dejections are discharged.

From these, numerous other branches proceed; the whole body being enveloped by the branches proceeding from the four lateral trunks. These are innumerable and terminate in open orifices on the surface, and convey perspiration, retain the body in a healthy state, and by their communications convey external applications into the system. By these vessels feeling is produced, and by them the oil or water is drawn into the system, and they cool, refresh, and clean it.

Srotá (*or Canals*).

These vessels convey prana or vital air; the food (*anna*); water (*uda*); chyle (*rasa*); blood (*rakta*); fat of the flesh (*mansha*); urine (*mutra*); feces (*purisa*); semen (*sukra*); and menses (*artobo*). From each of these numerous other vessels arise.

Should the two vessels conveying life (*prana*) be wounded at the root; which is in the heart, the person screams, bends forward, becomes delirious, shakes, reels, swoons, and often dies. Should the two vessels conveying food, the root of which arises from the stomach be wounded, the symptoms will be flatuleney, pain in the abdomen, loss of appetite, vomiting, thirst, blindness, and death.

There are two vessels, which convey *Chyle*, the roots of which are in the breast. It wounded the body dries up, and the same effects are produced as when the vessels conveying life are wounded; the person generally dies.

There are two vessels for conveying *blood*, the roots of which are in the liver and spleen, and if they, or the roots of the other blood vessels are wounded, the person becomes of a pallid or gray colour, with fever; much blood is lost, and the eyes become red.

There are two vessels for conveying *flesh*, the roots of which are the veins (*sirá*), and skin (*twak*), and the root of the vessels which convey blood which if wounded produce swelling, drying of the flesh, and enlargement of the vessels (*sira*) conveying blood (*aneurism*), and the person dies.

For *fat* there are two vessels, the roots of which are in the sides and loins, and when wounded produce perspiration, coolness of the body, the palate dries, the body swells, and there is thirst.

There are two vessels for conveying *urine*, the roots of which are in the bladder, and penis; and if wounded the bladder is distended by the collection of urine, and the penis swells.

There are two organs for containing *dejections*, one of which arises from *pakwásaya*, and the other forms the anus. If wounded costiveness (*ánáha*), and a bad smell are produced, and the intestines swell, or become knotted.

The *semen* has two canals the roots of which are in the breast; and two from the testicles. If wounded they produce impotency, and the semen is discharged very slowly, and is mixed with blood.

The *menses* have two canals, the roots of which are the uterus, and the *damanee* vessels, which convey the menses. When wounded, they produce barrenness, and the menses cease.

—:o:—

SECTION VIII.

Cellular tissue, and fascia of the Body (*kalá*).

The cellular tissue connects, and surrounds, the different parts of the body, and separates the seven essential parts from each other. The tissues which thus retain the different parts of the body together are of seven kinds:—

*1st. Mángsadhará** is situated between the muscles, and in which the vessels (rugs) pass, and divide into branches, to nourish the neighbouring parts, as the lily rises from the ground, and receives its nourishment from the water and earth.

2nd. Raktadhará† in which the blood is contained, in the spleen and the liver. They retain the blood, as the juice of trees is retained, and is discharged when cut into.

3rd. Medodhará‡ is the organ in which all the fat is retained, the chief place of which is in the abdomen (the omentum). When the fat is contained in the bones it is called *majá*.

---

* From Mangsa flesh, and dhara surrounds.
† Rakta blood, and dhara retains.
‡ Meda fat, and dhara retains. Maja brain, saroia marrow.

4*th*. *Sleshmadhará** which forms the bags containing the phlegm, with which the joints are lubricated, and rendered supple; as oil is applied for the movement of wheels.

5*th*. *Purishadhará*, in which the dejections are retained in the abdomen, it is attached to the *pakavása*, and is situated between the liver and the intestines.

6*th*. *Pittadhará*, or organ which receives from the stomach the four kinds of food, taken by sucking, dividing with the teeth, drinking, and licking. These kinds of food are digested by the heat of the bile (*Pittateja*).

7*th*. *Sukradhará* retains the semen, which is dispersed over all the body with other fluids, in the same manner as milk contains butter, or the juice of sugar-cane, sugar-candy. The principal seat of the semen, is too fingers breadth on each sides the neck of the bladder; and the semen passes along the urinary passages, and is discharged in a state of pleasure.

—:o:—

SECTION IX.

Organs or Receptacles (*ásaya.*)

There are seven of these receptacles, with an additional three in the female. They retain the Humours of the body in their respective situations; such as air, bile, and phlegm, blood, chyle, chyme, urine, and feces.

The receptacle of the blood is the heart; under which the organ of phlegm is situated. Still lower down (distid) is situated the stomach (*ámásaya*) between the breast and navel. Under which is the (*pittásaya*), receptacle of bile; below which is the receptacle of air (*pavanásaya*), or place for the excretions†; and below that is the receptacle of urine (vasti or bladder). The female has three more receptacles; the uterus, and two receptacles for milk, or the mammæ.

—:o:—

SECTION X.

Orifices of the Body. (*Bahisrota*).

There are nine orifices in the body of the male; the mouth, two nostrils, two ears, two eyes, the anus, and the urethra.

Females have the orifices of the two mammæ, and the vagina, more than those of the male.

---

* Sleshma phlegm, and dhara retain.

† Charaka divides these into large and small intestines, and gives each a name.

SECTION XI.

Skin. (*Twak*).

The skin is said to be in a state of health when it is soft, and has much hair. The skin consists of seven layers, or membranes; as milk when boiled, forms a coating like that of the skin. The skin gives the seven different kinds of colour to the body.

1st. *Avabháshini* (cuticle) this is the external layer, and is transparent. Its thickness is about the eighteenth part of a grain of rice.

2nd. *Lohita* is the sixteenth part of a grain of rice in thickness.

3rd. *Swetá* is a membrane of a white colour, and is the thickness of the twelth part of a grain of rice.

4th. *Támra* is of a copper colour, the thickness of an eighth part of a grain of rice.

5th. *Vediní* is the sensible part, and is the thickness of the fifth part of a grain of rice.

6th. *Rohini* is the thickness of a grain of rice.

These membranes are not found in the head or fingers, but are distinguishable when there is much flesh in the part examined, as the belly, extremities, &c.

7th. *Mangsadhará*. These parts of the body are innumerable, and retain the muscles in their places.

—:o:—

SECTION XII.

Supplimentary Parts.

Principal tendons (*kandará*) are sixteen in number :—

To each foot two ...	4
do hands	4
Neck, and front of the body ...	4
Back	4
	16

From the tendons of the extremities the nails proceed. Those of the neck bind it to the trunk, and it is a tendon which extends to form the penis.

The back and buttocks are bound together by mere tendons; which pass down and form the testicles.

There are also 16 *Jála* (like a net) and are formed of vessels, &c., which strengthen, and bind the joints; and six *kurcha* which form bundles of parts.

Sebani (sowing or sutors), there are five sutors in the head, one in the frenum of the tongue, and one in the frenum of the Penis.

——:o:——

SECTION XIII.

Dissection of the Human Body.

All the *Rishis* are said to have recommended the dissection of the human body, as proper and necessary. Menu, the great legislaton, and the one most respected by the Hindu sages, says (85) "one who has touched a corpse, is made pure by bathing;" and again (77) "should a Brahman touch a fresh human bone he is purified by bathing; and if it be dry by stroking a cow, or by looking at the sun, having sprinkled his mouth duly with water."

Charaka, one of the *munís*, and Physicians says, that a practitioner should know all the parts of the body, both external and internal, and their relative positions with regard to each other. Without such a knowledge he cannot be a proper practitioner.

Sushruta, a *Rishí* of the highest rank, says that a *jogí* (a holy man) should dissect, in order that he may know the different parts of the human body; and a surgeon and physician should not only know the external appearances, but internal structure of the body; in order to possess an intimate knowledge of the diseases to which it is liable, and to perform surgical operations so as to avoid the vital parts. It is by combining a knowledge of books with practical dissection, that the practitioner will alone attain an intimate knowledge of the subject of his profession.

The body which is to be examined by dissection should be that of a person who had neither been destroyed by poison, nor had died of a long disease, as the structure of the body will be altered by the deleterious substance taken, or destroyed by the ravages of disease. In like manner the person should not have been very old, and all the members should be in a perfect state.

When a proper body for the purpose has been selected, the dejections are to be removed, the body washed, and placed in a frame work of wood, properly secured, by means of grass, hemp, or the like. The body is then to be placed in still water, in a situation in which it will not be destroyed by birds, fishes, or animals. It is to remain for seven days in the water, when it will have become putrid. It is then to be removed to a convenient situation, and with a brush, made of reeds, hair, or bamboo-bark, the body is to be rubbed so as, by degrees, to exhibit the skin, flesh, &c., which are each in their turn to be observed before being removed. In this manner the different corporial parts of the body already enumerated will be exhibited; but the life of the body is too etherial to be distinguished by this process, and its properties must therefore be learned with the assistance of the explanations of holy medical practitioners, and prayers offered up to God, by which, conjoined with the exercise of the reasoning and understanding faculties, conviction will be certain.

——:o:——

CHAPTER V.

Vital Parts (*Marma*).

The description of these parts, and the consequences of their being wounded, afford a convincing proof of the great practical experience of the Hindu writers. The advantages of having a good and attentive medical attendant, compared with that of an ignorant one, is emphatically declared to be as great as the difference of the individual, being restored from weakness and deformity, or even from death after much suffering to perfect health.;

In Sushruta the dangerous parts are all named and described; and the necessity of avoiding them in operations pointed out. The consequence of wounds near the great toe in causing tetanus; in the palm of the hand, in producing such a degree of hemorrhage as will require amputation of the arm; of the effects of wounds of the testicle and groin, and of the fractured bones of the head and breast, which are to be raised or removed, &c., are all stated in this practical work.

There are five kinds of vital parts:—

Flesh has (*mángsa marma*)	1
Vessels (*sira marma*) have	1
Nerves and Ligaments (*Snáyu marma*) ...	1
Bones (*ostí marma*)	1
Joints (*sandhí marma*)	1
	5

The following are the varieties of vital parts:—

Flesh has	11
Vessels	41
Tendons nerves, and ligaments ...	27
Bone	8
Joints	20
Varieties of vital parts of the body.	107

These parts are also divided as follows:—

In each leg there are	11,	in both ...	22
In each arm	11,	do ...	22

In the abdomen (*udara*) there are 3, and in the thorax 9	...	...	...	12
In the back there are	...	...	...	14
Above the trunk	...	...	...	37
				107

Vital parts of the distid extremities.

1. *Kipra.* The space between the great toes, and the one next it, if wounded or bruised, the person will die with tetanus. Hence a bite of a serpent is very dangerous in this part.

2. *Talahridaya.* Under and behind the 4th and 5th toe. If wounded death will be produced with great suffering.

3. *Kurcha,* above the *Kipra,* and on each side of it. If wounded there will be an unsteadiness of the foot.

4. *Kurchasira,* under the ankles, it will produce pain and swelling.

5. *Gulpha,* the ankle joint, which produces pain, and the joint becomes stiff, and the person lame.

6. *Indrabasti,* along the anterior and posterior part of the leg. If blood flows largely, the person will die.

7. *Janu,* or vital part in the knee. When hurt, it will produce lameness.

8. *Ani Marma.* Three fingers in size above the knee. When wounded it will be followed by much swelling and stiffness of the joint.

9. *Urbi,* middle of the thigh. If wounded much hemorrhage will follow, with death.

10. *Lohitaka,* a little above the last, and below the groin. When wounded, from the great hemorrhage, paralysis of that side will occur.

11. *Vitapa.* If the part between the testicles and groin be wounded, the person will become powerless with a loss of semen.

Both upper extremities have the same vital parts as the lower, differing only slightly from each other.

Vital parts of the Trunk.

1. *Guda.* If that in the anus be hurt, it will soon kill the person.

2. *Basti,* or urinary bladder, if wounded the person will soon die, excepting after the extraction of the stone. If one side be wounded, a fistula will form, but the person will not die. Should the vital parts in both sides be wounded, the person will die.

3. *Nábhí*, between *Amasia* and *Pakasia*, when wounded where the vessels originate, the person will die.

4. *Hridaya* or heart, which is between the two breasts within the thorax. If wounded the person will soon die.

5. *Stanamula* is in two parts, situated below the breast; and is two fingers breadth in size. If wounded death will be produced by the severe cough, and asthma thus produced.

6 *Stanarohita*, above the breast two fingers breadth, if wounded severe cough and asthma will take place, by the visera being filled up with blood.

7. *Apalápa*, in the axilla. When wounded under the axilla, a great discharge of blood and pus will precede death.

Vital parts of the Back.

Should the loins on each side of the back (*Koteekotorna*) be wounded above the sacrum, from the blood lost, the person will become of a yellow or bad colour, and die.

1. *Apastamba.* The two vessels which convey *bayu* in the chest. If wounded cough and asthma will produce death.

2. *Kakundara.* The side of the spine near the buttocks when wounded is followed by a loss of feeling, and the person cannot move the inferior parts of the body, which become paralized.

3. *Nitamba.* When the sensible parts of the two buttocks have been wounded, the lower limb shrinks up, and becomes weakened, and the person dies.

4. *Parswasandu* is situated on each side of the trunk and lower part of the abdomen (iliac region); when wounded the person will die, from the flow of blood from the organs.

5. *Vrihati*, on each side of the spine, near the breast; the man if wounded there, will die from the great hemorrhage.

6. *Angsafalaka*, at the upper part of the spinal column, when wounded, the arm becomes insensible, immoveable, and dries up.

7. *Angsa.* If the shoulder joint be wounded it disables the arm.

Vital parts above the trunk.

There are 37 vital parts above the trunk; of which two are on each side of the trachea. There are four vessels called *neela* (blue) and two (*manya*); which if wounded or bruised the person cannot speak, or the voice becomes changed, and he loses his taste.

2. *Sira Matrika*, on each side of the neck, there are two vessels; if wounded the person will soon die.

3. *Krikatika*, or the joint between the head and neck, if wounded, the head is always in motion.

4. *Bidura*, under the lobe of the ear, if wounded the person becomes deaf.

5. *Fana*, should the inside of the two nostrils be wounded, he cannot smell.

6. *Apanga*, below the extremities or above the eyebrows, if diseased or wounded the person will become blind.

7. *Abarta*, above the eyebrows, if wounded, they produce blindness, and diseases of the eye.

8. *Sangkha*, the temples, if wounded the person will soon die.

9. *Utkhapa*, above the temples, if wounded, the individual will live as long as the instrument is in the wound, but if removed he will die. Should it be allowed to remain, and medicine be given to discharge the instrument it may drop out of the wound, and the person may live.

10. *Sthapani*. Between the eyebrows, the same effects will be produced as in the last case.

11. *Simanta*, the five joints of the head, if wounded, will produce fear, insensibility; madness, and death.

12. *Sringataka*, should the vessels at the union of the eyes, nose, ears, and tongue be wounded, the person will soon die.

13. *Adhipati*, inside of the upper part of the head, at the passage of the vessel along the bone (lateral sinus) wounds will soon destroy the person

In operations, sensible parts are to be avoided and a Surgeon and Physician should know all these parts.

When a member is cut off, the parts contract, and less blood will often flow; but if wounded in a vital part it will generally cause death, by the number of vessels that are divided, while the deranged air produces much pain. The person dies in such cases, as a tree will die if the roots be divided. Hence if the vital parts be wounded, as in the palm of the hand, the arm is to be amputated to save the individual's life. Should a person live after such injuries, the parts will be left in a state of weakness, and his recovery will depend entirely upon the skill of his medical attendant.

If a bone of the head or breast be broken, it is to be raised or removed by the assistance of instruments. Wounds of the legs or arms will not be fatal, if the vital parts have escaped. In these vital parts the qualities of the moon, air, strength (*tej*), and *raja*, *satwa*, and *tama gun*, and also life (*Jivátmá*) are retained in considerable quantities. Hence, the fatal effects which usually occur from injuries of these parts. The senses become imperfect or destroyed, the understanding becomes changed, and various kinds of pain ar produced in such wounds, followed by death. When the fatal termination of wounds of vital parts is prevented at the time of the injury, death will be produced, some days after, with much suffering and weakness. In those situations, where injuries do not produce fatal consequences, but an imperfect action of the part, they are cured by the skill and care of the surgeon By wounds in such situations death is produced on the instrument being withdrawn, by the escape of air (*váyu*), &c. If wounded near a vital part, and there is a bad surgeon, the person will become a cripple.

There are five varieties, or degrees, of vital parts. In one variety the person when wounded dies quickly, of which there are 19; another in a few days, of which there are 33; one when an external substance enters, it produces a fatal effect, as soon as it is withdrawn, there are 3 such parts; another kind produces lameness, 44 are of this kind; another produces only pain, of which there are 8.

When any of these parts are injured, it destroys the individual, from the portion of life it contains. Those that produce death suddenly, have the quality of fire and, like it, quickly destroy. The kind that destroy life only on the instrument being withdrawn, which had inflicted the wound, is in consequence of the part having the qualities of air (*váyu*). In this case, the external instrument closes up the air, &c.; and as soon as it is removed they escape, and the person dies. That which produces pain and lameness has the qualities of the moon; as it is cool, and steady, and retains life. That which produces pain has the quality of fire and air; by increasing which, the pain is produced. Some suppose that pain is produced by the injury of the five elements

When the five varieties of sensible parts, the vessels, &c., are wounded; the effect is increased by the number, and the person dies. If only four are wounded, he will live a few days. When three are wounded, and the instruments removed, the person will die soon after its extraction. If two are injured, an imperfect action of the part will be the consequence; and if only one be injured, there will only be pain.

These four varieties of vessels are generally contained in sensible parts; and retain the body in a healthy state: but if the sensible parts are wounded, the air is increased; it passes through the four species of vessels, produces much pain, and causes fainting, and death. Should an external substance be required to be withdrawn from a wound, the surgeon must first carefully observe the sensible parts, and then remove the instrument. If the vital parts are wounded towards their centre it will produce death in a few days; and it will produce an imperfect action of the part, when wounded on one side. Those vital parts which produce death on the instrument being discharged, when wounded near the edge, will give much pain. The other parts give much pain when wounded directly ; but will produce little pain if wounded on one side.

The same symptoms and consequences will take place should the parts be lacerated, crushed, or burnt, as when wounded with a cutting instrument.

——:o:——

CHAPTER VI.

Spiritual Part of the body.

Life (*Prána*) consists in the combination of the soul (*bhútátmá* purusha, *jivátmá*); the mind (*manah*); the five senses (*Indriya*); and the three qualities of goodness, passion, and inertness, (Satwa, Raja, and Tama).

The soul (purusha) is a shadow or emanation from God (Paramátmá, Ishwar), the eternal, who is without beginning or end, is invisible, immortal, and is only known by reflection. When it bedews the five elements it produces the living body, and becomes by its actions evident. It is liable to decrease, and is influenced by medicine. There is no difference between the human soul and the soul of the world; this being only the exterior and condescending manifestation of God, while the human soul is its reflection into itself, and its elevation above itself is the Divine soul. The presence of the soul is necessary to animate the body; is full of knowledge and happiness, and is possessed of judgment. It produces waking and sleeping ; and combined with mind is like a coachman who directs the senses, and regulates the body, suffering from its wickedness, or enjoying its beatitude. The soul is always in a state of purity, when separated from the body; but neither acts usefully, nor otherwise, useless when united with mind, and the female energy (*vrakriti*).

When the soul enters the embryo it forms the knowledge (*vidyá*), and ignorance (*avidyá*), wickedness, &c., of that individual. In some medical works the soul is represented to exist in beasts, animals, and demigods according to its conduct in former states of existence. When the soul (Jivátmá) has bedewed the body with its twenty four qualities, it performs all the corporeal functions, and sensible actions; as vision, hearing, touch, &c.; and by it we speak and act. If it acts on good works, the person will be good, and his soul will go to heaven after death.

When the soul is united with the mind (manah); it produces desire, activity, enmity, happiness, grief, misery, intelligence, exertion, judgment, memory, dexterity, and useful knowledge. It produces expiration and inspiration, closing and opening the eyelids, understanding, reflection, consideration, memory, the exercise of the arts, and performs the action of the senses.

The mind (manah) is a quality or power of the soul by which the person thinks and reasons. It is incomprehensible, and is known by its actions through those of the senses. As it is single only, one sense can act at the same time, as it requires the presence of the mind for the comprehension of any thing, and the understanding with ideas of its own operations.

The mind is chiefly situated in the head, between the eyebrows; others suppose that it is in the heart, and resembles the light of a lamp, by which the person knows, sees, hears, tastes, and moves. It proceeds from itself, as the silk worm weaves its thread from itself, and forms its own house, which it regulates, and in which the different qualities (*guns*) are produced. When, disposed to separate from the body it is drawn back by these qualities, as a loadstone retains a piece of iron, by their mutual influences; in which situation it remains immoveable. (Tantra).

Some say that the soul (Jivátmá), and the mind (manah) are the same essence; as there can be no soul without mind, nor mind without the soul.

The five elements from the five organs of sense, (Indriya) as the nose, ears, &c. ; the five objects of sense (Indriyártha), as sound smell, &c. ; and the five perceptive judgments. Above these is placed the mind, which is incomprehensible by them, and is alone rendered evident through the action of the senses. These are deranged by too great or too little exercise, while moderate exercise retains them in good health.

From these remarks it appears that the soul, the emanation from the deity, united with the mind and senses, perform all the vital actions of the body. The body, mind, and soul are considered, therefore, as the three pillars which support the living system.

——:o:——

CHAPTER VII.

Nature of Temperaments.

The opinion of the Hindus as to the formation, and condition of the world, afforded a natural means of explaining the temperaments, or peculiar qualities, of the body. The predominance of one or more of the humours; and the qualities of goodness, passion, and inertness, explained the peculiarities of habit, and character; and, as more shades were observed, in these the simple excess of one or more of these agents, were explained by their peculiar mixtures which produced the dispositions of the Gods, sages, demons, and the lower animals. The latter being only supposed to be inferior states of the animal body, which in a higher condition form man. These explain the theory of the temperaments found in our Medical works.

At the time of the mixture of semen and female blood whatever humour, whether air, bile, and phlegm, is in excess produces that particular temperament. Hence there are seven temperaments, one being produced by an excess of air, another of bile, and a third of phlegm; a fourth, fifth, and sixth, from an excess of two of these humours ; and a seventh temperament is produced by an excess of three humours, air, bile and phlegm.

1. When air is in excess the person is not inclined to sleep, or to become warm. His disposition is bad, and he becomes a thief ; is proud, and has no honour ; is always singing and dancing ; his hands and feet split, his hair and nails are dry, and he is always angry and boisterous. He speaks untruths, he is always grinding his teeth and biting his nails, he is always impatient, is not a firm friend, is changeable, and forgets good actions. His body is slender and dry, he always walks fast, is always in motion, and his eyes are always rolling. He dreams that he is flying about the air, friends are few and his riches of little value. Such persons as have an excess of air have the disposition of the goat, jackall, hare, camel, dog, vulture, crow, and ass.

2. A person with an excess of bile perspires much, and he has a bad smell. His skin is of a yellowish colour, his flesh is soft, his nails, eyes, pallet, tongue, lips, and the palms of his hands, and soles of his feet are of a copper colour ; his fortune is bad, and his hair becomes soon gray, the upper part of his head bald, and his skin wrinkled as if by age. He eats much, and dislikes warm articles of food, is soon angry, and is as soon pacified, is of moderate strength, and does not live long. His memory is good, he is a good man of business, and speaks accurately, and to the purpose. His appearance is fine, and in company he excells in speaking. He dreams of gold, and yellow flowers, fire, lightning and falling meteors, dislikes saluting a person, and is angry at others not doing so, is never content, &c. His disposition resembles serpents, owls, cats, monkies, tigers, and bears.

3. Phlegm in excess produces a light greenish or blue colour of the body. The person's fortune is propitious, he is pleasant to look on and handsome, likes sweet things, is grateful, constant, just, and forgiving, and is not covetous, is strong and understands with difficulty, and is an implacable enemy. His eyes are white, his hair is fine, black, and waving. He is wealthy, and his voice is strong and loud. He dreams of lilies, geese, and

large fine tanks. The angles of his eyes are red, his colour pleasing, and his members are well formed. His regard mild, his disposition is very good (*satwagun*), and he is charitable. He is active, honours respectable persons, and is kind to them; and knows the sciences. He retains his friend, and health remains constant; he is careful, but gives much. He is of the nature of Bramhá, Indra, Shiva, and Varuna; of lions, horses, elephants, cows, and bulls, and of the bird upon which Vishnu rides (*Garura*) (something between a man, and a bird like a goose).

When two or three humours are in excess, they are known by the combination of the two or three classes of symptoms.

Some suppose that the disposition is derived from the elements of the body. In this case air, fire, and water resemble the temperaments of air, bile, and phlegm; and the temperament of earth produces a large and strong body, and the person can suffer much. When there is an excess of pure ether the man is holy, lives long, and the external openings of the body are large. The disposition of individuals are either satwa, raja, or tama; that is good, passionate, or inert.

When the qualities of the Gods predominate in the embryo, the following will be the indications. When the qualities of the God Bramhá predominates in the body, the person will remain clean, religious, and learned in the *Vedas*; is charitable, hospitable, performs ceremonies, and prays to his Guru.

If the quality of *Indra* be in excess in the body at conception; the individual will be great, magestic, and powerful, and employs many dependants.

If the qualities of neptune (*Varuna*) be in excess he is always desirous of cool things, is patient under suffering, is of a yellowish colour, and his hair is like that of a lion. He speaks pleasantly or kindly.

The qualities of the God of riches (*Kuvera*) predominating, the person will be a peace maker, have much wealth, have many children, will be careful, rich, and fond of collecting wealth.

With the disposition of the God of music (*Ganddharva*) predominates. the person will have a desire for good smelling things, and flowers, and will be always wishing to dance, sing, and play.

The disposition of the angel of death (*Yama*), or judge after death, are as follows. The person acts agreeable to orders, and acts properly, has no fear, has memory, is always clear, is not angry, is not ignorant, has no hatred.

The person with a disposition of the sages *(Rishis)* is always pronouncing the names of the Gods; follows the orders of the shastras, and always remains pure and prays frequently. He has much knowledge, especially of the arts. When the satwaguna predominates in the embryo, the individual will possess these qualities.

The bad in disposition are those in whom the qualities of the demons (*Asuras*) predominate. These persons will be very rich, and inspire terror; they are great warriors, fierce, and always inclined to oppress people. They eat once a day, and require good things and never perform the usual ceremonies, on such occasions.

With the qualities of *Serpents*, such persons are always hot, are jugglers, fearful, fierce, forget persons, and do not act fairly.

Birds. A person with this disposition is not inclined to change his work; indulges in lust, is always eating, angry, and restless.

Rákhyasa or Giants. Such a person is constant to one work, he produces fear, and calumniates, acts unfairly to others, and has much pride.

Pihsách or devil. The person always wants to eat the fragments of others meals, is of a hot disposition; rejoices in wickedness, is courageous, and has no shame.

Preta (demon). His disposition is difficult to discover. The person is always lazy, and always wishing to act improperly, is covetous, and is not generous. The above six dispositions have much passion.

Persons with much of the qualities of *Beasts* (*Pashu guna*), have a bad memory and act badly; they are always dreaming that they are with women; do not work themselves, and entice others from work.

One with the disposition of *Fish* is always changing, has no sense, is always fearful, always wants water, and will injure others.

Men having the disposition of *Trees*, always wish to remain in one place, are always eating, will not work.

A physician is to notice such dispositions, and in his practice to act so as to remove an excess, or increase a deficiency.

———:o:———

CHAPTER VIII.

Ages.

There are three ages, childhood (bálya), manhood (madhya), and decrepitude (vàrddhakya).

1st. Childhood extends to the 15th year, and is distinguished by three stages:—

a. Period of suckling to 1 year.

b. The period in which milk and rice are the food; which extends to the second year.

c. When the food is rice; which extends from the 3rd to the 15th year, during which time phlegm is in excess.

2nd. Manhood (madhya) extends from the 16th to the 70th year; and is divided into four periods.

a. Vriddhi or growth, which extends from the 16th to the 20th year.

b. Jauvana. From the 20th to the 30th year.

c. Sampùrnatá, from the 30th to the 40th year; when all the humours, senses, strength, (bala) are in their full developement.

d. Háni, from the 40th to the 70th year; when all the powers of the organs are gradually diminishing. Bile is at this period in excess.

3rd. Decrepitude (*Várddhakya*) extends from the 70th year till the person's death; during which the humours, senses, strength, and animation diminish daily. The muscles become soft, and flaccid, the hair turns gray, and falls off, the body becomes bent, and the person is afflicted with coughing, asthma, and other such diseases. He cannot perform any work; and other signs of decrepitude appear; like an old house in the rainy season with many props. In this period of life, air is in excess, and nervous diseases prevail.

It is supposed the male at 25, and the female at 16 years of age, arrive at their perfection in figure and strength.

In youth and in old age, the application of fire, caustics (actual and potential cauteries), blisters, &c., and the use of strong purgatives are to be avoided; or when required they are to be administered in a weaker form than usual, and administered by degrees. There are likewise fat, thin, and middle sized individuals. In the first the humours are to be diminished; in the second increased; and in the third the humours are to be preserved in the same state. Some of these thin persons are strong, and fat individuals weak. Among all the principles of our treatment the strength of the person should first be observed; as without it, the administration of many medicines, and the performance of operations is improper.

——:o:——

CHAPTER IX.

On death (*Mrityu*).

Death is the separation of the soul from the body; of which there are one hundred and one ways in which a person may die; one of which at the time appointed, is natural death, which takes place about the hundredth year of age; the others are accidental, which occur from numerous causes, as bad living, intemperance, poisons, fire, lightning, drowning, sin, &c.; these are to be guarded against by care, medicines, and prayers. Man is like a coachman driving his own carriage; if this be well made, and if he continue to drive cautiously, it will go a long time; but, if he drives it upon bad roads, the wheels will get injured, and the carriage will be soon worn out.

Should he indulge too much in the gratification of the senses, he will die like a deer, which is supposed to be deluded to its destruction by the sweet sounds of the lute which the hunters use; should he indulge in lust, like the elephant; in sight, like the butterfly in approaching the lamp; in smell, like the bee which is inclosed and crushed in the flower, which has attracted it by its smell; in taste, like the fish by the fisherman's hook. So beware of indulging too much in any of the pleasures of sense, else it will lead, in like manner, to your destruction!

Death is always near; and when it occurs, nothing but the sins and virtuous actions which have been performed, accompany the soul*. "When a person leaves his corpse, like a log or a lump of clay, on the ground, his kindred retire with averted faces; but his virtue accompanies his soul. Continually, therefore, let him collect virtue, for the sake of securing an inseparable companion with which he may traverse a gloom, how hard to be traversed! For, in his passage to the next world, neither his father nor his mother, nor his wife, nor his son, nor his kinsmen, will remain in his company: his virtue alone will adhere to him. Single is each man born; single he dies; single he receives the reward of his good, and single the punishment of his evil deeds"

The wise and foolish, the great in rank, the low in condition, all die in the same way. As a rich man has more foresight than the poor and ignorant, so the former is more anxious about his death, which must happen to all; but it is the holy man who has least dread of its occurrence, as being more prepared than others for the necessary change.

After death, the body is like a house without a tenant; and the five elements slowly separate and join their like; the atoms of

---

*"A mansion infested by age and by sorrow, the seat of maladies, harrassed with pains, haunted with the qualities of darkness, and incapable of standing long; such a mansion of the vital soul let its occupier always cheerfully quit." Menu, ch. VI 77 p. 183.

† Menu Chap. IV 239, 240. 241, 243. The same idea is thus expressed in another sanskrit work. 'The wise man meditates on the acquisition of knowledge and riches, as if not subject to sickness or death; and cultivates virtue as if death had already seized him by the hair," (Hitopadesha).

earth join the earth, the watery mix with water, &c. Death is therefore called in Sanskrit *Panchatwa*, or separation and passage to the five elements. To promote this separation of the elements after death, which would be defiled if buried, and to purify them in their passage from the body, so as to enable the earth, air, fire, water, and ether, of which the body is composed, to join the mass of the same elements which compose the world, the bodies of Hindus are burnt. "What then dies? Not the body, for it only changes its form; and certainly not the soul! Why then regret the death of relations and friends, if they have passed through life with propriety! Such grief is indeed natural, for it is universal, but it is the offspring of our ignorance and our selfishness.

As the body is continually changing in its progress through life, so death is merely one of these changes. The body is frail, but the soul is incorruptible. Some say that an infant is born, that a person is dead; that this one is the murderer, and that body the murdered: but these are foolish exclamations! The body is alone destroyed, not the soul; as it only changes its position, like a person who casts off his worn-out garments. Cutting instruments may wound him, water may purify him, and air may dry him up, but the soul remains always the same. Those who are born must die, and whoever dies must be born again; and as the elements were invisible and separated, before the formation of the body, in like manner they are again separated and dispersed upon its dissolution.

At the moment of death the material elements of the body separate, and the vital soul, which has an invisible body (*linga sharira*), resembles the form of the body it had inhabited, and retains the organs of sense and of action. On separating from one, it joins itself to another, and according to the actions the person had performed in his former state of existence, so will be his future condition. As a seed of an inferior or superior order, so will the plant be; thus may the soul animate a man who will grow old in a deformed and diseased body; with a mind wicked and miserable. This union of the liberated soul, and its juncture with the seed of another body, takes place immediately; as a leech on leaving one piece of grass, must immediately attack itself to another. Thus that immutable Power, by acting and reposing alternately, revivifies and destroys, in eternal succession, this whole assemblage of immoveable and locomotive creatures.

Beatitude is to be obtained by the coercion of the members, by abstaining from hurting and afflicting, or giving pain to sentient creatures; when the individual becomes fit for immortality." Menu, $ 60. When the vital soul has been purified by the good deeds which have occurred in the body, it is absorbed into that supreme essence, the divine soul of all beings, which withdraws his energy, and placidly slumbers. Menu adds.—"Let him not wish for death let him not wish for life ; let him expect his appointed time, as a hired servant expects his wages." (Chap. VI. $ 45, page 178).

—:o:—

THERAPEUTICS.

The Hindu sages suppose that diseases are either produced by sins committed in a former state of existence ; by derangements of the humours ; or by the combination of these two causes. The former class can only be removed by certain sacrifices, prayers, penances, and gifts ; the second class only, are those which may be removed by the employment of remedies. By this means, the physician knows that when a disease does not yield to the employment of proper remedies, it must belong to the first class of diseases, and will be only cured by the means prescribed in such cases. The third class of diseases are produced by a combination of sins and derangement of humours ; these require for their cure the employment of prayers, and of a proper course of medicine.

The means employed by the physician for curing diseases, will be considered under the following heads.

1stly—*Hygeology* or regimen.

2ndly—*Materia Medica* and *Pharmacy*, or preparation of Medical agents ; and,

3rdly—*Surgery*, or all manual applications for the cure of injuries and diseases.

—:o:—

CHAPTER I.

Hygeology.

The Hindu Legislators appear to have been convinced, at a very early period, of the importance of a knowledge of the means of preserving health, as we find various laws were enacted for this purpose ; and in order to enforce these precepts among a rude people, incapable of appreciating their importance, and disinclined to obey them, religion was employed to afford its powerful assistance. This explains the numerous precepts of Hygeine which we find in the sacred works of the most ancient people ; and which necessarily vary in their nature with the climate, and the character and habits of the people. In the sacred works of the Hindus, these laws are so numerous that it is impossible that any single individual should follow them. On this account they are probably more generally neglected than they would have been had the catalogue been less numerous. A fact much to be regretted, since the climate requires so much more attention to Hygeine than a more temperate one. The most important Hygeian precepts will be considered under the heads of relative and personal precepts.

——:o:——

SECTION I.

Relative duties.

Climate of India.—The extensive country known among the ancients by the title of *India* within the Ganges, has been famous, from the earliest ages, for the wisdom of its sages, the richness if its productions, and the fertility of its soil. It is now named Hindusthan, and is bounded by the River Indus on the west, and north by the Himalaya mountains; on the south by the Indian ocean, and on the east by the hills and forests of Assam. From the magnificent range of Mountains in the north, Hindusthan consists mostly of extensive plains, which posses a rich and black loam, consisting of clay with a considerable proportion of silicious sand, fertilized by various salts, and by decayed animal and vegetable matter where it is watered by the Ganges. In other parts of the Panjab, in Bengal, and the adjacent provinces, there is a considerable extent of clayey soil. In Sind and Guzerat the soil is sandy, and in Malwa a rich deep black mould prevails. The soil is generally unproductive in Gundwana, and Orissa; and near the coasts, of the Malabar and Coromandel sides, the soil is sandy and generally very poor, while the Table land of the Peninsula of India is generally fertile. The eastern part of Hindusthan is intersected by numerous branches of large rivers, which irrigate the rich plains of Bahar, and at not a very distant period seems to have formed, from its rich deposits, the large, flat and fruitful province of Bengal, to which the following remarks principally apply:—

In the Hindu medical works three climates are mentioned, the moist, the hot, and the mixed, or temperate.

The moist country (*Anúpa*) is distinguished by having much water upon its surface, by being intersected by rivers and being irregular in its surface, with high mountains, and tall trees. In such a climate the air is cool, and the wind temperate. There lillies and other water flowers abound; geese, ducks, cranes, and other such birds are common; and fish and serpents are numerous. In such a situation the inhabitants are unhealthy, and are short-lived.

There diseases of air and phlegm abound, and the inhabitants are fat, indolent, and weak. In such situations the juices of the body require to be dried by the use of hot, dry, and light food, in small quantities; so as to strengthen the internal fire.

The second or Hilly country *(Jángala)*, is characterized by the heat of the air, and by the prevalence of hot winds, by large and arid plains covered with dwarf trees and prickly shrubs, growing at a distance from each other. In such a country there is little water upon the surface, and it can only be obtained by digging wells. In such a climate the bamboo, the *ákanda* (Calotropis gigantea), the *kul* (Zizyphus Jujuba), *yagyadumur* (Ficus glomerata); the *Gáb* and *Kenduka* (Diospyros glutinosa and Diospyros melanoxylon), and the like trees are found. The inhabitants of such climates are remarkable for having little muscle, for having large bones, and being good workmen. The diseases of air and bile are most frequent; but the climate is healthy, and the inhabitants are long-lived.

When the two above climates are found in the same country it is called mixed, or temperate (*Sádhárana*). The heat and cold are more equable, the derangements of the air, bile, and phlegm are equalized, and the climate is favourable to life. The inhabitants of such a fortunate region are stronger, more vigorous and healthy, than in either of the other two climates. It is, however, worthy of remark that a person who is attentive to his regimen may live with impunity in any of the above climates.

When a person is born in a particular climate, and has air, bile, and phlegm deranged, on going to a worse one, the derangement of the humours increases and will destroy the person; or if he journies to another and better climate the tendency to disease will be removed.

Whatever is the custom of a climate as to food, clothing, &c., is to be followed, when the change will not produce any bad effect. If the disease is recent, and the individual strong, it will be cured easily; but this will be retarded or promoted, by the predisposition of the climate and season to affect such diseases. A complicated disease will always be cured with great difficulty. When one remedy does not produce the expected good effect, another should be substituted for it. But if a remedy does some good, it should be continued, in preference to a hundred others which have not been tried. If no other treatment can be devised in such severe diseases, the one adopted should be continued. The remedies must be varied according to the climate, season, age, and constitution of the affected person. If this is not observed, bad effects will follow, and other disorders will be produced.

Time (*Kàla*) like a God is produced perfect in root, stem, and branches. It has neither beginning nor end; or is like a wheel which is always turning. It produces life and death, and the good and bad qualities of every thing, excepting that indistinguishable something, called the ultimate elements of the world (*Paramánu*), from whence another world will be ultimately formed.

2nd. Of time and of the seasons. Time is divided as follows:—15 winks of the eye are equal to a *káshthá*; 30 *káshthá* 1 *Kalà*; 20 *kalás* 1 *Muhúrta;* and 30 *Muhùrtas* to a day and a night; 15 days 1 Pakhsa or fortnight; one of which is the dark (*Krishna*) and the other light (*Shukla*)*; 2 Paksha* 1 month (*mása*); 2 months are equal to one *Ritu* or season; 3 *Ritu* 1 Ayana; 2 Ayana 1 year; and five years make one Yug. The sun forms the distinguishing qualities of the seasons. It dries the earth, which is softened by the moon; and with the assistance of wind it promotes the growth, and life of organized matter.

Seasons (*ritu*) are divided into *Uttaràyana,* when the sun is supposed to be north of the equator; and *Dakhsináyana,* the six months when it is supposed to be south of the equator.

The seasons are six in number, each consisting of two siderial months each The succession of them is always the same; but the vicissitudes of climate in them will depend on the position of the Equinoctial colure. Sometimes the year is reckoned by *Ayana,* from September (*Shràvan*), and January (*Màgha*).

a. Cold Months, Shishira, (Mágha and Phálguna or January and February), during which warm clothing is to be used. Air is in excess during this season; when the broths of animals, fish, amphibious animals, and substances mixed with ghee, are to be taken. The wine called *Sídhú* is to be used, and honey mixed with water; milk and different sweetmeats; fat, and new rice; and warm water is always to be used. The body should be well rubbed with oil, which should also be applied to the head. The person should sleep in a room near the centre of the house, so as to be warm, and removed from the wind. Warm clothing should always be used during this season. The food should be in small quantities, and hot and dry substances should be avoided.

b. Spring Months, Vasanta (March and April). All organized bodies are generated during this, or the spring season. The air is then clear, flowers are numerous, and the country looks beautiful, with the new leaves on the trees; and man is cheered by the song of birds and the hum of bees. The south wind now begins to blow. In this season the phlegm predominates, and its diseases appear. The internal fire is diminished. Emetics and purgatives should be employed, and heavy, oily, and sweet substances are to be avoided, and sleeping in the day time should also be guarded against Bodily exercise should be used. Tepid water should be used for every purpose, and the body should be rubbed with sandal and other fragrant woods. Use barley and wheat, the flesh of deer, hares, and wild fowls. Drink *Sidhu* and *Mada* (wine) and reside in a garden with women.

c. Hot Months, Ghrishma, (May and June). The hot season, in which the rays of the sun are powerful, with warm wind from the south, which makes this season oppressive and unpleasant, increases air, produces debility, and affects even the understanding. The earth becomes hot and dry, the rivers diminish, the water is warm and light, and the earth appears to smoke. Birds and deers proceed in search of water; and the juice of plants is raised, and their qualities are diminished; creepers, grass, and the leaves of trees are diminished and fall off, dried and decayed.

During this season the diseases of air prevail. In it use cool liquids and food prepared with ghee. Drink different sherbets, and use broth of wild animals and birds; eat rice with milk and ghee; by which means a person will not lose his strength. Little wine is to be used, and always mixed with much water. Salt, acid, and hot things are to be avoided. Do not take much exercise. Reside in a cool garden with a large tank and flowers; avoid excesses in venery. Sleep during the day in a cool room, and at night repose in the upper rooms, and use the hand *pankha* (fan) sprinkled with sandal wood and water.

d. The *Rainy season, Varshá* (July and August). During this season the sky is loaded with clouds; the wind easterly, with much lightning and thunder; new grass and leaves appear, the rainbow is beautiful; numerous graceful creepers of the class of convolvulus appear, of various colours, white, blue, and pink. The banks of the rivers, and the trees upon them are broken away by the force of the torrents; the tanks and lakes are adorned by varied coloured lilies; much clear water continues upon the surface of the earth, and vegetation proceeds rapidly. There are many clouds which obscure the sun and planets, and much rain falls. Towards the end of the season there is little thunder. The clouds diminish the light and heat, and with the water of the moon (dew), reduce the juices of living animals, and their strength. Water is impure, during this season; the body is soft, the cold damp air affects the strength of the internal fire, and the food is burnt in the body, by the increased quantity of bile.

In *Varshá* the appetite is diminished by the derangement of the humours, caused by the heat and moisture; and new water has an acid quality. The food should be sparingly given, and should neither be too hot nor very cold; sleeping in the day time and exposure to the climate are to be avoided, as also the use of river water. Too much exercise, exposure to the sun, and venery are to be avoided. Water mixed with honey is to be used, and in a cloudy day take food mixed with salt, acids, and ghee ; barley, wheat, and old rice are to be used, with the broths of wild animals and fowls. The wine of grapes, and fresh water which has been boiled, are to be drunk. Anoint the body with fragrant oil, and bathe daily, use light and white clothes, and live in a high and dry house.

5. The *Moist Season, Sharat,* (September and October). During this season the sky is overcast with white clouds, and the tanks are full of water lilies. The earth is covered with *salt,* and many trees are rooted up and die. The surface of the earth appears irregular.

During this season the sky is clean, with white broken clouds ; the air is sultry, the moisture on the ground dries, the sun's rays increase in strength ; and by the changes in temperature bile and cough produce diseases. In this season the water is pure, and may be used freely for bathing, and for drinking. Vegetation is vigorous, the country beautiful ; and food produced during this season is not good, but is improved by keeping, if it admits of this. The lakes are covered with lilies, reeds, and white flowers. Ducks, &c., abound.

Diseases of the Bile prevail in this season. The food and drink to be used should be light, cool and sweet ; with tonic and bitter articles. Such food as wild fowls, hares, and animals of the same kind ; mutton is also good, with rice, barley, wheat, and the like. Use purgative medicines and blood-letting ; while exposure to the sun and heat and night air are to be avoided, more particularly the east wind ; sleeping during the day, too, is to be avoided ; as also fat, oil, fish, the flesh of amphibious animals, and acids. The clothes should be light, and clean.

6. *Cold season, Haimanta* (November and December). The water during this season becomes clear, cool, and heavy. The rays of the sun diminish in influence ; and phlegm is increased, as is exemplified in its discharge from the nose, from colds.

The Bilious diseases, which were common during the last season, diminish during the present, in which healthy, cool, northerly airs prevail. A mistiness hangs over tanks and rivers, like clothes which cover the body. The cows, sheep, buffaloes, and elephants look clean, and several trees such as priyangu, punnága, &c., are in flower.

The seven last days of one season, and the seven first of the new one, are called *ritusandhi* (the junction of seasons). During this time the regimen of the former is gradually to be left off, and that of the succeeding one substituted.

Diseases from Bile are cured by the cold season; those from phlegm diminish in the hot season, and from air during the moist months. The morning is like the spring season, noon like the hot, and evening like the rainy season. The same changes occur in the night; the first watch being like the rainy season; the second like the moist; and the morning watch, like the cold season. In these times, air, bile, and phlegm increase like the seasons; and in the process of digestion they increase in the same manner; during the first stage phlegm predominates, then bile, and lastly air.

The irregularities of the seasons produce an unfavourable effect on health, and both food, water, and medicines lose their good effects, and various diseases are produced. It is during these irregularities that plagues appear, devils rage, and sin prevails. Poisonous air often produces the same effects. The odours of flowers mixed with poisonous air produces derangements of phlegm, difficult breathing, vomiting, discharges from the mouth and nose, headache, and fever. There is an influence of planets and stars, from the bad situation of dwelling houses, the place in which persons sleep and sit, and the diseases of the horse upon which he rides, is liable to effect the rider. These are to be prevented by changing the person's residence, by prayers, by the removal of sin, by different sacrifices and ceremonies, by the intercession of Brahmins, and by visiting holy places.

When a disease continues long, the situations of planets and stars are calculated; by which the long continuance of the disease is explained, and for the relief of which certain ceremonies and gifts are performed.

The heat of the fire cures diseases of air and phlegm. It also removes passing pains. It promotes the dejections, and removes shivering and discharges from the nose, mouth, and eyes. It increases the diseases of blood and bile, and during sleep retains the humours in a good state; it improves the colour of the body, strengthens it, removes dozing, and promotes happiness and internal warmth.

The heat of the sun when very strong, is drying; and promotes perspiration, faintness, giddiness, thirst, and the heat of the body. It increases the bad smell of the body, deepens the dark colour of the skin; and increases the diseases of the bile, and blood.

Shadows remove the bad effects of heat, as they have a sedative, cooling, and pleasant quality.

The smoke of fire increases bile and air.

Dew and mist increase phlegm and air.

Moonlight cures diseases of blood and bile.

Rain increases strength, is cooling, increases semen, sleep, languor, phlegm, and air.

Easterly wind increases phlegm, is cold, has a saltish quality, and is heavy. It diminishes appetite, increases laziness, the heat of the body, and strength. It produces diseases of the blood and bile, is bad for those with sores, or who are affected with poison, and diseases of phlegm. It removes the derangements of air. It is good for persons fatigued, and it diminishes the form of consumption produced by phlegm. It also give strength, and softens the body. A Southerly wind is pleasant, does not produce heat, and has a light and sedative quality. It is good for the eyes and strength, it cures diseases of blood and bile, and the air is not deranged by it. Westerly wind increases internal heat, dries the body, and diminishes the bulk of the body and strength; it produces a roughness of the skin, diminishes the strength, and health. It dries up phlegm and fat. Northerly wind is soft, cooling, light, agreeable, and slightly sedative. It promotes the dejections, and increases diseases of air, bile, and phlegm. In healthy individuals it increases the phlegm, and the strength. It is good for severe cough with bloody sputa, for diseases from poisons, and does not derange the humours.

The air from Pankhas, removes faintness, thirst, perspiration, fatigue, and heat. The Tál Pankha (common hand pankha) and chowry and cloth pankhas, cure deranged air, bile, and phlegm; are cooling, and increase happiness.

There are three prevailing seasons in Bengal, the cold, hot, and rainy seasons. From the end of February, and during March and a part of April, may be considered as spring months, and are the most agreeable of any of the year. Towards the end of March, and during the months of April, May, and a part of June the weather is very hot; and in the northern and more inland provinces a violent hot wind blows from the west, loaded with almost imperceptible particles of sand. In this season the weather is so oppressive as to confine the inhabitants to their houses, during the great heat of the day. Vegetation is destroyed, and these provinces are reduced to a burning tract of sand; while the air of the neighbouring mountains remains cool and pleasant, during these hot months

In the upper provinces the rains begin in April and May; but in the plains they do not commence till the beginning of June, and continue to full till the end of July. The rain disperses the accumulated heat, which would otherwise be insupportable. During the months of August and September the rain falls less frequently and copiously, and the long day and high altitude of the sun, with an atmostphere loaded with moisture, render the weather excessively oppressive and sultry; particularly when the air is calm, which is of frequent occurrence, as the Monsoon changes at this time. The cold season commences in the month of October, when dews are heavy; the cold increases, and during the months of November, December, and January, it is often intense in Bengal and Behar. In these provinces the cold has generally a damp disagreeable feel, whereas, in the northern and western provinces, snow and ice are common on the mountains, and the air is dry and bracing.

From such an extensive country, and variety of soil and climate, the vegetable and animal productions are of the most varied description in the different latitudes, heights, and exposures; and man himself affords great varieties in his physical and mental powers in the different situations and climates in which he resides. In general the head and face of the Hindu are small and oval, the nose and lips prominent and well formed, the eyes black, and the eyebrows regular, and full. The females are distinguished for the gracefulness of their forms, the softness of their skins, their long and black hair, dark eyes, and delicate persons. These peculiarities are marked in youth, but rapidly fade. The fairness of the skin also differs—depending on that of the parents, and on the occupation and exposure of the individual to the sun, &c.

——:o;——

SECTION 11.

Personal Duties.

The practitioner should give instructions to persons not only as to the manner of curing, but also of preventing the occurrence of disease. *

The following remarks will be considered under the heads of; duties—*a* rising from bed in the morning; *b* cleaning the mouth; *c* anointing the body; *d* exercise, shampooing, and rubbing the body; *e* bathing, *f* clothing, *g* food, and *h* sleeping.

a. It is proper to rise from bed sometime before sun rise, to perform the duties of nature, with the face towards the north.

b. After these duties the teeth are to be cleaned with a piece of a fresh branch of the nim or catechu tree, and the mouth and eyes and face are to be cleaned with water. Should these not be got, branches of any other kind of wood, not hollow, may be used.

* Bodies are cleansed by water, the mind is purified by birth, the vital spirit by theology and devotion, and the understanding, by knowledge. Manu P. 161 Ch. V.109.

Persons are not to clean the teeth when it produces vomiting, when the food is not properly digested (*ajirna*), in diarrhæa (*atisár*), in *shúl*, in diseases of the teeth, during the first eight days of fever, in asthma (*shwása*), when the mouth is dry, in cough, in epilepsy, in fainting, in headache, and in diseases of the eyes. The teeth should not be cleaned before the tenth year of the child's age.

When a powder is used for cleaning the teeth it is to be formed of honey, long-pepper, black-pepper, and dry-ginger, &c. This is used daily, and a soft brush of the above wood may be used. Cleaning the teeth promotes appetite and happiness.

For cleaning the tongue, a piece of gold, silver, or wood ten finger's breadth in length, with a thin edge, may be used as a scraper

The mouth is to be washed with water, ghee, oil, or the like; which strengthens the teeth, and promotes appetite.

c. The Hindus, and all Asiatics, anoint their bodies daily with oil, more especially their heads, ears, and feet; which they suppose is conducive to health, by increasing good fortune, improving the colour and softness of the skin, increasing happiness, sleep, life, strength, and curing perspiration, bad smells, and lassitude. It also diminishes the diseases of air and phlegm, increases the seven *dhátu*, and improves the marrow, and the colour of the skin, and the organs of sense. It also cures diseases of the feet, prevents painful cramps of the fingers; and as long as the head is kept moistened with oil, it prevents headache, improves the hair, and prevents its becoming gray. In all cases in which bathing is to be avoided, the anointing of the body will be advantageous to the person's health.

Mustard, or any other fragrant oil, is used for anointing the body. Anointing the face with sweet smelling oils, as females often do, retains the eyes healthy, and the face soft and pure, the mouth and lips like the lily, the eyelashes beautiful, and the skin clear like light. Using such, increases riches, children, and other desirable objects. Anointing the ears prevents deafness, &c., and the diseases of the nape of the neck, and of the condyles of the jaw. Anointing the feet improves the eyesight, and prevents the feet from cracking. The body should not be anointed at the beginning of fever, when the food is not digested, or after purging, vomiting, and enemas. The Hebrews, in like manner, especially their females, made much use of oil; and it was considered by them as a mark of esteem, and honour to offer oil to those that went to see them, so that they might anoint their heads. * The modern method of anointing the head at the coronation of kings is derived from this custom

* See Luke VII. V. 46.

The hot climate and slight clothing, and exposure to a burning sun, increases the action of the cutaneous vessels, and renders the skin hard and dry; and if perfect cleanliness is not observed, it becomes incrusted with its own discharges, and with foreign matter which erritates the part, and prevents the proper action of this important organ To prevent such a consequence, oil is ordered to be rubbed over the surface before it has been washed, by which it is rendered soft, and pliant; it also promotes an equable perspiration, and an excessive degree is avoided which would weaken the body. In this case the oil was mixed with other vegetable oils to render its effects more permanent. The metallic oxyds were sometimes, added so as to form ointments, liniments, and plasters. The latter medicines giving them a due consistence by their drying effects on the oils.

Several oils are prepared with those medicinal plants which are used internally, and are applied externally in different cases of disease; especially in old fevers, spasmodic, paralytic, rheumatic diseases, in affections of the mind, as madness, &c.; and these oils are supposed by the Hindus to be thus used more advantageously than when given internally. Medicines keeping the feet and the outlets of the body clean, promote health, and are good for the eyes and skin. After the person has adjusted his dress, prayers are to be offered up to the gods.

d. Exercise increases strength, prevents and cures diseases, by equalizing the humours; it prevents fatness and laziness, and strengthens the firmness of the body. It removes grief, increases the internal fire, and the body becomes lighter, more vigorous, and ready to work. It daily used, it prevents the bad effects of indigestible and unusual articles of food, and fat food so desired. Walking is always to be used, particularly by those persons who live on rich food; such exercise is to be used evening and morning, especially in the cold and spring months, while fatigue is avoided.

Persons with diseases of the blood and bile, with fever, difficulty of breathing, dizziness, asthma, fatigue, and all kinds of cough, and dryness of the body, should avoid exercise. When the mouth is always dry, with difficulty of breathing; in diseases of the air and bile, in boyhood and old age, after eating, and before the food is thoroughly digested, or when there are sores upon the body, exercise is to be avoided. When reduced in flesh by lust, such exercise tires and increases fever, phlegm and thirst; and increases diseases of the blood and bile. Should much exercise be taken, it produces cough, fever, and vomiting; after exercise quietude is proper, as it increases strength, cures a superabundance of fat, and removes the feeling of fatigue.

e. Shampooing cures diseased phlegm, air, and fat; the members are retained healthy, as well as the skin, and it increases internal heat. *Rubbing* the body is pleasant, cures *amasia*, improves the skin, and the body feels light; it also cures itching, small pimples, diseased air, and impurities in the abdomen. If the body be rubbed with a brush, the fire of the skin will be increased and perspiration then cures itching, and small tubercles. The nails, beard, mustachoes, and hair are to be cut every fifth day. The hair is to be combed and cleaned, which improves health.

f. Bathing. There are several kind of baths (*Snana*). The following are the most common:—1st. Cold bathing removes the inordinate heat of the body, fatigue, perspiration, itchiness, thirst, and promotes happiness and pleasure. It removes the impurities of the body, clears the senses, removes drowsiness and sin, increases semen, retains the blood pure, and increases the internal heat. If warm water is poured on the head, it is not good for the eyes: but the use of cold water strengthens vision. Bathing in very cold water in the winter deranges phlegm and air, and during the hot season warm bathing increases bile and blood. Bathing is not proper in diarrhœa (*atisár*), in the beginning of fever, in diseases of the ear, or in those of the air, in swellings of the abdomen, in indigestion, and after eating. Bathing the feet is to be used for removing impurities, local diseases, and fatigue It retains the eyes clean, increases semen, and prevents the approach of devils. Independent persons, such as rich merchants, bankers, talukdars and others, generally bathe at 10 or 11 o'clock, and after performing their ceremonies they breakfast. Shop-keepers, day-labourers, &c. eat, at 1 or 2 o'clock, and do not generally bathe till after 12 o'clock. There are some who bathe twice or thrice a day, but they are few in number. This description applies to the male inhabitants of towns. The higher class of females seldom bathe in rivers, but do so in tanks, in their respective gardens; or in warm water, between 10 and 11 o'clock. Widows of the lower class are not strict, and do not observe the rules of the *Shástras* regarding bathing.

The cold bath is used in some inflammatory fevers, and in madness (*unmáda*); and locally in some external inflammatory swellings (*vrana*).

2nd. *Avagáha snana*, or warm water bath. It is prepared with several medicinal plants, and is used either locally or generally; for relieving pain, in different kinds of fevers, spasmodic affections, &c.

3rd. Vapour Baths (*Ushmá snana*) are much employed by the Bengalis, more particularly for removing pain. They are made by heating a quantity of water in an earthen pot, over which a lid had been placed. The patient is first well rubbed with oil, and then sits on a chair over the pot of hot water, with a covering of clothes thrown over both. When any particular part of the body is pained, this only is exposed to the steam bath, and in other cases medicinal plants are added to increase the good effects of the remedy, as milk, *nim* leaves, and other such drugs.

4th. *Upanáha sweda* or hot cataplasms of medicinal plants. These are made into a paste, heated, and applied locally to relieve pain. In other cases these medicines are applied locally, with hot vapour. A tube is used to convey the vapour to the diseased part.

5th. *Tápa sweda* is the frequent application of a hot hand, a heated cloth, or a bag filled with hot sand or salt.* It is used for relieving local pain, and for promoting the warmth of the body, when it becomes cold, in any disease.

After bathing apply *Súrmà,* or antimony, to the edges of the eyelids ; which improves the sight, clears the itchiness, or any unhealthy humours of the eyes, and prevents the bad effects of the glare of the sun, and the diseases of the eyes in general. Persons should not use *Súrmà* who have sat up during the night, who are much fatigued, who have vomited, who have eaten recently or are feverish. Medicines are sometimes added for increasing some particular effect.

g. Clothing. After bathing, the body is to be well rubbed with a piece of clean cloth, which produces a good colour of the skin. Silk, and warm *red* clothes diminish the diseases of air and phlegm, and should be used in the winter season. The clothes should be light, cool, and thin during the hot weather In rainy and cold weather, warm *white* clothes of a medium thickness are to be used. Care must be taken always to wear clean clothes, which is good for the skin, looks well, and promote happiness and longevity.

A piece of cotton cloth tied round their middle is all the clothing the poorer classes have ; it is only when they appear in public that they add the turban, or piece of cloth to cover their heads and shoulders. The turban defends the head from heat and cold, and prevents the determination of the humours to the head. If the person uses it continually he will live long, and his head will remain clear, and cool. A single piece of coarse cotton cloth, several yards in length, is the usual dress of females. Such clothes, particularly with the addition of ornaments, prevent the approach of the Rakshyasas or devils, increase strength (*ojas*), improve good

* In some cases the earth is heated, and a plantain leaf is extended over it, upon which the person lies.

fortune, and retain the heart happy and contented. Sandals are to be put upon the feet to strengthen, and to protect them.

A paste of sandal wood, and other fragrant drugs, is then to be rubbed over the forehead, chest, and upper extremities. A prayer is offered up to God, and gifts presented to the *Bráhmins*.

The *Umbrella* protects the person from rain, wind, and dust; it diminishes perspiration, protects him from the influence of dew, retains the colour of the skin and eyes, and promotes health. A stick protects the person against beasts, and it prevents fatigue.

h. The *houses* are well adapted for the climate, being raised from the ground by prepared earth; with which the walls are likewise formed, and a thick thatch covers it, and extends beyond the walls so as to form a protection from the heavy rains. They are usually well ventilated in consequence of a space being left between the walls, and the thatch. These houses are divided into apartments to suit the convenience of the family, and the mud walls and thatched roof keeps them in an equable temperature. In some country, the houses of a family or tribe are usually built in the form of a square, or a series of squares, for their mutual protection. The open central space is usually kept clean, and is covered above, in days of festivity, when the prescribed ceremonies are performed. In some parts of the country their houses are made of sun-burnt or fire-burnt bricks, and the houses are often two, or more stories high. In many parts of the country the houses or villages are fortified to protect them from wild beasts, and from their enemies.

i. Diet. The Hindu medical writers usually commence the cure of a disease by arranging the diet that is to be followed by the sick person. So much do the Hindu Physicians rely upon diet that they declare that most diseases may be cured by following carefully, dietetic rules; and if a patient does not attend to his diet, a hundred good medicines will not remove the disease. The generality of diseases being supposed to be produced by derangement of the humours, if one or more are morbidly increased in quantity, their indications of cure are commenced by promoting the just balance of the elements and humours, by a judicious choice of aliments, and by such means as assist the vital principle on the completion of the assimilation. On this account they have not only been careful in describing the regimen, but also the food and drink for the different seasons, and even the vessels in which they should be kept.

Food gives strength, and colour to the body, and the essential part of life (*ojas*). It also supports the heat of the body, increases and diminishes the humour, retains these in their equilibrium; keeps the person happy, the senses active, and the memory retentive, while it supports life, and promotes longevity.

The different articles of food which are employed to nourish the body will be considered under the head of general remarks on food derived from the vegetable, and animal kingdoms; with a few remarks on condiments; under which will be considered articles derived from the mineral kingdom, including water and medicinal liquids. The form in which food is taken into the body will vary its effects upon the system; but some articles of food are always wholesome, even from birth to old age; as water, milk, rice, ghee, &c. A second kind is always dangerous to health as fire, escharotics, and poisons; the one burning the part, the second destroying it, and the third killing the individual.

Some substances are injurious to the system when mixed and prepared in a particular manner, when they become like poison. Thus pumpkins, mushrooms, bamboo-shoots, plumbs, dried vegetables, unleavened bread, goats or sheeps flesh, pigs flesh, salt spirits, when eaten, or drank with milk, resemble poison. Some, times articles of food act on the humours favourably or unfavourably, according to the state of the body. One article will be good for deranged air, and another bad for deranged bile, &c. Again the state of the article will modify its effects. Red rice, which grows in the cold season, wheat, barley, and other grain of the same kind are good, and preserve health; whereas rice which has sprouted, *másh kaláy* (Phaseolus radiatus), fat, honey, milk, jagree, when eaten with the flesh of domestic or amphibious animals, or with fish, are so bad as to resemble poison. Milk with honey, and vegetables in general should not be used together. Pepper and a kind of vegetable called *kákámáchi* are not to be used; as also honey, and hot water. When animal food is to be used, the bile is to be carefully evacuated, or it will derange the person's health.

Butter-milk, with honey, ghee, a variety of fishes, and the flesh of deer, are not to be eaten together; fish and milk, or its preparations or fish and sugar, and its preparations; hogs-flesh prepared with honey, are to be avoided; plantains with butter milk, curdled milk, or milk with sour fruits, before or after eating, are improper. Pigeons fried with mustard oil; honey mixed with rain water, and kept in brass pots for ten days, should be avoided. These remarks are particularly applicable to boys and strong persons, and those who take violent exercise.

2nd. Food may act unfavourably by the quantity which is taken. Thus honey and ghee, oil and marrow, or honey and water, oil and ghee, or fat, are bad when eaten in large and equal proportions.

3rd. The following mixtures of articles possessing certain tastes are improper, as sweet and sour articles, sweet and salt, sweet and pungent, sweet and bitter substances, or bitter and salt articles. Such mixtures should therefore be carefully avoided; as they form bad chyle, and thus the appetite &c., is deranged. Such mixtures, however, will not injure the health of the young and strong, those who live in a pure air and take much exercise; and those accustomed to their use, by whom they may be eaten in small quantities with impunity. But in ordinary circumstances, when their bad effects are felt, recourse must he had to the use of emetics and purgatives, and such medicines as have a tendency to equalize the humours. The articles of food which are wholesome from mixture, and preparation; are those which derange air, and diminish bile. The opposite articles of food which moderate air, and derange bile, are unwholesome. By improper mixtures wholesome articles of food may become as poisons. But the kind of food to be used must be varied according to the age, habits, and seasons as well as to the individual's idiosyncrasy.

There are four forms in which food may be taken—one kind is taken without being chewed as drinks (pita); another is lapped (lírhá); another sucked (chúshya); and another kind of food is chewed (kátita).

According to Charaka there are six varieties of food.

1. Soft food (bhojya) as rice, &c.
2. Soft sweetmeats (bhakhya).
3. Hard food (charbya), that requires chewing to prepare it for digestion.
4. Drinks (Peya).
5. Liquids that are lapped (lehya).
6. Food that is sucked (chúshya), such as mangoes, sugarcane, &c.

Food and medicines are also divided into six different classes, according to their effects on the senses. These are into sweet, acid, salt, bitter, pungent, and astringent. These tastes are however, modified by disease.

a. Sweet articles of food increase the semen, the milk, and the fat; while they improve the eyesight, asthma, worms, and affections of the throat. They also increase phlegm, the strength of the tissues, and humours; retain the body in health, and promote longevity. These substances are good for the soul, and cooling for the body. They cure derangements in air and bile, promote appetite, and are useful in correcting the effects of poison.

b. Acid articles of food promote appetite, are cooling before, and heating after eating. They are agreeable to the taste, promote digestion, and increase bile and phlegm. They increase the blood, and restore irregularities and derangements in the air, bile, and phlegm. When they have been often taken they produce weakness, and emaciation of the body, and sometimes they produce blindness (nyctalopia). Acids act quickly, and produce itching, eruptions over the body, a palor of the skin, and a swelling of the body, with thirst, fever, and boils.

c. Salt articles of food relax the bowels, promote digestion, and increase appetite. They also promote perspiration, remove derangements of the air, bile, phlegm, and blood; produce a glossiness of the surface of the body, diminish or cure aphrodisia, are cooling, and heal sores. They are, however, bad for the eyes; and if long continued, they derange the humours; the skin becomes covered with irregularities upon its surface, followed by leprosy, weakness, and by symptoms produced by poisons having been taken (visarpa).

d. Bitter food is not pleasant to the taste, but is dry, and light to the stomach; increases bile and air, and produces dryness, heat, and diseased milk. If taken before eating it improves the appetite, removes worms, thirst, poison, leprosy, epilepsy, nausea, heat of the body, and fever. It corrects too much bile, and phlegm. It also improves the flesh, fat, marrow, urine, and dejections; increases memory, is cooling, and is good for the palate and throat. But if always eaten it has a bad effect, deranging the humours, and producing diseases of air.

e. Pungent articles of food are of a drying nature, increasing the appetite and milk, and diminishing thirst and fever. They cure diseases of phlegm, diseases of the throat and head, itchiness, and internal pain. But if eaten for some time in considerable quantities they produce thirst, weakness, shaking, pain over the body, and derange the spleen.

f. Astringent articles of food are cooling, and cure diseases of the bile and phlegm. They increase air, particularly flatulence, they clear the blood and flesh, and are heavy to the stomach. They produce costiveness, and stop diarrhœa, and thicken the dejections; they remove diseases of the skin, and heal wounds and sores. But if taken for some time they produce costiveness, a swelling of the abdomen, thirst, and weakness, and retard the circulation of fluids in the body.

For ensuring good digestion the patient's passions must be regulated. He must sleep at night in a protected room; must use warm water to bathe with, and take bodily exercise. Such observances are considered to be most necessary to health.

1. *Articles of food derived from the Vegetable Kingdom.* There are seven parts of vegetables employed for food. These

are the leaves, flowers, fruits, wood, branches, roots, and mushrooms. They are more easily digested in the above order, which is followed in the Hindu Medical works.

Fruits. The form and size of fruits would soon fix the attention of mankind, and with the culmiferous and leguminous vegetables would form the primordial food of man. In Hindustan there are a great variety of indigenous specimens of these articles of food The following are the principal :—

English.	*Scientific.*	*Sanskrit*
Pomegranate,	Punica Granatum,	Dárima.
Myrobalan,	Phyllanthus emblica,	Amalaká.
Custard apple,	Annona squamosa,	Sleshmátaka, orátá
Plumbs,	Prunus,	Badari.
Apples,	Pyrus,	Simbítiká.
Quince,	Pyrus Cydonia,	Táhár.
Wood apple,	Feronia Elephantum,	Kapittha.
Lemon,	Citrus acida,	Mátulunga
Mango,	M Mangifera,	Amra.
Hog plumb,	Terminalia Chebulá,	Harítakí.
A Species of Bread fruit tree,	Artocarpus Lacucha,	Lakucha.
Karinda,	Carissa Carandas,	Karamarda.
Guava,	Psidium pyriferum,	Párábata.
Tamarinds,	Tamarindus Indica,	Amliká.
Rose apple,	Eugenia, Jamborosa,	Jambúl.
Jack fruit,	Artocarpus Integrifolia,	Kanthaphal or Kántál.
Pine apple,	Bromelia Ananas, *Palms*,	Shátanetra.
Cocoanut,	Cocos Nucifera,	Nárikela.
Date tree,	Phœnix dactylifera,	Karjúra.
Fan Palm,	Borassus flabeleiformis,	Tàla.

Pamplemus, Plantain, &c., &c.

The following varieties of oranges, lemons, citrons, &c., are indigenous to Hindustan, and were well known to the Greeks and Romans. They increase bile, improve the appetite, and cure dyspepsia.

There are several varieties of oranges (Kamalá), but they are not distinguished by different names.

There are different sorts of Lemons, (Nebu) such as Limpáka, Kágaji, Nárángi, Batábi, Kamalá, &c.

Drupes. These fruits are of the genus Amygdalus, &c.

Prunes.—Apricot, Prunus Armenaica ; Cherry, P. Cerasus &c.

Cucurbitaceous fruits or Gourds.

Water Melon,	Cucumis Melo,	Kharbuj.
Sweet Melon,	C. Momordica,	Phutí.
Common Cucumber,	C. Sativus,	Sashá or Khíra.
Bottle Gourd,	C. Lagenaria,	Laoo.
Pumpkin,	C. Pepo,	Kumrá.
Squash Gourd,	C. Melopepo,	Saphari Kumrá.
Fig tree,	C. Citrullus,	Tárbúj.

These fruits have from the earliest times constituted an important part in the diet of the Hindus.

Vegetables. In general vegetables are not easily digested, as they increase air, bile, and phlegm, produce worms, and constipate the bowels. They are rendered more wholesome when boiled and seasoned. If employed alone for food they derange the system, affecting particularly the colour of the skin and eyes, and diminishing semen, blood, and memory.

The leaves of the *chilu, bastaki, sunishannaka, tanduliyá,* and *mandúkaparni,* are considered the most wholesome kind of vegetables. They are usually prepared by being boiled in water, fried in ghee, and then seasoned with salt. In some cases they are dressed with butter, and tonic compounds called Ticta barga: such as Prapunnára (a kind of Cassia), Somarájí (Serratula Anthelmentica), Patola (Tricosanthes diœcia), Várttákí, (Solanum melongela) or the egg plant, &c.

The *Esculent roots* are very numerous. The following are the chief varieties. The Arum Colocasia; A. Marcrorhizon, and A. Peltatum; the roots of the different varieties of lotus (Nymphœa Lotus), &c. (Shálúk) Nelumbo (Padma); Yams (Dioscorea); Spanish potatoes (Convovulus Batatas), beet root; onion; garlick; leeks; white and red carrots; raddishes, &c.

The generality of European pot and salad herbs are found indigenous in Hindustan. The following are a few of these:—

Cauliflower (Brassica), broccoli, parsley (apium petroselium), spinage (spinacea oleracea), common lettuce (Lactuca sativa). Garden cress (Lepidum sativum), endive (cichorium endivia), mustard (Sinapis nigra et alba), with many others. The properties of each of these are given in the Hindu medical works, with their effects on the different humours, and on diseases.

The *Graminivorous* seeds form a numerous class which afford the chief article of diet to a large proportion of the inhabitants of Asia. The principal varieties of corn and pulse were derived from Asia, and they are peculiarly fruitful in Hindustan, and from their hard consistence they may be kept in a good state for long periods. Rice (oryza sativa) in the form of paddy, when covered with its husk, in a dry situation will keep for years perfectly fresh and good, and may be transported from one part of the country to another with great facility. A large population almost entirely live on this grain, of which there are numerous varieties. The *Shâli* rice, when of a red colour, cures diseased air, bile, and phlegm, clears the eyes, increases the strength, semen, and urine, and removes thirst, Atapa, or Sun-dried rice, increases the diseases of air, bile, and phlegm; is heating, increases the perspiration, alvine evacuations and urine. It is considered indigestible, and weakens the body. When the plant has been transplanted, the rice is rendered lighter, and more easily digested.

New rice is heavy, increases phlegm, gives an oleaginous appearance to the body, and promotes the secretion of semen.

Old rice is pleasant to the taste, is drying, improves the appetite and internal heat. It is light, and increases air. The rice of sixty days growth, which is produced in the rains, or in the months of August and September, is considered as forming the most wholesome food; and is called *Shashtiká*. A small red rice, called *Raktashâli*, is considered wholesome; and the kind called *Kanguka*, is considered good. There are twenty other varieties, which are distinguished by the size, and colour of the grain.

Parched rice is much used, and is considered nourishing, increasing appetite, and curing the diseases of phlegm. When the parched rice has been preserved unhusked (khai) it is considered more wholesome, increasing appetite, removing thirst, vomiting, dysentery, and great fatness. It also removes the diseases of bile and phlegm.

Rice-water, and rice and milk, are also considered very wholesome. The particular qualities of each preparation are given at length in the Hindu Medical writings.

Wheat (*Godhuma*) has been used, and has been an article of food from time immemorial in Hindustan. Several varieties are cultivated with success. It is considered nourishing; increases the appetite, flesh, and strength, and the seven humours, improves the general health, and increases the semen. It cures the diseases of air and bile, and increases phlegm.

Barley (Yava) is considered nourishing.

Sesamum seed (Til) is now principally used as a condiment.

Leguminous seeds, or Pulse. The list of these seeds is very long; the following are some of them:—

Pea, matter (Pisum Sativum,); Bean (vicia); the different varieties of Dolichos, the black seeded (D. Lablab,) the D. Labea, the D. biflorus, or horn-grain, and the D. Catjang. The Phaseolus communis (common bean), and the P. maximus; P. nanus; P. minima; P. mungo, &c. The chick pea (cicer arictinum); the Cytisus (caja 1) ;the Frigonella (Tænum Græcum) are enumerated with many other excellent varieties of pulse. They should be eaten after being well boiled, or in the form of porridge, or soup.

Animal food.—It is probable that for many ages the use of the flesh of animals was unknown, from the want of weapons and the strength and activity of the animals; but when this kind of food was brought into use, it seems to have been considered as a great luxury. In these ancient times, the chief of the household usually acted the parts of the butcher and cook. The flesh of animals was then considered as agreeable to the taste, increasing the bulk of the body, and the strength, and curing the diseases of air. It is also said to be heavy to the stomach, and when digested is sweet. The writers of the more ancient shastres lived in a cool air, and were accustomed to an active life, which required the use of more animal food than is proper in Bengal. This was probably one reason of the superiority of the ancient Brahmins over their more degenerate descendents; who are small in stature, and incapable of those mental and corporeal exertions which raise a people in the rank of nations. The indigestible nature of the flesh of some of the animals of the country, with their unclean habits, rendered them objects of disgust. Pork, even in Europe, is sometimes unwholesome, producing diarrhœa, griping and vomiting, and sometimes resembling the effects of the most violent poisons. The flesh of this and other animals is not so digestible as in more temperate climates, where their food is of a superior quality. The want of exercise and food during the greater part of the year, renders the flesh of such animals peculiarly unwholesome; and seems to have induced the Hindu Legislators to inculcate the transmigration of souls. Such an opinion must at once have prevented the general use of animal food. It was most probably introduced in to Greece by Pithagoras.

It is stated that, during the three first Yugas, cow's and buffaloe's flesh were used for food. Its prohibition is thus accounted for:—A prophet had a favourite cow killed by his scholars during his absence. On his return he was much displeased, and directed that, in future, should a Hindu use the flesh of the cow during the Kali Yuga he should loose caste. Another legend states that a prophet, in performing a religious ceremony which required the offering of cow's flesh, with gur, honey, and oil, used such powerful prayers that the cow rose up out of the sacrificial fire. It was, however, found that a part of the animal was wanting; on enquiry the Brahmin's wife confessed that she had taken a part of the sacrifice to eat it. On producing it, two vegetables were found growing from it (the Lashun, garlic; and Pyáj, onion). The flesh thus recovered was put up on the cow, and it adhered and completed the animal, which was, in consequence, directed not again

10

to be eaten. Cow's flesh is said to cure the diseases of bile, sores in the nostrils accompanied with want of taste, and prevents relapses in fever. The flesh of calves cures the diseases of air, and increases phlegm. Besides the flesh of cows and buffalows, deers, hares, hogs, goats, and sheep were used by the ancient Hindus as food. The flesh of animals are digestible in the following order, the first being the least so; the pig, tiger, cow and deer.

Flesh boiled with oil is heavy, increases bile, and is heating. Dried flesh removes fatigue, is of use in diminishing bile, in curing the diseases of phlegm, and sores in the body.

The flesh of domestic animals was not given to the sick as it was considered heating. On this account the flesh of wild animals was substituted, as they were supposed to be more wholesome, such as deer, of wild fowls, &c; the fat in these cases being carefully removed. Animal fat and marrow were supposed to cure diseases of air, and increase the diseases of blood, bile, and cough. *Broths* were made of the flesh of these animals, and given to invalids; they cured old fevers and increased strength, improved the voice and eyesight, increased the strength and semen, and cured boils. They strengthen the joints, and promote their cure when wounded. If given with rice, broths cure old fevers, strengthen the individual, while they lighten the heart, and cure the diseases of bile. The Hindus are directed, at the same time, to abstain from hard and indigestible food, such as curds, milk, oil, jagree, with various kinds of pulse and leguminous plants.

Animal Secretions.—*Milk* is heavy, cooling, and sweet, gives a shining appearance to the skin, strengthens, fattens, and increases semen; it cures the diseases of air, bile, and phlegm. *Goat's Milk* is sweet and cooling; it is binding, promotes the internal heat; cures *raktapitta* (Hœmorrage) and diseases of air, bile, phlegm, and blood; as Goats eat many medicinal plants, drink little water, and are very active. *Sheep's Milk* is sweet and heavy, and increases phlegm and bile. *Buffalo's milk* is drying and heating, but cures swelling of the abdomen, and diseases of air and phlegm. *Mare's milk* is saltish, sweet, and light. *Woman's milk* strengthens the soul, increases flesh, and the consistence of the circulating fluids: it should only be drunk fresh. *Cow's milk* is pleasant, and very wholesome. It is cooling, sweet, promotes semen, cures diseases of air, blood, and bile, and promotes memory, strength, and longevity. Early in the morning this milk is heavy, and constipating. It is not good when the cow is near calving, or when there is no calf; the best milk being when the calf and mother are of the same colour, particularly when of a white or of a black colour, with erect horns; and when the cow has eaten the leaves of the sugar-cane. Milk that has been kept a day is heavy, and constipates; and fresh milk increases the secretion of phlegm from the nose. When boiled and drunk warm, it cures diseases of phlegm and air; when allowed to cool, it cures the diseases of bile. The milks of goats and asses are not so wholesome as that of the cow. They should not be drunk fresh; and salt may be added or the milk may be boiled.

2. *Curdled Milk* is formed by adding a little sour milk, or *dai*, to milk which has been boiled and cooled. It should be allowed to stand for a night before being used. It is cooling, increases the internal heat, and is useful in the cure of agues, diarrhœa, dyspepsia, and strangury; it increases the phlegm, and the secretion of semen.

3. *Butter-Milk* (Ghol) is made by stirring about curdled milk until butter is obtained; or this is produced in the ordinary way. It is good for persons who take poison, who are labouring under diarrhœa, dyspepsia, vomiting, strangury, jaundice, piles, spleen, or ague. It diminishes fat, phlegm and air. *Fresh Butter* is sweet and nourishing; it is cool, agreeable, diminishes bile and air, and promotes the secretion of semen. It cures consumption, chronic cough, asthma, ulcers, piles, and tetanus. It increases strength, and is good for children. *Ghee* is made by boiling butter for a few minutes to dissipate the watery part, when it may be kept for a long time. It is sweet, and softens parts. It is useful in madness, epilepsy, and ague. It diminishes air and bile, and improves the appetite, memory, and the beauty of the body. It also promotes longevity, and preserves the eyesight. Ghee which has been kept ten years and upwards is called old ghee, which is said to cure sudden blindness (timira), morbid discharges from the nose, eyes and mouth; difficulty in breathing, fainting, leprosy, and epilepsy; diseases of the vagina, pains in the ears, eyes, and head; old fevers, carbuncle, and diseases of air, bile, and phlegm.

Flesh of Birds. Their general properties are, that they cure the diseases of air, bile, and phlegm; improve the colour of the skin; are slightly heavy, and sweet; increase the semen, memory, and appetite; and give consistency to the alvine evacuations. The principal of these are partridge; jungle-cock; common cock; peacock; pigeons; water-wagtail; taylor-bird; duck; paddy-bird, &c.

The flesh of animals and birds is not good the second day, when they are tainted. Such as have been drowned, or killed with an arrow, as this may have been poisoned, are digested with difficulty, and produce diseases, particularly of air, bile, and phlegm.

The upper (atlanted) part of the male, and the lower (sacral) part of the female are the heaviest. The flesh of female quadrupeds, and male birds, is the lightest. The flesh of large animals which work much, and eat little, is heavy, in the following order: head, shoulders, spleen, skin, liver, fore-feet, and hind-feet, tail, testicles, abdomen, and urinary organs. The humours are heavy in the following order:—blood, flesh, fat, bones, marrow, and semen.

Such birds as live on flowers are thin, and increase the bulk of the body; such as live on fish, increase bile; and such as eat rice, remove the diseases of air.

Flesh should be eaten the same day it has been killed; rice should be prepared rapidly, and a man should live with a *young* wife, use milk, ghee, and boiled water which has been allowed to cool, as they promote health and strength. The opposite articles have a contrary effect on the health; as putrid flesh, exposure to the morning sun, new curdled milk, sleeping in the morning, &c.

Fish produces a shining appearance of the body, is slightly heating, and sweet; and increases the air, urine, and alvine secretions. When white, fish increases the strength, phlegm, and bile; it is of advantage to health when the person labours under diseases of air, when used by wrestlers, by those accustomed to violent exercise, and those who are tired. Black and small fish are light, and constipate. They increase the appetite and strength, cure air, and are of use during convalescence. White fish increases air, bile, and phlegm, gives a shining appearance to the skin, is digested with difficulty, and produces a laxative effect upon the bowels. Fish ruis are pleasant and increase air, phlegm, and semen, diminish the appetite, and produce a bitter state of the stomach.

Fish when boiled is heavy, and cures the diseases of air; it increases the strength, removes fatigue, enlarges the muscles, and improves vision. Dried fish constipate, and weakens the body, and is digested with difficulty; when roasted, fish is heavy, increases the semen, flesh, and strength. In such cases fish should be prepared with oil. These properties of fish are increased and modified, by mixing them with other articles of food, as with the leaves of certain trees, pumpkins, &c. *Rui* is the best of all fish, and others in the following order; Vetki, Bhangun, Parshia, Tupsia, Chital, Shol, Ilish, Baul, Gágará, Garká, Balsguni, Chenga, Kai, Punti, Tetí, Chuná, Chándâ, Dáinkona, Chingri. Turtles were used, and were stated to cure diseases of air, to increase strength, semen, and memory, and to improve the eyesight.

The following are supposed to be the proportionate nutritive qualities of certain articles of food:—

Rice is eight times lighter than cakes.

Milk is eight times lighter than flesh.

Flesh „ „ „ oil.

Sugar, Saccharum, Officinarum, has been known in the east from the earliest antiquity;. it is the sweet cane of Scripture "brought from a far country," and offered up by the jews among other sacrifices to Jehovah (Isa. xlv. are 24.; Jer vi. 20.) The fresh juice is cooling, increases semen and urine, is pleasant, increases strength, and cures the derangement of air; it improves the dejections, and diseases of blood and bile, is sweet, gives a shining appearance to the skin, increases happiness and flesh, and is heating.

After the juice has been exposed to the air for some time, it is heavy to the stomach, is heating, cures derangements of the air and phlegm, and increases the shining appearance of the skin. *Gur* or the inspissated juice, is sweet and pleasant to the taste, and gives strength and a shining appearance to the skin. These qualities are improved by keeping, when it removes derangements of the air and bile, and purifies the blood. It is heavy to the stomach, increases semen, purifies the urine, increases the strength and flesh, and produces intestinal worms. Sugar is of use in diseases of the blood and bile, in fainting, vomiting, and thirst.

Oils.—There are numerous plants which furnish a large supply of oil from their seed, which is extensively used. Besides the oils extracted from the different palms, and the *madhurá,* (Anise) it is obtained from the almond (Pistachavera, or Pistachio nut); sesamum indicum; sinapis alba et nigra, or mustard oil; S. Orientale, the til oil; Ricinus of Palma Christi, the Rám Tila of the Hindus, and the Huts-elli of the Mussulmans, &c., *i.e.* castor oil; the tillee, or linseed oil; curumbo oil; and Coringa oil. Other oils are also used in medicine, but they possess the same qualities as the seeds from which they are extracted On this account they are used for some diseases. Vegetable oils are bitter and sweet, and are good for the skin, and alleviate all diseases. Oil is heating, when taken internally; it increases the diseases produced by bile, and constipates the bowels, and lessens urine.

Liquids.—These may be considered under the heads of water, and medicinal drinks.

Water.—The Hindus were very careful about their drinking water, and ascribed the appearance of many diseases to bad water. Pure water has no taste and is considered is cooling, relaxing the body, and improving the senses, and the general health. They considered the water of wells, or natural springs in the sandy beds of rivers, as the most wholesome, as they promote digestion and strength; the river and fountain water at the bottom of high hills, was considered less wholesome ; and the most unhealthy was considered to be the water from brooks, and the stagnant water of tanks, and reservoirs: this water was supposed to produce indigestion, obstructions, and lethargy, with a predisposition to fever.

Rain water, when preserved in a clean vessel, was supposed to cure the diseases of air, bile, and phlegm, and improve the health. It keeps the mouth clean, and improves the state of the tongue, teeth, and memory. It was considered to be heavier during the rains than in the cold, and hot weather. Hail-water was considered peculiarly wholesome.

Water was supposed to be improved by boiling, and its effects were varied according to the quantity dissipated by evaporation. Water which has been boiled and drunk cold cures air, bile, and phlegm, also cough, fever, and constipation. It removes great fatness, and increases the internal fire.

Water mixed with the other elements produces six tastes, or sweet, sour, salt, pungent, bitter, and astringent. When the food contains a large proportion of water and earth, they produce a sweet state of the stomach. The sweet, sour, and salt articles, diminish air, the sweet, bitter, astringent, diminish bile ; and the pungent, bitter, and astringent, diminish phlegm.

Medicinal drinks.—The usual *drink* for the sick, is water in which a little of the infusion of cinanmon and cassia has been mixed. By others the drink is varied with the nature of the disease. When *air* is deranged, water in which the infusion of such medicines as cure this class of diseases, as long as black pepper, sugar, &c. is to be added. When *bile* is deranged, pure water is either given, or its cooling qualities are increased by the addition of the infusion of ushira, or kaskas; gandhatrina, a fragrant grass; sugar-cane, Ikhyu; kusha, a kind of sacred grass &c. When *phlegm* is deranged, the infusion of cinnamon black or long-pepper, cloves &c., is to be added.

In fever, produced by derangement of air, bile, and phlegm, the fresh juice of the kau, a kind of grass, is recommended instead of water.

In hemoptysis (Rakta Pitta), the fresh juice of the Káshanda (pumpkin) and pomegranate are the best additions to the drinks. In cases of swelling, or *dropsy*, an infusion of dry raddish (múlaka), ginger, soot, &c., are to be used. In *leprosy* the infusion of catechu (khadirá) is to be used, with the infusion of black pepper, and sugar-candy.

Condiments.—In weak digestion, water mixed with camphor, or infused in native mint (Padina) is to be used. Beetle-nut, camphor, cloves, long-pepper, pepper, dry ginger, and other spices are mixed with slacked lime, surrounded with the leaves of *pán*, and chewed as a condiment. It cleans the throat and voice, promotes digestion, keeps the breath sweet, improves the senses, and gives an agreeable appearance to the person. It increases semen, and should be used after vomiting, bathing, and sleeping. The Hindus also use as condiments, nutmeg, cloves, cardamum seeds, cinnamon, turmeric, mustard, sandal-wood, debdaru-wood, ginger black, and long-pepper, capsicum, coriander-seed, aniseed assafœtida &c.

Wines.—Within the first year after the debarkation of Noah from the Ark, he made wine from the grapes of Mount Ararat (Gen. IX). The wine also thrives well in the Northern parts of Hindustan, but not in Bengal. It is only in the northern parts of Hindustan that the grape is sometimes converted into wine, from the fermentation being too quick, and from the heat and moisture of the lower provinces. The grape is considered cooling and aperient. All wines are moderately strong, and are divided into sweet, and sour. They all increase bile, and dir ''sh phlegm, and air. They are also tonic, stimulating, increasi.. ..e acuteness of the senses and appetite, and promoting digestion and health, when properly used. There were different kinds of wines used by the ancient Hindus, which received different names according to the fruits, flowers, and other substances from which they were derived. The wine which was made from the grape was called *Siddha*; from the raisins (kismis) *márdhwika*; from the flowers of the Bassia latifolia, madhwaka; from jagry or gur, *goura* or *surá*.

In the *Veda* shástras the use of wines and spirits are forbidden; but in the tantra they are allowed, and the worshippers of *Kali* indulge in their use.

When digestion has been completed, the state of the stomach will depend on the qualities of the food or medicine which has been taken. When bitter and astringent articles of food or medicine have been eaten, they produce a bitter state of the stomach; sour food produces a sweetness after digestion; and sweet and salt food produce sweet eructations from the stomach.

During the rains, light and stomachic food with bitters should be preferred, while liquids and oils are not to be used too freely; the drinking water should be boiled, and drunk with a little honey. In cloudy days exercise is not to be taken in the open air; the bed-room should be warmed with fires, and all persons should sleep upon a chàrpoy, during the night. In Autumn (sharat) bitter and sweet articles of food are to be preferred, and light and clean water is to be used freely for drink. Exercise is to be taken in the evening; and deranged bile is to be cured by bleeding or purging. Sherbets and spirituous liquids, especially such as relieve the increased secretion of bile, are be used.

In winter (Shishira) saline, bitter, pungent, and warm articles, prepared with ghee and oil, are to be taken for food. Meat is to be used, and the drink warmed, and accompanied with spirituous liquors. The warm bath and frictions with oil are to be used, and exercise taken in the morning.

In spring (Vasanta) sour, sweet, oily, and saline articles are to be used. The drinking water is to be boiled, and spirituous liquors are to be mixed with it, to diminish the increased phlegm. The warm bath, and foot exercise are also to be used.

During the hot season (Grishma), sour, pungent, and strong warm substances are to be avoided, and rice, barley, and curries of light vegetables are to be used. Food possessing warm qualities is to be avoided, and the breakfast should consist of cooling fruits and sherbets. The cold bath is to be used, and thin light dresses are to be worn. The surface of the body is to be smeared with cooling aromatic applications, cool water should be used for drink and sleep is to be allowed during the day.

The highest classes of Brahmins, as officiating priests, attend rigidly to the performance of religious ceremonies, and generally bathe in the morning at sun rise. After performing the ceremonies of their guardian Deity, they take for breakfast small sweet cakes, or a handfull of moistened rice, at 10 or 11 o'clock; as they must always purify their body by washing, before eating. They dine on boiled rice, peas, and vegetables, and some of them have fish curry at 1 or 2 P. M.*

From eight to eleven o'clock, supper is prepared, and consists of the same food as at dinner. The middling and higher classes mix a small quantity of milk and ghee with what they eat at dinner and supper.

In some houses instead of boiled rice at night, unlevened flour-cakes are eaten, with a little ghee spread over it. They are often eaten with vegetable curries or boiled peas, or with the flesh of kids, pigeons, and other birds. These are often eaten with butter by the rich. Shop-keepers eat late, and sleep for an hour or two after midday. Their drinks consist of plain water and sugar-candy, or sugar and water, to which lime-juice is sometimes added.

The principal precepts with regard to personal duties are—use boiled water for drink, sleep all night in a cool, dry and elevated situation, and take exercise; wash the eyes with cold water, which will keep them cool, clean, and diminish heat; and anoint and

* The months of October, April, and January are considered holy, when not only the priests, but many others, who are desirous of an easy entrance into heaven, repair to the river-side to bathe, immediately before sun rise, and to perform the morning ceremonies.

keep the body clean by frequent bathing. Rest after labour will increase strength, prevent fatigue, and promote the freshness of the body.

The diet of the sick is to be regulated by the nature of the sickness, the constitution and strength of the individual, and the situation, period, state of the appetite, &c.

k. Sleep. "Early to bed and early to rise," is one of the old and most approved maxims of the Hindus; which indeed is peculiarly applicable in a hot enervating climate like Bengal, where the night air is so pernicious, and the mornings so cool and healthy. The Hindus sleep on a pretty large mat, with a small sized pillow for the head, generally upon the plain ground, or upon a charpoy. The mat is to be soft and clean, and not circular; the head is to be turned towards the east, or rising of the sun; or south, towards *Yama*, where the person goes after death, and where is the residence of the gods. Care is taken not to turn the feet towards their father or mother, or superiors. To have refreshing sleep, the mind of the person should be tranquil and contented. This will also be promoted by music, and rocking; by anointing the body with oil; by the use of the bath; by eating new rice, milk, ghee, and the like; by sherbuts and spirits, and such articles as improve the health; by sleeping upon a large mat, in a comfortable house, and at the accustomed time. Sleep keeps the humours in a healthy state, improves the colour of the skin, the health, appetite, and strength.

Watching increases air, dries the body, and diminishes cough and fat, and retards the action of poison. Sleeping during the day increases cough and fat, and should be avoided in those in whom phlegm is increased, and during the spring, in the rains and winter months, &c. It may be indulged in during the hot season, when the habit has been acquired and when the air is deranged.

The Hindus generally rise at 6 o'clock in the morning; but before getting up in the morning and going to sleep, they repeat certain prayers. The person next proceeds to perform the duties of nature, and then washes his face, mouth, &c. They brush their teeth with a small fresh branch of a bitter tree or plant; afterwards they change their night-clothes, and go to their business. The smoking of tobacco is used morning and night, at bed time, and after dinner and tiffin. It should be smoked slowly by means of a long tube.

——:o:——

CHAPTER II.

Materia Medica.

The following remarks on Materia Medica will be arranged under the heads: 1st, general remarks on simple Medicines; and 2nd, regarding the most common preparations and uses of Medicine.

—:o:—

SECTION I.

General remarks on Simple Medicines.

The Hindu medical writers have recorded many observations on the properties and choice of medicines, the situations in which they are to be found, the time at which they possess their peculiar properties in the highest degree, and the manner of preparing and preserving them. These medicines are very numerous.

The following remarks will be arranged under the heads of the vegetable, animal, and mineral kingdoms. A list of the principal medicines will be given in the next chapter, arranged according to their effects.

A. *Simple Medicines from the Vegetable Kingdom.* The belief of there being a remedy for each disease, led the Brahmins to make a very careful examination of the vegetable kingdom; and a large number of Medicines were discovered, some of which were very powerful. The success which followed the employment of these remedies in the cure of diseases was invariably supposed to rest on individual sanctity, and the divine pleasure which imparts it. Hence the great difficulty of obtaining information; as it is believed that if such secrets are revealed to others, the medicine loses its effects, not only in the hands of the person to whom its qualities have been revealed, but also of the person who had known them before. I must remark here that it is from such selfish motives the properties of many valuable medicines have been lost. There are nine such secrets which should not be revealed to any one:—these are the age of a person; his wealth; family occurrences; his bad actions; or those which reflect shame, or dishonour upon him; his intercourse with his wife; his prayers to his tutelar gods; his charities; and the virtues of nostrums the ingredients of which are known to him.

The simple vegetable medicines are procured from the bark, roots, leaves, flowers, fruit, seeds, juices, gums, and wood of plants. These medicines are arranged in the following order:—

1. *Bánaspáti,* or those trees which contain fruits without flowers.

2. *Vrikshya,* those which contain both flowers and fruit.

3. *Virut,* creepers with flowers in clusters.

4. *Oshadhi,* those plants which die after the ripening of their fruit, as rice, &c.

The effect of medicines from the vegetable kingdom will vary with the period at which the medicine is gathered, according as the air is agitated with wind or not, as it is in the sun or shade, as taken during the day or night, during the cold or hot weather, during dry or rainy weather, and also according to the interval between the time when the medicine is gathered and that when it is used.

Medicines from this kingdom should not be procured either from the jungly, or from a country covered with water; neither from a dry and sandy ground, nor from one that is unequal or has many holes, stones, or broken vessels upon it. Situations in any way destroyed by insects, or in which white ants have their nests, as these are supposed to remove the strength of the earth, or where water drops from a choppered roof, where bodies have been burnt or buried, where persons have died, or sacred situations are not proper places for raising medicinal plants. Soils in which there is much salt are also unfavourable for the growth of medicines; and plants that grow at unseasonable times, or when very old, and those which water forms, or insects have injured are to be thrown away.

The soil most favourable for the growth of medicines is of a soft black, yellow, or red colour; is equal, or heavy; is situated near water, and where trees grow luxuriantly, and the grain is moist and glistening: in such situations the soil has its proper quality of taste. Those of water are found where the place is sweet, and the plants glistening. The qualities of fire are greatest, when the soil has several colours, and where the earth is light, the trees small and growing at a distance from each other, and where the young leaves of grass, as they burst through the earth, are of a light yellow colour. The qualities of air predominate in dry places, of a grayish colour, like the ashes of wood. In such situations the earth is light, the trees are few, small, dry, and have holes in them, with little juice. The qualities of ether (akásh) are in excess in such situations as are of a greenish colour, are soft in the centre and equal, with many holes. The water in such situations is without taste, and the mountains and trees are large.

The rays of the sun and moon produce the colour, &c., of plants. Thus the yellow colour of trees is produced by the sun, and such medicine should be gathered during the hot period of the day. Emetics are to be gathered at such times, from soils possessing the qualities of ether and air. The moon produces the white and cold plants, which should be gathered during the cold season, when the qualities of these plants will be most energetic. They will then be sweet, moist like oil, and cold like water. Purgatives are thus to be gathered in a soil possessing the qualities of taste and smell.

The physician should observe the lucky days and hours, and the most favourable period of the moon's age, in order to ensure the cure of the disease. The stars which are predominant on particular days are to be observed, particularly those which occur on odd days. Medicines which are to be exhibited internally, are to be taken for the first time on Mondays, Thursdays and Fridays. They are also to observe the most favourable period of the moon's age, and that fortunate stars are in the ascendant.*

Before a medicinal plant is gathered in the morning, a prayer should be said by the person with his face to the north. The following is such a prayer, which is supposed to remove any devils which may be hiding near.

'O God! If any devil be lurking here—begone! whether it be Vetal, Pishácha, Rákshas, or Shrisarpa (the devil of serpents). As the shrub is being gathered, the person is to say: 'O, shrub! as Bramhá, Indra, and Vishnu plucked you, for the same reason I now remove you.'

B. *Simple Medicines derived from the Animal Kingdom.*

These are skin, hair, nails, blood, flesh, bones, fat, marrow, bile, milk and dejections. These medicines should be obtained from healthy animals, which are neither very old nor very young. The urine and other dejections should be obtained from the female.

a. Skin, nails, and *hair,* are used for fumigations in intermittent fevers, &c.

b. Blood. When there has been a great loss of blood, it is sometimes exhibited internally.

c. Flesh is mixed with oily and other medicines, and vegetables; and is given in weakness, phthisis, and in nervous diseases.

d. Bones. The ashes of bones, mixed with other medicines, are exhibited in nervous diseases and those of children. They are also used to fumigate.

e. Fat is used principally externally, as in the form of ointment, &c.

* There are twenty-seven stars, one of which presides over each day of the week.

f. Marrow is used externally in the form of ointment, and internally in cases of weakness.

g. Bile is considered a stimulant, and is used in fever; also as an external application, as to the eye.

h. Milk is one of the principal articles of food It is used in combination with decoctions, and given internally in diseases of children, and for nervous diseases. It is often used with oil as an external application.

i. Urine is pungent and slightly bitterish and saltish to the taste. It is slightly laxative and cures diseases of phlegm, air, worms; and diseases produced from poison: it is also of use in leprosy, and in dropsical swellings, jaundice, and dyspepsia. Cow's urine is generally preferred.

k. Dung. The moisture contained in cow's dung is used in inflammation, and in discolouring of the skin. It is also given internally, and prepared with other medicines.

C. *Simple Medicines derived from the Mineral Kingdom.*

These consist of metals, (*Dhátu*) and inferior minerals (*Upadhátu*).

Of *salts* (Lavana), Saindhava is the best form of Rock-salt.

There are four kinds of *kshára,* 1 Java, (saltpetre) 2 Sarjiká (natron) 3 Páksham (Bitlavana) 4 Tankana (Borax).

1. To Yavakshár, add Sajimáti (natron or alkali) and Sohága (borax), &c.

Sámudram, or, common sea-salt, is less powerful than the black salt (bitlavana). It is stomachic, and cures air and indigestion.

Sarvakshár or Sachal, (an impure soda) is used in spleen (gulmo), colic (shúl), and dyspepsia. There are other salts, such as Vámaka, Udhada, &c.; but their qualities are the same as above.

Salt increases. appetite; produces diseases of the blood and bile. It cures gulma, piles, dysentery and stone.

Metals (*dhátu*).—Iron and tin were the only metals used internally by the Hindu Physicians; but in the more modern works the other metals are described, and were probably introduced into Hindustan two or three hundred years ago, probably for mercenary purposes; as the Physician, before the recovery of his patient, only received his recompense for the medicine he prescribed.

The metals now used in medicine are as follows :—Quicksilver, gold, silver, copper, iron, lead and zinc.

1. Mercury (Sútam, Rasa or Párada).

Quicksilver is found in Thibet; in the form of cinnabar, and in its native state in Nepal.

Shiv declared to Durga that, if properly prepared, quick silver will cure all diseases, even should they be of a fatal nature. Quicksilver is used either in its metallic state, or reduced so as to lose its peculiar properties. In both forms it is useful for the cure of diseases.

Quicksilver is often in an impure state, as when it is mixed with black lead, stone, poison, tin, or other impurities of the same kind; another bad quality is when it resembles fire, and when it disperses in different directions. Good quicksilver is of a slight blueish colour, like water internally and externally, and bright like the sun at mid-day. It is also good when it has a brownish, or whitish colour; but if it has a mottled appearance it is not good.

To purify quicksilver from lead; mix it with rice-water and expose the mixture to fire, which will remove its bad ingredients. To purify quicksilver from tin; mix it with the powder of Vishál (Cucumis colocynthis) and *Ankotha* (Alangium hexapetalum), and then expose the mixture to fire. To remove the other impurities, add the juice of Cassia fistula. To purify quicksilver when it separates into globules; mix it with the juice of datura and lime, and then expose it to heat. To destroy the poisonous qualities of quicksilver mix the three kinds of Myrobalan, and then expose it to heat. It is thus fit for use.

Quicksilver is the semen of Shiv; and being difficult to prepare, the practitioner is first to pray to Vishnu, &c., on a lucky day; and agreeable presents are to be made to virgins, and families of Brahmins before the process is commenced. The following prayer is then to be offered up to Shiv.

'O Ugra (wrathful one)! I salute you! and O Ugra, I pay my reverence! Goraksha, Ishwara, Sarva, Shiva and Bhadra; I salute your different forms; and ask your gracious assistance in rendering this medicine successful.' The quantity of mercury to be prepared should not be less than one pala; and some say when only a small quantity can be obtained, prepare two tolás.

To purify mercury so as to render it fit for being used as medicine, take of turmeric, brick-dust, suet, the juice of lemons (or congee, if limes are not procurable), and the wool of sheep, of each one chhatak, and mix it with one seer of quicksilver. The mixture is to be well rubbed in a mortar, for one day, and wash the product carefully with water.

Another means of purifying mercury is to place it in a bag which is then to be immersed in congee, and exposed to heat. This is called a dolâjantra. By this means the quicksilver is completely purified.

Another way of purifying mercury is by sublimation. The apparatus is called *Urddhwapátanajantra*; and is used in this manner. Take vermilion and the juice of lemons; dry it in the sun and then sublime. It is then to be rubbed with more of the lime, or the juicc of the Páribhadra (the coral tree or Erythrina fulgens) and nimba (Melia azadirachta). They are to be mixed for three hours and again sublimed.

Quicksilver is also purified by evaporation, by means of Vakajantra.

Before quicksilver is mixed with sulphur the following prayer is to be offered up. 'O Shiv, may you so order that this preparation may be so made as to enable it to cure all diseases.' When such prayer is offered up with faith, by a holy Brahmin, it will be granted. Then mix six parts of sulphur with one of quicksilver, put it in a crucible* with its opening properly luted, place this in a sand bath, and apply heat slowly. When the mixture is completed, take the crucible off the fire and break it; the contents may then be used for medicine.

There are four forms in which quicksilver is used in medicine; the black, white, yellow and red forms.

The *black* kind is formed by dissolving equal parts of sulphur and quicksilver over the fire, when the residue will assume this colour which is the most common form in which mercury is used in practice.

To form *white* mercury (hydrargyrum precipitatum album). Take of Borax, honey, lac, and the wool of sheep; mix, and add the juice of the 'Bhringaraja (Verbesena scandens); then add sulphur, and mix for one day; after which expose it to the heat of a sand bath until it is reduced to ashes. It will be white like pure camphor, and will resemble the corrosive sublimate. Another kind of white mercury is made by mixing turmeric, brick-dust, suet, amalakí, (phyllanthus emblica or emblic myrobalan) boirá, (beleric myrobalan) and haritaki, (chebulic myrobalan) chítá (treacle), congee, and the juice of the ghritakumárí, or Indian aloes, mix for one day, and then add half the weight of prepared sulphur.

Another form is made with rock salt, blue vitriol, sulphur, chalk, alum and quicksilver in equal quantities; mix the whole with the juice of the lemon. This is to be put in an earthen vessel over which another is to be placed and the juncture luted.

---

* The crucible is made by mixing two parts of the ashes of paddy, one of the earth of white ants, one pint of iron cinders, one part of white stone and one part of hair; mix with goat's milk, and beat half a day. The crucible is then to be formed, and dried in the sun or fire, for use.

The mixture is then to be exposed for a day to the action of fire, when the mercury will be white and prepared for use.

The use of the white form of mercury is very important. It cures rheumatism, and the eighty diseases of air, as well as the diseases of bile and phlegm. Should it affect the gums, a gargle of curdled milk should be employed. This preparation of mercury will also be found useful in shúl, (colic,) fistula-in-ano, in diseases of the eye, in diseases of the arms, and in general debility; as it increases strength, appetite, and the general colour of the body.

The *yellow* preparations of mercury are made in the following manner. Mix equal parts of sulphur, quicksilver, and the sundu plant and myrobalan. Dry the mixture and put it in a sand bath, and apply heat for twenty four hours. When properly prepared it has a yellow colour. This preparation increases the appetite, and cures dropsy and dyspepsia.

Red Factitious cinnabar or red sulphuret of mercury, when in powder vermilion (Hingula) is prepared as follows: mix one pala of sulphur, and one pound of black lead with the juice of the ghritakumárí; place it in a clean vessel, put a lute or coating of mud and cloth, or a mixture of lime and chalk over it. It is to be exposed in a sand bath for three days, when it will be found of a red colour

It cures all diseases, even of the fatal kind. It removes weakness, improves the appetite and memory, diminishes fat, and cures leprosy. It requires to be given a proper menstruum and mixed with other medicines. The dose is then one gaňja.

Another form of mercury is prepared by mixing the black preparation in an iron spoon. Add a little ghee, and then expose it to heat. When melted throw it into a leaf of the plantain. It is then called Rasaparpatí or *cake* mercury and is very useful in dropsy, chronic dysentery, and as an alterative.

2nd. *Gold.* This, as well as the other metals, is first to be reduced by beating to small thin plates. These are to be exposed to a red heat, and in this state cooled separately in oil, curdled milk, cow's urine, conjee, and a decoction of kulattha (a kind of pea). This process is to be repeated seven times in each liquid. The metal is then considered as prepared for use. Some only quench the hot metal in the above liquids three times. It is also recommended that metals should be cooled twelve times in a mixture of the juice of the leaves of the tuk and àkanda trees, with brim-stone. In other cases three parts of the metal are mixed with one of quicksilver and exposed to heat. Other mixtures are recommended by different authors for oxidizing the metal.

The preparations of gold are considered as most valuable medicines, curing nearly all diseases, even those in which other medicines have been used without any good result. The general effect of these preparations is to increase memory, and restore the vigour of manhood.

The usual manner of preparing gold for use is to mix sixteen times the quantity of the gold plates to one of lead, and add lemon juice and *gritakumári*, or Indian aloes. They are to be rubbed together, exposed to heat, and made into boluses of the usual size. Or take of the mass of gold plates, mix with quicksilver and sulphur, add a little water, or the juice of *ghritakumári*, make it into a large mass; put it in an earthen pot with a mouth well secured, surround the vessel with a mixture of clay and cow-dung, and expose it to the sun to dry. It is thus to be exposed to the fire twelve different times, until it is reduced to powder. Some practitioners mix lead, sulphur, and quicksilver together with the gold, and the mixture is then prepared as above. The oxide of gold thus prepared is often mixed with other metals; and is considered a valuable medicine in chronic diseases, in intermittent fevers, in gonorrhœa, and in diseases of the spleen. It is considered an excellent tonic, improving vision, reducing the bulk of the body, and is good for consumption, and pregnant women and children. It is useful in diseases of air, bile, and phlegm.

Silver. This metal is prepared by mixing two parts of it reduced to small thin plates, with one of brimstone. These are to be well mixed, lemon juice is to be added, and the whole surrounded by a mixture of cow-dung and clay, and exposed to a high heat in a furnace, in the same manner as that in which gold was stated to be prepared. This preparation is sour, cooling, and astringent; and it cures deranged air, promotes appetite, strength, digestion, and the colour of the skin. It also lengthens life, and is of much use in all chronic diseases, as it purifies the body and the dejections.

Copper. This metal is found in the north of India. It is purified by boiling for three days with a strong heat, the small thin plates in cow's urine. The metal is then to be mixed with two parts of brimstone and one part of rock-salt, to which the juice of the lemon has been added. The mixture is then to be surrounded with a coating of cow's dung and clay, and exposed to the fire of a furnace, when it is ready for use. To prevent its producing vomiting and purging, put the mixture into a bulbous root called *Súrana*, which has been hollowed out; it is then to be covered with a mixture of dung and clay, and exposed to heat.

The sulphuret of copper (Tútaka) is prepared by mixing two parts of the thin plates with one of sulphur. It is then to be exposed to heat for two hours. The medicine will neither produce giddiness, vomiting nor purging.

These preparations of copper are found useful in fevers, particularly the intermittent kinds, diarrhœa, spleen and diseases of the liver and blood. It is also, useful in leprosy, colic, piles and indigestion.*

Lead (sisaka). This metal is found in many parts of Hindustan and is prepared for use by mixing it with the juice of the *ákanda*, tree. It should remain immersed for three days; then wash the metal in water, and mix it with the juice of the leaves of the vásaka tree (Justicia ganderussa) and sulphur. Put it into an earthen vessel, and expose it to a high heat. It is then ready for use, and is recommended in gonorrhœa, chronic diarrhœa, in leprosy and in ulcers.

Tin (Trapu and Ránga). One part is to be mixed with the same quantity of sulphur, mix it with the milk of the arka tree (calotropis gigantea), and the dry bark of the Banian tree. Rub them together in a hut mortar for many days.

It is then prepared for use, and is bitter and sour to the taste. It diminishes fat, the diseases of phlegm, is an Anthelmintic, and cures gonorrhœa and jaundice. It is to be avoided in diseases of air.

Zinc, and other metals are prepared in the same way as copper, and their effects upon the system are the same.

Sulphuret of Antimony (Rasánjana Sanvira) is generally obtained from Nepaul or Siam. It is prepared for use by placing it in lime water, and exposing it for several hours to the sun. It is exhibited in diseases of the eye, in the form of a collyrium, mixed with the juice of the ripe pomegranate. It is applied to the edges of the eye-lid to increase the brilliancy of the organ; and it is also used as an emetic in the first stage of the fever, and in combination with other medicines.

Iron (Lauha), is found in many parts of Hindustan in the form of oxide, in ochres, bog ores, and other friable earthy substances. The two following ores are almost commonly used by the Hindus as medicines:—

Sulphate of Iron (káshisha). This is prepared for use by macerating it in a decoction of the leaves of hemp. It is bitter to the taste; and is useful in epilepsy, in white leprosy, in diseases of the eyes, in diabetes, in amenorrhœa, and in phthisis. It is considered tonic, amenagogue, anthelmintic. An *Iron Oxide* called *Sarnamanku?* is prepared by mixing two parts with

* This preparation is also used for strengthening the teeth, and for cleaning and improving their colour.

one part of rock-salt, and with lemon juice in an iron vessel. Apply heat, and rub it with an iron pestle, until it becomes of a fine red colour. It is then slightly bitter and sweet; and is of use in gonorrhœa, in diseases of the urine, in worms, and in various diseases of the bile and phlegm. It is usually exhibited in combination with other medicines for improving the strength.

There are also other varieties of iron. The Kanta (steel?) is the best, and is prepared as follows:—The iron is to be made into three small plates—exposed to heat, and quenched in the juice of the plantain tree. Repeat this seven times: make a furnace by digging a hole one cubit in depth, and the same in circumference—fill it with live charcoal, mix the iron with half its weight of (Swind Maaker) the common Pyritic iron ore, mix them in the juice of the three Mirabuli—add one-fourth of red arsenic (Manahshilá), rub them together with sour congee—expose them to heat in the usual manner with a blast furnace, which is to be well covered; remove the iron when in a red hot state, and quench it in a mixture of the three Mirabuli—beat on an anvil to separate the oxidized part. Again expose the iron as before, so as to reduce all the iron to this oxide, which is used by rubbing it with cow's urine; make it into small boluses, put them in an earthen vessel, and expose the mixture to the heat of a fire of cow's dung. Repeat this a number of times—from 10 to 1,000.—It should never be used unless prepared at least with an exposure to heat more than ten times, and it will be so much better if repeated a great many more times. In this state it does not sink in water, and there is no alterative so good as this. It is an excellent tonic, improves digestion and removes all diseases

When iron has been exposed for many years in the earth it is changed to a red colour, easily powdered. It is called mondulo, and is used for the same diseases as the above preparations of iron.

Arsenic.—The *yellow* sulphuret of *Arsenic* or *yellow Orpiment* (Haritála) is brought to India from China and the Burman dominions; is purified by boiling it in the water of a kind of gonaro Kushundo; in lime water; in oil; and in sour congee, for two or three hours in each. This medicine is also purified by mixing it with four parts of nitre, and then subliming it. This is done by placing it in an earthen pot with another over it, and applying heat for a day and a night.

This is a very celebrated medicine in the black leprosy, and in fever. It also improves the colour of the body.

Red Arsenic or *red Orpiment* (Manahshila) is brought from Japan and is prepared by macerating it in the juice of the Boke tree, or in the juice of the fresh ginger. It is tonic, and is used for removing diseases of phlegm, for Asthma, &c.

White oxide of *Arsenic* (Daarmuch) is prepared by being macerated in the juice of the lemon, and then boiled in the juice of the plantain tree. It is used in doses of the fourteenth part of a grain, in conjunction with aromatics, to check obstinate intermittent fevers, in glandular and leprous affections, in the same way as the yellow Arsenic.

Minerals (*Upadhátu*).

The minerals which are employed in medicine are mica, diamond, precious stones, brimstone, ammonia, a particular shell, and the fragrant earth obtained from Surat.

1. Mica (abhra) is first to be exposed to a high heat, and then thrown into the juice of the *Justicia Gandarussa,* rub them together, and expose the mixture to a high heat. This is to be repeated ten times; when it is considered ready for use. It is reduced to powder, and is then said to cure all diseases. As it increases the secretion of semen it is used for curing impotency, lengthens life, and strengthens judgment.

2. *Diamond* (híraka, vajra) there are four varieties; white, yellow, red, and black. The first is said to resemble the Brahmin class, the second the Kshattriya; and the other two Vaishya and the Shúdra. The large, soft, round, square, and bright, without inequalities or cracks, is considered masculine; the small, hard, five angular, and cracked diamond is considered feminine, and the oblong and triangular kind is considered as neuter. The first is the best kind, it alone should be used in medicine.

It is prepared by being covered with clay and cow-dung, and exposed to heat for a day and a half. Soak it then in the urine of a horse, expose it to heat seven times, when it is considered prepared for use.

Use. It lengthens life, and improves the strength and colour of the body; and cures many diseases.

Precious Stones (mánikya)—these are pearls, and corals. They are prepared by mixing them with lemon juice for a day. Then boil them in a mixture of the juice of the three mirabuli. This is done by exposing them in a bag, covered with a coating of clay and cow-dung and reduce the medicine for use. It is considered a good tonic, and cures many diseases.

4. *Sulphur* (gandhaka) is prepared by mixing it with lime, water, oil and congee, and exposing it to heat, upon an iron vessel, for three hours. It is then ready for use as a medicine, and is administered in combination with other metals.

5. *Ammonia* (nishaadul) is prepared by mixing it with lime water in a bag (golaaguntro) for several hours. It is u^ed in

preparing mercury, and some other medicines It is not used by itself.

6. A shell called (shankanábhi) is sometimes used as a medicine, in combination with others. It is prepared by being macerated in lime-juice.

7. The fragrant earth obtained from Surat called Saurásthtra-mátí is prepared by macerating it in the juice of the lemon for several hours, and then drying it. It is of use in cases of chronic diarrhœa, and dysentery. It is generally given in combination with other medicine.

——:o:——

CHAPTER III.

Pharmacy, or the Preparation of Medicines.

In this Chapter, the weights and measures, with the preparation, and forms, and doses of medicine will be considered.

——:o:——

SECTION I.

Weights and Measures.

Weights and measures were reduced to a more exact form by the celebrated Madhuvakara, who is the author of the work named Paribháshá which treats of this subject. Four of the particles of dust which are seen floating in the sun's rays as it enters a dark room make one likshá ;—

6 Likshás are equal to		1 Sorroko or Mustard-seed.
6 Mustard-seeds make		1 Yava, or Barley-corn ;
3 Barley-corns make		1 Gunja (or seeds of Abrus precatorius.)
3 Gunjas are equal to		1 Tolá.
10 Gunja	,, ,, ,,	1 Pranaka.
4 Másá	,, ,, ,,	1 Saanoo.
2 Saanoos	,, ,, ,,	1 Tolá or Weight of a Rupee.
2 Tolás	,, ,, ,,	1 Karsha or Aksha.
2 Karsha	,, ,, ,,	1 Shukti.
2 Shuktis	or	8 Tolás equal to 1 Pal.
2 Tolás*	,,	1 Karsha or Aksha.
2 Palas	,,	1 Prasrita (handful.)
4 Palas	,,	1 Kudava or ½ a Seer.
8 Palas	,,	2 Kudavas=1 Mansko or Sharáva or a Seer.
6 Palas	,,	1 Prastha or 2 Seers
4 Prasthas	,,	1 Pátra or 8 Seers equal to 1 Adhaka,

and 4 Adhaka make 2 Dronas equal to 1 Shúrpa or 64 Seers

2 Shúrpas make 1 Ghonee or 128 Seers; and 16 Chonies make I Kharee; and 100 Palas are equal to 1 Tolá.*

Some authors say that there are 5 Ratís in 1 Másha (Sushruta) others that there are 8 or 10 Tolás in 1 Másha. In general Practice 5 Ratís are equal to 1 Másha in making pills, extracts, and powders. In decoctions and infusions 10 Ratís are equal to 1 Másha, 8 Másha are equal to 1 Tottah or 64 Jungahs, is equal to and 8 Tolás are equal to 1 Pala. These are the weights which are used for dry medicines. Several other varieties of weights are given in other books.

Double the weight of moist medicines should be taken beyond the dose of dry articles; until the weight exceeds a Khoorubo, 32 Tolás, or half a seer in weight, when the dose in both should be the same. Should the juice of the vegetables be very strong, half the dose of the dry medicine should be given. Lists of medicines are then given in the medical works, with the dose of each variety.

The Fluid measure consists of a pot made of bamboo, wood, or iron, four fingers breadth in depth, and one in circumference. It is called korobo or fluid measure.

Before a medicine is exhibited to a sick person, the physician should examine the state of the air, bile, and phlegm, the internal heat, the individual's strength, the age of the person, the cause producing the disease, and lastly the ingredients of which the medicine is composed. He is next to note whether or not the intestines have been cleared out, and after the best consideration the medicine is then to be administered.

—:o:—

SECTION II.

Preparations of Medicines.

Pharmacy, or the preparation of medicines, is treated of in four Books, stated to have been derived from the great God, *Ishwara.*

The compound internal medicines are usually stimulants, such as infusions of pepper, ginger, &c. Limes are the common acids which are used.

All kinds of medicines are best recent, with the exception of honey, ghee, ginger, long-pepper, and belongo. These medicines should be kept some time before they are used as medicine. All other medicines should be used fresh, and have the proper smell,

* A Tolá in the Sanskrit MSS is equal to ½ Tolá of the modern weights in Medical works.

and when they are a year old they are to be thrown away. Plants obtained from the Himalaya Mountains are the best, and the juice of plants is usually the strongest; cowherds, hunters, &c., may be employed to collect medicinal plants. A Brahmin, however, is preferred, who is poor, and has performed the necessary ablutions and prayers.

Medicines from the animal kingdom are to be taken for young subjects—and secretions, such as milk, urine, &c., are to be taken after the digestion of the food of the animal

The effect of these remedies is either to increase, diminish or cure deranged air, bile, and phlegm; of these diseases, or those of the compound parts (dhátu) of the body. The simple forms of medicines are sometimes applied externally, but they are very seldom administered internally. When a medicine was discovered to possess some property its effects were not tried, but it was usually combined with numerous other remedies of the same kind, in the hope of augmenting the efficiency of the remedy by multiplying the ingredients. On this account the individual articles of the Materia Medica were rarely employed singly!

Medicines should be prepared in a good house, and in a retired situation. If prepared in open situations, in boats, in bazars, and by the sides of roads, their qualities are liable to be injured by unfavourable influences. Should a bad woman, or one menstruating, touch a medicine it will lose its qualities.

Medicines given in too small doses will be like throwing a little water upon a large fire that rather increases than diminishes it. In like manner too large doses of medicine will increase the diseases, and will be liable to produce other diseases.

There is no medicine with one quality, so there is no disease in which there is only one humour affected; medicines, should therefore be mixed according to the state of the patient, the term, and the virulence of the disease. If a medicine consisting of one or two ingredients is not found useful, other ingredients should be mixed with it; and in other cases some of the ingredients should be removed from the prescription.

——:o:——

SECTION III.

Forms of Medicines.

The Hindu Physicians arrange Medicine, in the following order:

1. *Jívaníya,* or that form which gives longevity.
2. *Vrihaníya,* those which give strength, and corpulency to the body.

3. *Kshinakar*, those which make the body thin.
4. *Rechaníya*, those which produce a laxative effect.
5. *Sandániya*, sedatives.
6. *Dípaníya*, stimulants, increasing the internal fire, appetite, &c.
7. *Valíya*, tonics, or those which increase strength.
8. *Varníya*, that improve the colour of the body.
9. *Kanthya*, expectorants, or those which clear the throat.
10. *Hridya*, that give a good relish.
11. *Triptighna*, those which diminish appetite.
12. *Arshaghna*, those which cure piles.
13. *Kushthaghna*, those which cure leprosy.
14. *Kandúghna*, which cure itchiness.
15. *Krimighna*, anthelmintics.
16. *Vishaghna*, antidotes for poison.
17. *Stanyajanana*, which increase the secretion of milk.
18. *Stanyashodhana*, which purify the milk.
19. *Shukrajanana*, which increase the secretion of semen.
20. *Shukrashodhana*, that purify the semen.
21. *Snehopáya*, that produce smoothness and softness of the skin.
22. *Swedopáya*, which produce sweating.
23. *Vamanopáya*, emetics.
24. *Berasjanopáya*, purgatives.
25. *Hasthápanapáya*, enemas of oil, ghee, &c.
26. *Anuvásanapáya*, oily do.
27. *Surabhirachana*, errhines.
28. *Chardanigrahana*, those which stop vomiting.
29. *Trishnánigrahana*, those which quench thirst.
30 *Hikkánigranaha*, those which cure hiccough.
31. *Puríshanigrahana*, those which stop looseness.
32. *Mútrakrichraníya*, diuretics.
33. *Káshahara*, those which cure cough.
34. *Shwásahara*, those which cure asthma.
35. *Sotahara*, those which cure swelling or dropsy.
36. *Juarahara*, febrifuge remedies.
37. *Shramahara*, those which produce tranquility of the humours and remove fatigue.
38 *Dáhaprashamana*, which diminish the burning of the body.
39 *Shiaprashamana*, which stop shivering.
40. *Udoowoprashamana*, those which remove temporary swelling, as urticaria.
41. *Angamarshaprashamana*, that remove pain as rheumatism, &c.

42. *Shúlaprashamana,* which cure colicky pains.
43. *Shonitásthápana,* that stop hemorrhage.
44 *Sangasthápana,* those which restore the senses.
45. *Bedanásthápana,* those which remove pains produced by external causes, as injuries, &c.

This is the division which is followed in Charaka, and under each class simple medicines are arranged. They are all given in the form of decoction.

Susruta again divides medicines into two classes, the *Sangshodhana,* or those which evacuate had humours from the body ; and *Sangshamana* those which diminish the exalted action of the humours and restore them to the healthy state.

The *Sangshodhana* are divided into two classes, *viz.,* purgatives and emetics.

1.—*Powders* (*Chúrnah*). Powders, or dry medicines, are often used instead of green herbs on account of their scarcity.

For preparing such medicines, dry the vegetable in the sun or over the fire, powder it in a pestle and mortar, and clean the powder by passing it through a sieve.

The usual dose of such powders is from one másha to half a tolá, and it is usually administered with water. They are usually employed in diarrhœa and dysentery, and as a purgative, emetic, &c.

2.—*The fresh juice of Plants.* (Swarasa.) This is a frequent form of exhibiting medicines. The juice, generally of the leaves, is obtained by boiling and then straining.

3.—*Pastes.* (Kalka.) These are prepared by grinding the medicine between two stones.

Forms of Medicines.

The manipulations are performed with that useful instrument the mortar, which is used either hot or cold. The qualities of the different medicines are modified by exhibiting them in the Pharmaceutical forms of infusions, extracts and mixtures, &c.

These preparations are divided into medicines used externally, and those which are used internally. Of the former class are ointments composed of oil, ghee or the like, with the juice of the leaves of trees, &c.

The internal preparations are formed of various ingredients, and are administered without any reference to the circumstances of their administration, their comparative efficacy and proportions, or the stages and modifications of diseases in which they are to be employed. Some of the simple medicines are very powerful and their action is too little known.

13

Internal Medicines are usually given in the form of 1 powders, 2 fresh juices (swarasa); 3 pastes (kalka); 4 Decoctions, &c. (kwátha, shíta) infusions (phánta); 5 Extracts (phanita); 6 Roasting (Pátrapáka); 7 Spirituous mixtures (Arishta, Asava and Surá) 8 Pills (Vatiká); and 9 Electuaries (Avaleha); 10 Oils (taila).

4.—*Infusions and Decoctions*, &c. *Infusions* are prepared by mixing one part of the medicine with four parts of boiling water. They are to be infused four hours and the water strained for use.

For *decoctions* (phánta, kwátha, shíta kwátha) take two tolás of medicines to half a seer of water, or one part to sixteen parts of water: boil down to one quarter; strain and take this quantity twice a day. Some recommend eight parts of water to one of the medicine, which is to be boiled down to one quarter. These decoctions are made fresh as required and a little honey is usually added. Weak decoctions are prepared by adding to two tolás two seers of water, which is to be boiled to one half the quantity. This is to be taken several times a day. Sometimes medicinal powders are added to the decoction.

Paníya, is a weaker form of decoction, which is frequently administered to afford immediate relief, seven symptoms such as Shaianga Páníya which is prepared in the following manner:—

Take of Musta (Cyperus rotundus)
Parpatíka (Oldenlandia biflora)
Chandana (Sandal wood)
Kuskus (Cuscus grass)
Bhala Shunthí (dry ginger) of each an equal quantity. Two tolás of this to be mixed with two seers of water and boiled down to one seer; *dose*, a chhaták occasionally. This is an excellent drink to check thirst.

Panchana is another form of decoction. It is formed by decocting two tolás of certain drugs in a pint of water, and reducing it to one quarter; *dose*, a chhaták twice a day in cases of fever, dysentery, &c.

Prakapah is another form of decoction in which medicines are added in powder to increase the strength of the decoction.

Sometimes the medicine is recommended to be prepared for use by *Maceration* (shítakwátha) for a night in cold water. The water is then strained for use.

The fresh juice of plants is considered the strongest form of medicine. The decoction is next, and those obtained by maceration and by infusion are the weakest.

5.—*Extracts (phánita)*. Make a decoction of medicine, mix it with jagree, boil until it becomes thick, or until a small portion when thrown into water does not mix for some time, nor swim in the water; or when a piece of it sticks upon a board when thrown upon it. The extract is then prepared for use. Too much boiling should be avoided, as it by this means loses its peculiar qualities.

Bhávana is made by reducing the medicine to powder and mixing it with a decoction of the same drug, and then exposing it from time to time to the influence of the sun.

6.—*Roasting* (*Pâtrapàka*). These medicines are prepared by crushing them between two stones with the addition of water. When in a state of pulp, wrap them in the leaves of the blackberry or Indian fig-tree, tie it tight with a string and cover it with a coating of clay an inch thick. It is then to be exposed to the fire of cow dung until the clay is red. It is then ready for use, and may be exhibited in the form of powders or pills.

7.—*Spirituous Mixtures or Wines* (Arishta, Asava, and Surá) are often recommended by the other writers on medicine.

8.—*Pills* (*Vatiká*). Pills are prepared in different ways; some are made by rubbing the medicine between stones, others by macerating or grinding to powder. The powder is then to be mixed with water or syrup, and then placed in an open place at night. Other pills are formed by boiling and allowing the mixture to stand in the air or in the sun, and then forming it into balls or pills, which are called Modaka and Gutiká. Each should weigh from one half to one quarter of a tolá. They have different names and measures for preparing them according to the nature of the medicine and the manner in which it is to be used.

9.—*Electuaries to be swallowed* (*Kavalíya*). These preparations are made by boiling down the decoction of the medicine to one quarter, mix sugar with it and again boil for some minutes, and when it has arrived at the consistence of congealing quickly on being removed from the fire, add the usual powders.

Electuaries to be sucked (*Lehya*). These medicines are made with syrups, powders and certain other medicines. They are very useful in curing dysentery, cough, hœmoptysis, &c.

10.—*Oils* (*ghee*). Oils are usually prepared by mixing four times the quantity of milk, whey, cow's urine, &c.; boil, and when the watery part is evaporated, certain fragrant medicines are added, and it is then strained through cloth. These oils are used as external applications. Several such preparations of oils are used, as errhines.

Medicine should be administered according to the strength and age, to the stage and nature of the sickness, and to the kind of medicine as specified in the shástras. It is also very necessary in preparing medicine that the exact proportion of the different ingredients be observed; for if more or less of any one of the ingredients be used than specified, it will have a tendency to increase rather than cure the disease.

Should the sick person be strong, and not too young, a whole dose of the medicine may be given. Thus, with such a person, when oil, decoctions and the like are to be given, one *pala* is the dose. To a moderately strong person three fourths of a dose are to be given, or 3 *akshas* or 6 *tolas*. Should the sick person be in a state of weak health, or be old, or an infant, half a dose should be given or five *ratis*, or one *masha*, whether it be made of oil, ghee, a decoction, or any other medicine. Of electuaries and syrups one or two *karshàs* may be given, according to circumstances. The dose is afterwards to be increased or diminished according to the circumstances of the case, such as the frequency and consistence of the dejections, &c.

——:o:——

SECTION V.

Administration of Medicines.

The Hindus used either iron or stone mortars, warmed or cold. The hot mortar was prepared by exposing it to a fire made with the dry litter of goats and the husks of rice. The Pestle was made of iron or earthenware. It requires to be quite clean and of a sufficient size to hold by the hand. A prayer should always be said over the mortar before the medicines are mixed in it.

The *Menstruum* in which medicine is to be given is water, honey, sugar, &c.; or such substances as speedily act on all the body. When *Váyu* (air) is deranged, cooling and heating things are to be mixed with the medicine; for deranged phlegm, warm and dry things—and for deranged bile, sweet and cooling substances.

In diseases of the chest, such as difficult breathing, cough, ulcers of the thorax, of the nose, affections of the voice, the above menstruums are not proper; as the medicines, such as expectorants, &c., must be taken frequently so as to keep up their action.

The time for administering medicines is important, some requiring to be given before, others during, and a third kind after eating. The general opinion is that medicine should be taken on an empty stomach as it is then soon digested; and like a drop of oil let fall upon water is taken into the system and diffused quickly over it. The following precepts should be recollected in the administration of medicines:—

1. In short and acute diseases the medicine is to be taken without food.

2. The medicine may be taken in some cases with advantage before eating.

3. One half of the medicine should be taken before, and another after food.

4. By the old and weak the medicine should be taken with the food.

5. By others after the food.

6. Another kind should be taken with a covering.

7. When the disease is in the middle of the body, the medicine is to be taken between the two periods of eating.

8. Another kind is to be taken with each morsel of food.

9. Another kind is to be taken after each morsel of food.

10. For asthma, cough, thirst, a vomiting medicine is to be administered frequently.

In treating some diseases, rice is sometimes excluded; and in other diseases, rice alone is allowed after the medicine—in other cases more rice than usual is to be taken; in another form the rice is mixed with the medicine when the person is strong, with powerful internal heat. Medicine should not be given after drinking water, after long fasting, nor in great weakness.

When no liquid for drink is mentioned, water is intended; when no part of the vegetable is stated, the root is to be used; and when no time is stated, the medicine is intended to be taken in the morning.

Before administering medicine the following prayer is to be offered up:—

"Oh! Bramhá! Daksha Ashwiní Kumára[2]—Shiva, Indra, Prithiví,[3] Chandra, Súrya,[5]—Oh! Dhanwantari,[6] Divyadása,[7] Kâshi Rái,[8] Nakula,[9] and Sahadeva[10]—Oh! Váyu,[11] Mala,[12] and all sages and indigenous situations of medicines, and every kind of devil! Cure this disease: and Oh! prophets, like *Rasáyana*,[13] and Mriti which cure weakness and all diseases, may the present prove such: and Oh! Vásuki,[14] endue this medicine with the property of restoring health."

---

1. Son of Bramhá to whom he first gave the Ayurveda.
2. The Physician of the gods.
3. Earth.
4. The moon.
5. The sun.
6. One of the first great Physicians among mortals.
7. Ditto.
8. Ditto.
9. Son of the Physician of heaven.
10. Ditto.
11. Air.
12. Fire.
13. Water of immortality.
14. The great serpent and author of a medical work.

To the medicine the person says—"You are Bramhá and Vishnu, and like Shiva and Durgá, may you cure diseases! May the energy of the east (Indra) and that of the south-east (Agni), the south (Yama[1]), of the north-west (Marut[2]), of the west (Varuna[3]), of the north-west (Nairit), of the north (Kuvera[4]), and of the south-east (Isháua) approach to bestow the qualities for the cure of diseases."

The patient must carefully avoid making faces when he takes a medicine, as this is like Bramhá and Shiva; and it is sinful so to act. As soon as the medicine is taken the vessel which contained it should be turned upside down. The patient is then to wash his mouth and a little sweatmeat is to be taken to remove the taste.

When the medicine is digested, it produces languor, heat, and weakness, giddiness and faintness, diminishes memory, &c. It sometimes produces intoxication and thirst.[5]

Care should always be taken, that a second medicine is not given until the one previously taken has been properly digested otherwise it will not cure the disease.

———:o:———

SECTION VI.

Uses of Medicines.

Charaka arranges simple medicines under the following heads. They were all exhibited in the form of decoction:

1. *Jívaníya*, or that form which gives longevity.
2. *Vrihaníya*, those which give strength, and corpulency to the body.
3. *Kshínakar*, those which make the body thin.
4. *Rechaníya*, those which produce a laxative effect.
5. *Sandáníya*, sedatives.
6. *Dípaníya*, stimulants, increasing the internal fire, appetite, &c.
7. *Valíya*, tonics, or those which increase strength.
8. *Varníya*, that improve the colour of the body.

---

1. The judge of men after death.
2. God of air.
3. Of waters.
4. God of wealth.
5. A medicine is known to be properly digested when it acts in the usual manner, and appears in the motions—while the body feels cold and light, with appetite and thirst, and occasional belching, when the person is in good spirits and the senses are acute.

9. *Kanthya*, expectorants, or those which clear the throat.
10. *Hridya*, that give a good relish.
11. *Triptighna*, those which diminish appetite.
12. *Arshaghna*, those which cure piles.
13. *Kushthaghna*, those which cure leprosy.
14. *Kandúghna*, which cure itchiness.
15. *Krimighna*, anthelmintics.
16. *Vishaghna*, antidotes for poison.
17. *Stanyajanana*, which increase the secretion of milk.
18. *Stanyashodhana*, which purify the milk.
19. *Shukrajanana*, which increase the secretion of semen.
20. *Shukrashodhana*, that purify the semen.
21. *Snehopáya*, that produce smoothness and softness of the skin.
22. *Swedopáya*, which produce sweating.
23. *Vamanopáya*, emetics.
24. *Berasjanopáya*, purgatives.
25. *Hasthápanapáya*, enemas of oil, ghee, &c.
26. *Anuvásanapáya*, oily enemas.
27. *Surabhirachana*, errhines.
28. *Chardanigrahana*, those which stop vomiting.
29. *Trishnánigrahana*, those which quench thirst.
30. *Hikkánigranaha*, those which cure hiccough.
31. *Purìshanigrahana*, those which stop looseness.
32. *Mútrakrichraníya*, diuretics.
33. *Káshahara*, those which cure cough.
34. *Shwásahara*, those which cure asthma.
35. *Sotahara*, those which cure swelling or dropsy.
36. *Juarahara*, febrifuge remedies.
37. *Shramahara*, those which produce tranquillity of the humours and remove fatigue.
38. *Dáhaprashamana*, which diminish the burning of the body.
39. *Shiaprashamana*, which stop shivering.
40. *Udoodoprashamana*, those which remove temporary swelling as urticaria.
41. *Angamarsha prashamana*, that remove pain as rheumatism, &c.
42. *Shúlaprashamana*, which cure colicky pains.
43. *Shonitásthápana*, that stop hemorrhage.
44. *Sangsthápana*, those which restore the senses.
45. *Bedanásthápana*, those which remove pains produced by external causes, as injuries, &c.

Sushruta again divides medicines into two classes, the *Sangshodhana*, or those which evacuate bad humours from the body, as purgatives and emetics; and *Sanjshumana* those which diminish the exalted action of the humours and restore them to the healthy state.

Medicines may be arranged according as they are supposed to cure air, bile or phlegm, or according to their action on certain organs. I shall now give a list of the principal simple remedies in each class, according to their supposed effects.

The following are the principal simple medicines which are employed for the cure of deranged air, phlegm, and bile :—

1. List of Simple Medicines used for the Cure of deranged váyu, (air.)

	Sanskrit.	*Scientific Names, &c.*
1.	*Badarà,*	Zizyphus jujuba or scandens.
2.	*Dàru,*	Pinus Devadaru.
3.	*Kushtha,*	Costus speciosus.
4.	*Haridrà,*	Turmeric.
5.	*Varuna*	Capparis trifoliata.
6.	*Mashà,*	Phaseolus radiatus.
7.	(*Màsh Kalai ?*)	(Dolichos pilosus ?)
8.	*Shringára, Bhojapatra,*	Betula Bhoorja.
9.	*Balà,*	Sida cordifolio.
10.	(*White*) *Balà,*	
11.	*Dási,*	Barleria cœrulea.
12.	*Kachchhura,*	Dolichos carpopogon.
13.	*Shonaka,*	Bignonia Indica.
14.	*Virataru,*	Pentaptero Arjuna.
15.	*Shana,*	Crotolaria juncea.
16.	*Agnimantha,*	Premna spinosa.
17.	*Vatsádaní,*	Menispermum glabrum.
18.	*Eranda,*	Ricinus communis.
19.	*Ashmabhed,*	Plectranthus scultellaroides.
20.	*Shatamúlì,*	Asparagus racemosus.
21.	*Punarnava,*	Boerhavia diffusa & V. alata.
22.	*Vasuka,*	Asclepias gigantea.
23.	*Vasira,*	Pothos officinalis.
24.	*Kánchanaka,*	Michelia champaca.
25.	*Vardhaka,*	Siphonanthus Indica.
26.	*Kàrpasi,*	Gossypium hirsutum.
27.	*Brischikali,*	Tragia involucrata.
28.	*Patúra,*	Pterocarpus santolinus.
29.	*Badarà,*	Mimosa octandra.
30.	*Yava,*	Hordeum hexastichon.
31.	*Kola,*	Piper chuvya.
32.	*Kulattha,*	Dolichos biflorus.

33.	*Vidàri,*	Hedysarum gangeticum.
34.	*Kuveràkshí,*	Bignonia suave-olens.

2. *Simple Medicines used for the Cure of deranged Phlegm.*

1.	*Kaliyaka,*	Curcuma xanthorrhiza.
2.	*Aguru,*	Aquilaria agallocha.
3.	*Tilaparní,*	Pterocarpus santolinus.
4.	*Kushtha,*	Costus speciosus.
5.	*Haridra,*	Turmeric.
6.	*Shita,*	Marsilea quadrifolia.
7.	*Shiva,*	Mimosa suma.
8.	*Shatapushpa,*	Anethum sowa.
9.	*Sarala,*	Pinus longifolia.
10.	*Ràsna.*	Mimosa octandra.
11.	*Prakírjya,*	Cœsalpinia bonducella.
12.	*Udakírjya.*	Galedupa arborea.
13.	*Ingoodi,*	The name of a plant commonly called Ingua.
14.	*Suvarna, Dhattúra,*	Datura Metel.
15.	*Kàkadúnì,*	Cannabis sativa.
16.	*Làngalika,*	Gloriosa superba.
17.	*Hastikarna,*	The castor oil tree.
18.	*Munjàtaka,*	Munja grass.
19.	*Làmajjaka,*	The root of the Andropogon muricatum.
20.	*Vrihati,*	Solanum melongena.
21.	*Mushka,*	Cyperus rotundus?
22.	*Surasa,*	Vitex trifolia.
23.	*Arakvadha,*	Cassia fistula.

3. *List of Simple Medicines used for the cure of deranged Bile.*

1.	*Chandana,*	Sirium myrtifolium.
2.	*Kuchandana,*	Pterocarpus santolinus.
3.	*Hhrívera,*	A drug and perfume commonly called *Bála.*
4.	*Ushìra,*	Andropogon muricatum.
5.	*Manjishthá,*	Rubia manjith, Bengal madder.
6.	*Payasya,*	Asclepias rosea.
7.	*Vidàrí,*	Hedysarum gangeticum.
8.	*Shatàvari,*	Asparagus racemosus.
9.	*Gundra,*	Saccharum sara.
10.	*Shaivála,*	Vallisneria octandra.
11.	*Kalára*	Nymphæa lotus.

12.	*Kumuda,*	Nymphæa esculenta.
13.	*Utpala,*	Nymphæa cerulea.
14.	*Kadali,*	Musa sapientum.
15.	*Kandalì,*	Banana or Plantain.
16.	*Dúrvá,*	Panicum dactylon.
17.	*Mūrvà,*	Sanseviera zeylanica.
18.	*Kakola,*	Cocculus Indicus.
19.	*Nyagrodha,*	Ficus Indica.
20.	*Panchamùla,*	This is prepared by the mixture of five roots, the Bel, Premna longifolia, Cassia, Gmelina arborea, and the Trumpet-flower.

Actions of Medicines.

There are five principal actions of medicines; or *diaphoretics, emetics, purgatives, (enemata) errhines,* or *stimulants.*—Before any of these medicines are given, the body should be relaxed by rubbing oil upon it externally, and giving some oleaginous mixture internally.

1. *Diaphoretics.*—There are four kinds of them:—

1.—*Tàpasweda,* or the application of heat.

2.—*Ushàsweda,* or the steam of hot water.

3.—*Upanahasweda,* or the application of certain warm poultices or plasters made of different medicines; and,

4.—*Dravasweda,* or fomentations with various decoctions.

Of the medicines for relaxing the body; ghee, oil, charbi, marrow, and such like are to be used; of these ghee is the best, as it is produced from milk, which is obtained from the cow. This milk first yields curdled milk, then butter, and with the assistance of fire ghee is produced. Nothing else can be obtained from ghee, so that it may be considered as pure. For diseases of the bile, ghee only is to be given; of air, ghee and salt mixed: and for diseases of phlegm, ghee, long-pepper, pepper, dry ginger and nitre mixed together. A weak person with a bad memory and digestion, should use ghee to cure them. In certain cutaneous diseases, for open boils, and for worms, oil is useful, particularly when the phlegm is deranged. To fat people, particularly when the air is deranged, oil should first be given, particularly when the dejections are not natural. Lard (charbi) is most useful for diseases of the joints, bones and sensible parts.

Perspiration should not be promoted in the scrotum, throat, or eye.

When air and phlegm are deranged in a place, or when only air or cough is deranged, perspiration alone is to be invited to such places. When air and phlegm are deranged, medicines that contain the qualities of coldness and heat, are to be used. When air is deranged, cooling medicines alone are to be used.

Perspiration is not to be encouraged in very fat, very thin, or debilitated persons, when affected with diseases of the blood or air, when the diseases are incurable, in dysentery, or when the person is afflicted with large sores over the body (*Kotha*). Nor will perspiration be proper after poisons, or drinking; when given to the blind, when the abdomen is swelled, or in Erysipelas (*visarpa*), or Leprosy, or in a bad state of the blood. In such cases milk, ghee, curdled milk, and honey should be given after purgatives.

It is improper to give diaphoretics when the body is burnt; in diseases of the anus, in grief or fear-producing diseases; in passions, in hunger, in thirst, in weakness, in jaundice, in gonorrhœa, in hemoptysis, pulmonary consumption, dysentery, during the flow of the menses, or after taking much wine; in pregnancy, particularly near its termination, in diseases of air, or in fatal diseases. When diaphoretics are used under such circumstances they will do harm, or their peculiar effects will not be produced.

In general, emetics are recommended when the stomach is surcharged with phlegm, and purgatives when the intestines and bile are deranged.

Emetics. After the oleaginous or relaxing remedies, and the exhibition of diaphoretics, the five varieties of the other remedies are to be used. The first of these are *emetics*.

When the practitioner has decided on the necessity of giving an emetic, the preliminary relaxing medicines with honey and *Sainphal* (an impure kind of salt,) are to be exhibited. This is usually done the day before the exhibition of the emetic, more particularly when the strength and internal heat of the person are great. A quantity of whey, congee water or the like, should be taken, and the warm hand be applied frequently to the abdomen for an hour to soften it.

The usual emetic is then to be given with the proper prayer. If it cannot be taken for the taste, in the usual way, it may be sucked through the stalk of a hollow reed, so that it may be thrown down the throat. The emetic should be taken in the morning. The person is to place himself upon a stool, with his thigh parallel to the floor, and his head back, and sides supported by friends. He will first feel sick, then saliva will flow from his mouth, and tears and mucus from his eyes and nose, followed by vomiting. The vomiting will be promoted by thrusting a finger or the stalk of a lily down the throat. The vomiting is to be encouraged until the stomach is completely emptied; this is known not to be the case by the discharge of saliva, by the bad breath, and by the body being itchy.

Emetics are to be used when the air is deranged.

Among emetics, madana fruit is the best—and may be administered in the form of powder or decoction with honey and rock-salt.

Emetics may be given in diseases of phlegm, inflammation or internal abscesses, when the bile is deranged, &c.

If the emetics do not act freely, use warm water internally mixed with long-pepper.

The following emetics are to be used when the phlegm is deranged.

White-mustard, rock-salt, and long-pepper; repeat the dose frequently until the desired effect is produced. There are various emetics which are exhibited in the form of powder or chocolate; use warm water after these. The dose of the emetic should be varied with the strength of the individual.

When an emetic has acted properly it first produces an evacuation of phlegm and bile without pain; the breast, neck, and head feel clear, and the body light. The vomiting may be stopped by snuffing sweet smelling mixtures up the nostrils. One kind of emetic acts as a purgative, another restores irregularities of the humours (dhàtu), and retains the body soft.

Vomiting should not be excited in cases of sparks being seen, or sudden blindness, or great fatigue, in spleen, or in jaundice, when the abdomen is swelled, for very fat or thin persons, for infants or for very old persons, particularly when afflicted with piles, sores or diarrhœa, in tetanus, for persons with hoarseness, with hemoptysis or after great losses of blood, nor for pregnant women. When emetics act as purgatives and not as emetics, in the same way as purgatives, when they produce emetic effects, they are unfavourable. The kind of emetic must be varied according as the air, bile, or phlegm is deranged; and various diseases are supposed to be produced when the emetic effect is not produced, such as a bad mouth, fœtid breath, &c. In such cases the person is not to eat, and the emetic must not be repeated that day. Should the vomiting be too severe, it will be repressed by anointing the body with ghee, by cold bathing, and by taking internally a decoction of rasins (kismis) with sugar and water, and other agreeable drinks. In the afternoon, a warm bath is to be given, and light and nourishing food, such as ground pulse of different kinds with the broth of wild animals. An aperient is then to be given to act on the bowels, and food is to be taken in small quantities, to renovate the internal fire and thus repress the vomiting.

Emetics are very useful in diseases of the phlegm, in cases in which poison has been taken—in diseases accompanied with much thirst—in diseases of the internal heat—in diseases of the mammœ

—in madness, in epilepsy—in elephantiasis—in diseases of the humours—in fevers—in want of appetite—in boils—in diseases of the stomach (àmàshay)—in dysentery—in diseases of the chest—in large secretions of saliva—in sickness—in difficulty of breathing—when the person has lost his sense of smell and taste—in diseases of the lips and mouth—when pus is discharged—in diseases of the throat—and in bloody discharges by stool.

The following is a List of the principal Emetics:—

1.	*Madana,*	Vangueria spinosa.
2.	*Kutaja,*	Echites antidysenterica.
3.	*Jimútaka,*	Andropogon serratus.
4.	*Ikshyàku,*	A bitter gourd.
5.	*Dámurdava,*	Achyranthes aspera.
6.	*Ketavádana,*	A plant with white flowers. Pandanus?
7.	*Sarshapa,*	Sinapis dichotoma.
8.	*Garuga,*	A vegetable and medicinal substance.
9	*Pippalî,*	Long pepper.
10.	*Karanja,*	Galedupa arborea.
11.	*Prapunnàda, padmáta,*	Cassia tora.
12.	*Kavidàra,*	Hedysarum alhagi.
13.	*Karvúdára,*	Barleria cerulea.
14.	*Nimba,*	Melia azadiracta.
15.	*Ashwagandhà,*	Physalis flexuosa.
16.	*Vetasî,*	Calamus rotang.
17.	*Bandhujîvaka,*	Pentapetes Phœnicea.
18.	*Sità,*	Clitoria ternatea.
19.	*Shatapushpiká,*	Anethum sowa.
20·	*Vimbikà,*	Momordica monadelpha.
21.	*Vachera,*	Acorus calamus.
22.	*Mrigahbojani,*	Colocynth or bitter apple.
23.	*Chitrá,*	Plumbago Zeylanica.

These medicines not only act as emetics, errhines, &c., but cure all the bad humours from the stomach upwards. From *Madana* to *Prapunnáda*, the fruits alone are used for producing the above effect, and from *Karvadàru* to *Chitrá* the roots are to be used for the same purpose. Sometimes they are used simply, more commonly in combination.

Purgatives, (*Virechana*) and *Enemas* (unávávana or vastí).

Purgatives.—The day before a purgative is exhibited the patient is to eat light food in combination with warm water, so as to remove any disarrangement of the phlegm; the next morning the body is to be anointed with oil and exposed to heat, so as to promote perspiration; after which the purgative is to be given. Should a purgative be given without the preparatory medicines, the person's constitution will be broken, like dry wood at the time it is warping. These will vary according to the intention of the practitioner, and the state of the bowels, which are to be evacuated. There are three such situations:—

First: the *Mridu Kashta,* in which there is much bile and a state of looseness; when if the bile is required to be evacuated, a small quantity of the medicine should be given cold.

The second state is called *Krúrá Kashta,* in which the air and phlegm are deranged, producing costiveness, and the medicine acts with difficulty. In this case the medicine should be given warm and in a strong dose.

The third state is named the middle state or *Madhya Kashta,* in which the air, phlegm and bile are in equal proportions, and accompanied with a state of bowels neither relaxed nor costive. In this case the medicine should be given of a temperate heat and of a middle quantity and quality.

The dose of medicine should vary with the age, &c., of the patient. To infants give sugar with honey. When a purgative has been administered in the above form its action should not be suddenly stopped. The patient should stay in a closed room, and he should not take cold water, nor use force in the evacuation.

When the purgative has not produced the desired effect, it will produce derangement in the bile and phlegm. The body is hot, there is no appetite—and there is a heaviness in the belly, uneasiness in the breast, itchiness of the arms, and there is not a free evacuation of the urine.

When purgatives act too powerfully, they produce fainting, frequent mucous stools, prolapsus ani, and pain in the belly.

When the purgatives act properly, the patient feels easy; and air, phlegm and bile pass freely, and he feels happy and light; air passes by the anus in the usual manner. After the action of purgatives, the patient should take thin and light food—as congee, and sometimes broths.

If purgatives are taken from time to time in a proper form, they clear the understanding and senses, improve the strength of the organs, and of the body. They also improve the appetite and retain the humours in a healthy state, and retard the approach of age.

In infancy a mixture of honey, sugar and trivrit (Teori—Convolvulus turpethum) is to be given, in the form of a powder.

When a purgative acts too strongly with a discharge of blood; in such cases pour cold water upon the body, and give an emetic, with congee and honey; or give the oily or mucilaginous liquids. The enema should be prepared with honey and ghee; animal and vegetable broths should likewise be given.

Purgatives should not be given during the beginning of fever: that is while the patient feels a slight appetite, and his bowels are not very costive. For infants and old or very fat people, purgatives are to be avoided, especially when the body is very hot or much fatigued—in bloody stools, and immediately after labour; also when the appetite is bad, in derangements of the blood, bile and air, when there are sores on the body, or internally, when there is great thirst, after loss of blood—and in diseases of the lungs. Should a quack give purgatives at an improper time he will kill the person.

Purgatives should be used in fevers, in diseases from poisons, in piles, in swelling of the glands, in jaundice, in epilepsy, in diseases of the heart, in fistula-in-ano, in vomiting, in diseases of the vagina, in colicky pains, as costiveness, and in cholera (vishúchikà) in disease of the belly (alasaka), in leprosy, in eruptions, in gonorrhœa, in the enlargement of the spleen, in hydrocele, in ophthalmia, and in general in diseases of the eye, especially in purulent ophthalmia, in diseases of the head, ear and nose—in those of the anus and penis, in worms, in diseases of the bile, and involuntary discharges of semen, &c.

The discharges produced by purgatives are first, urine, fœces, bile, the medicine, and lastly phlegm.

Of the purgatives the *Trivrit*, or as it is usually called Teorí (Convolvolus turpethum), and Harítakí (Chebulic myrobalan) are considered the best. Of the oily purgatives, the castor oil is the best. In diseases of air, give Teorí in powder (6 annas weight for a dose) with the juice of the sugar cane.

In diseases of the bile, the medicine is administered with milk, and in diseases of phlegm, the same medicine is given with the decoction of long and black pepper and dry ginger.

The covering of the Harítakí, is to be used like the teori, in the same form and dose—and to cure the same diseases.

Castor oil is prepared by gathering the seed at the proper season, drying it for seven days, and taking the kernels and boiling them in water—the oil is to be removed for use—in other cases the oil is got by pressing the seeds between weights. This oil is to be given to children from birth to the tenth year. It is also given to old and weak and delicate persons.

Purgatives may be prepared and exhibited with ghee, oil, milk, wine, cow's urine, broths and certain forms of food.

The action of purgative medicines will be increased by using warm water with some infusion, the warm or vapor bath, and friction with the warm hand. When the laxative effect is not sufficient, it is not to be repeated till the next day; but when a sufficient effect has been produced the purgatives should not be repeated for ten days.

The internal fire is diminished by purgatives, and as soon as the action is produced, light food is to be given, and a little mango bark mixed with congee water is to be used internally, and externally friction so as to increase the internal fire.

The efforts of nature should not be resisted; but when the person is weak, and the bowels loose, the medicine is to be given in small quantities and frequently repeated. When the bowels are loose, and the patient either weak or strong, purgatives are to be given, and when in that state if the bowels are not freely evacuated the collection of the bad humours, if retained, will produce other diseases.*

A small dose of the purgative should be first given, and when the individual's constitution is better known, a stronger one may be given.

The following are examples of purgative mixtures: take of Harítaki (yellow myrobalan) salt, and long-pepper in equal proportions; grind them into a paste with water; dose three drams.

Or take of Harítakí, (yellow myrobalan), amlakí (emblic myrobalan), vibhítakí (Beleric myrobalan), in equal parts. Three tolás of this mixture are to be boiled in 48 of water until reduced to 12 tolás. To six tolás of this infusion add three of castor oil.

Or take three tolás (9 drams) of castor oil, with six of milk.

When the purgative is required to be taken, for diseased bile the following mixture is recommended:—

Take of	Garatwak (cassia bark) ...	...	¼ tolá.
	Tejpátá (cassia leaf) ...	...	¼ ,,
	Pepper	...	¾ ,,
	Teori (convolvulus turpethum),	...	¾ ,,
	Sugar	...	¾ ,,

pound and mix with hot water.

When the phlegm is diseased:—

Take of	Pippalí (long-pepper) ...	...	¾ tolá.
	Shunthí (ginger) ...	...	¾ ,,
	Yavakshára (nitre) ...	...	¾ ,,
	Shyámalatá (Echites antidysenterica	...	¾ ,,
	Teori (Convolvulus Turpethum	...	1 ,,

pound and form an electuary with honey.

---

*This is known by symptoms of derangements of phlegm and bile, by the loss of appetite, and heaviness and itchiness, heat of the body, and a diminution of the internal fire. The dejections are constipated in such cases.

Purgatives, or those medicines which clear the body of diseased humours below the stomach.

1.	*Trivrit*,	Convolvulus turpethum.
2.	*Shyáma*,	Panicum frumentaceum.
3.	*Dantí*,	Croton Polyandrum.
4.	*Dravantí*,	Anthericum tuberosum.
5.	*Saptalà*,	Abrus precatorius.
6.	*Shankhini*,	Cissampelos hexandra.
7.	*Vishàniká*,	Asclepias geminata?
8.	*Vavàka*,	Clitoria ternata.
9.	*Shavalantari*,	A kind of Convolvulus.
10.	*Shatraha*,	
11.	*Suvarnaka*,	Cassia fistula.
12.	*Chitraka*,	Plumbago Zeylanica.
13.	*Kinihí*,	Achyranthes aspera.
14.	*Kushà*,	Poa cynosuroides.
15.	*Kásha*,	Saccharum spontaneum.
16.	*Jelaka*,	
17.	*Kampílaka*,	A variety of *teori* (Convolvulus turpethum.)
18.	*Ramàkà*,	
19.	*Pátálá*,	Bignonia suaveolens.
20.	*Haritakí*,	Terminalia Chebula.
21.	*Nílinì*,	Indigofera tinctoria.
22.	*Eranda*,	Ricinus communis.
23.	*Kuthika*,	Costus speciousus?
24.	*Aragvada*,	Cassia fistula.
25.	*Mahàvriksha*,	Euphorbia.
26.	*Saptacheda*,	
27.	*Arka*,	Calotropis gigantea.
28.	*Jatísatí*,	Halicacabum cardiospermum.

From *Trivrit* to *Kásha*, the roots are used: and from *Jelaka* to *Pàtàlà* the bark is used, from *Harítàkí* to *Eranda* the fruits of the tree, the leaves of *Kuthika* and *Aragvada* are used; and the milk of the other medicines of this list is used for producing their purgative effect.

There is another class of medicines which produce both vomiting and purging, they are:—

1.	*Kashàtakí*,	Several sorts of cucurbitaceous plants.
2.	*Saptalá*,	(Abrus precatorius.)
3.	*Shankhiní*,	(Cissampelos hexandra.)
4.	*Devadàlí*.	
5.	*Ravílikà*,	(Momordica Charantica.)

The juices of these plants are used for producing their effects, as the organs of speech for the articulation of vowels and Sibilants.

Enemata (anuvásana). This is considered as the best manner of exhibiting purgative medicines in diseases of the lower part of the abdomen, and lower extremities. Medicines may be mixed with these so as to cure diseases of air, bile and phlegm, as the medicine enters the system like water poured at the root of a tree. These medicines were much used by the ancient practitioners.

The general effect of enemas is to strengthen the muscles, and to lessen fat. They retain the eye and surface in a healthy state—and will retain the body healthy till death, or even lengthen the period of existence.

The bladders of pigs, buffalos, goats, &c., are used for these injections. For this purpose the animal should be healthy and of full age. Should bladders not be found a leather bag may be substituted.

The injecting pipe should be made of gold, silver, copper, iron, hard wood or ivory. It should be smooth, strong and tapering like the tail of a cow, with a slightly tuberculated extremity, six fingers' breadth in length to the cross piece, from the first to the eighth year of age; eight or ten from the 9th to 16th year; and afterwards somewhat longer. During the first year, the tube should be the size of the little finger, afterwards of the ring finger, then of the middle finger; and after the 25th year, the size of the thumb. In administering enemata care must be taken not to introduce it in an oblique direction, nor too far or too short a distance, and not to press it on one side. The cross piece is likewise varied in length at the different periods of life. The size of the injection should also be varied according to the size of the patient's hands.

For the very young two handsfull of the liquid is to be used; for a child of eight years four, and of from 16 upwards eight handsfull.

There are two varieties of glysters. one without (asnehaka) and another with oil (snehaka).

The following is offered as an example of a glyster in costiveness, piles, dyspepsia, intermittent fever, in diseases of the loins, back, and intestines. It should be prepared as follows:—

Take of the decoction of, Suttee.—

Pushkara,	A kind of Costus.
Krishnapàka,	Carissa carondas.
Madana,	Datura metel.
Dubdáru,	Uvaria longifolia.
Kushtha,	Costus speciosus.
Yashti madhu,	Liquorice.
Villa,	Assafœtida.

add ten parts of milk and four of oil; mix and administer warm. Various other glysters are prepared in much the same way.

This form of administering medicine is very useful when not too frequently used, in fever, diarrhœa, and dysentery; in diseases of the head and eyes, in tetanus; in convulsions, and in many nervous and other diseases.

Enemata are not proper in madness, in piles, jaundice, in fainting, for the timid or those labouring under grief, in indigestion, in vomiting, leprosy, dropsy, asthma, cough, diseases of the throat, diseases of air, such as swelling of the extremities, before the third or fourth month of pregnancy, and in the very young and old, or when afflicted with nervous diseases.

Two thirds of the usual quantity of food should be taken before the glyster is to be administered; before or after eating they will produce vomiting.

Before the injection is administered the body is to be cleaned and anointed; the patient is to rest in the lap of a large man in a clean situation; where there are no currents of air; he is to recline on his left side, and in an hour the enema will operate.

If the enema does not operate properly, it will diminish the internal heat, increase the urine, and will not purify the body. It first discharges the dejections, the bile, phlegm and air. In this manner it purifies the body.

Injections by the urethra (uttaravastí).—These should be used by a tube fourteen fingers breadth in length, or the length of the penis, with an opening of the size to allow a mustard seed to pass. For the female the tube should be four fingers breadth in length and the opening capable of allowing the passage of a small pea (mudga). For young girls the tube should be two fingers breadth in length. The tube should be covered with oil and gently introduced, and by pressing the bladder fixed at one extremity; crosses should be fixed on the tube to prevent its being introduced too far. The injection should be two tolás in size. These injections are used for diseases of the semen, the bladder and the uterus.

When there is a burning in the bladder, an injection of honey, sugar, or a decoction of liquorice and cold water is given. In some cases injections of ghee are used; and in others astringent injections, such as decoctions of the bark of the vata tree (ficus indica) and banian tree.

After the introduction of the injection the patient should take liquid food such as barley water, congee or animal broths.

After the evacuation by purgatives, emetics, enemata, or blood letting the patient is left with the internal fire diminished, and on that account heavy food should be diminished still more—and light and nourishing food should be taken.

4.—*Errhines.*

This is a large class of local irritants; and they are used with the intention of producing sneezing and exciting a discharge from the nostrils, by which the head is supposed to be cleared from the presence of bad humours.

There are five varieties of fumes used as errhines:—

1.—*Prayojika,* or those forms of smoke which are taken by the nostrils at three efforts. For this purpose different spices are made into a powder, and a tube twelve fingers breadth in length, its size of the small finger, and to taper to the end which should be the size of the thumb. The aperture should be the size of a (Kobo) or small pea; for eight fingers the tube is to be surrounded with silk cloth, over which the medicine is rubbed. The candle thus prepared is to be set fire to, and the fumes are to be drawn into the nostrils.

2.—*Snaihika,* are prepared by oily substances. They are made with wax—different gums, such as gaguli (gum resin) with ghee. This is to be lighted and the fumes are to be introduced into the nostril.

3.—*Varechanika,* those which clear the head. They are made with medicines which irritate the nostrils, such as black pepper, long pepper, and *Aguru* a kind of fragrant wood. They are to be made into a paste, with which the tube is to be covered and then lighted. The fumes produce the effect desired.

4.—*Vámaníya,* which cause vomiting. They are found by burning the skin and hair of animals—dry fish and flesh, and other substances which produce vomiting. The smoke should be taken in first by the mouth and evacuated through the nostrils, and when taken by the nostrils it should be passed through the mouth.

These are the usual forms in which expectorants are given for promoting the secretion of the nervous membrane of the glottis, trachea, and air cells of the lungs. These are rarely used. In diseases of the throat and chest the smoke is to be taken by the mouth, and by the nose for those of the head, nose and eyes.

Káshaghna, which cures cough. The usual manner of exhibiting it is prepared with medicines which cure the cough, such as,

Vrihatí (Solanum melongena).
Kantakáriká (Solanum jacquini).
Long pepper.
Black pepper.
Dry ginger.
The root of the Kankataka Shringhí.

The proper errhines are five:—

1.—*Nasya,* is prepared with ghee, oil, and decoctions of vegetable errhines. It is usually used in diseases above the neck, from derangements of the air and bile.

2.—*Shiroveshaníya,* is prepared with medicines which clear the head of pent up humours—accompanied with weight and pain of the head. This form is likewise used in diseases of the throat particularly swelling—when worms infest the head and nose, in jaundice, in polypus of the nose—when the person can neither distinguish taste nor smell; oily substances are usually employed. It is used in diseases of the mouth, eye, and ear, caused by derangements of the phlegm.

3.—*Pratimarsha,* is prepared with those errhines which clear the head, and is used in the form of powder. It is used in health in the following cases,—after waking from sleep, after fatigue, eating both in the morning and evening. This medicine cures diseases above the neck and retards the marks of old age.

4.—*Avapira* is prepared with sugar, the juice of the sugar-cane, milk, ghee and animal broths, and those errhines which clear the head. It is used for diseases of the heart, as in fainting—for weak and delicate persons.

5.—*Pradamna* is prepared with those medicines which clear the head in the form of powder, and is introduced into the nostrils by means of a tube. It is used in epilepsy, apoplexy and other diseases producing a loss of sense.

When phlegm is deranged the errhines are to be given in the morning; when bile, at noon; and when the air is deranged, in the evening.

Errhines should not be employed in Raktapitta, Virakti, after emetics and purgatives, in swelling of the abdomen (Udara) in involuntary discharges of the semen, in sudden blindness and when the air is deranged, after eating much food, or drinking wine, after poisons, wounds or injuries of the head, in jaundice, when the person cannot sleep, and when very thirsty.

Errhines for clearing the head of humours.

The following is the list of medicines used as *errhines* to clear the head:—

	Sanskrit.	*Scientific and other names.*
1.	*Pippalí,*	Long pepper.
2.	*Viranga,*	A vegetable and medicinal substance.
3.	*Apangaka,*	Achryanthes aspera.
4.	*Shigru,*	Morunga guilandina and hyperanthera.
5.	*Siddhárthaka,*	White mustard.
6.	*Shirísha,*	Acacia sirisa.
7.	*Marícha,*	Pepper.

8.	*Karavíra,*	Oleander or Nerium odorum.
9.	*Vimbí,*	Momordica monadelpha.
10.	*Girikarnikà,*	Hedysarum alhaji.
11.	*Kinihí,*	Achyranthes aspera.
12.	*Vacha,*	Orris root.
13.	*Jalashúlí,*	Halicacabum cardiospermum.
14.	*Karanja,*	Galedupa arborea.
15.	*Lashuna,*	Garlick.
16.	*Ativisha,*	Atis or Betula.
17.	*Shunthí,*	Ginger.
18.	*Talísha,*	Flacourtia catáphracta.
19.	*Tamála,*	Xanthochymus pictorius.
20.	*Surásarjaka,*	
21.	*Ingudí,*	Name of a plant called Ingua.
22.	*Mesha,*	A sort of small cardamum.
23.	*Sangí,*	Betula Bhoorja.
24.	*Mátulunga,*	Citrus medica.
25.	*Murangí,*	Hyperanthera morunga
26.	*Phalí,*	Blossom of the Sacharum Sara.
27.	*Jati,*	Phyllanthus emblica.
28.	*Shála,*	Ophiocephalus?
29.	*Tála,*	Borassus flabelliformis.
30.	*Madhuka,*	Bassia latifolia.
31.	*Lákshá,*	Shell Lac.
32.	*Hingu,*	Assafœtida.

Sores are frequently recommended to be fumigated. For this purpose a tube is used eight fingers breadth in length and the fumes of the medicine are to be conveyed so as to be brought into contact with the surface of the sores.

Gargles. The quantity should be such as can be moved in the mouth. The patient should stand erect. He should attend to what he is doing, and when it is mixed with the bad humours of the mouth, nose or eyes, it is to be evacuated and another portion is to be taken into the mouth. Gargles usually consist of astringent decoctions with honey or urine of cows, or the juice of acid fruits, black pepper, long pepper, dry ginger, vacha, mustard, harítakí raví balm, mixed with oil, vinegar, wine, cow's urine, salt or honey, according to the disease, &c. They may be used either hot or cold, and when properly employed they cure diseases of the mouth, clear it and produce easiness of the part.

6.—*Emmenagogues.* The remedies for restoring or bringing on the menstrual discharge are vinegar and acids, cow's urine, curdled milk, khito (a kind of pea), cow's urine and wine. These medicines are not often used, and as the irregularities are often produced by weakness, tonics are frequently given.

7.—*Diuretics.* This class of medicines are used in strangury, in pain of the bladder, in scanty urine and in gravel and stone. The principal of these medicines are :—

Víratarv,	Barleria longifolia.
Sahachara,	Yellow Barleria.
Darbha,	Poa Cynosuroides.
Lavang,	Nutmeg.
Kusha,	Plant called maukátha.
Kásha,	Saccharum spontaneum.
Ashwavedhaka,	Plectranthus sculellaroides.
Agnimantha,	Premna spinosa.
Vasuka,	Sesbana graudiflore.
Vasira,	Pothos officinalis.
Ikshu,	Sugar-cane.

These medicines are either used in decoction or in powder. For this purpose the following decoctions are used with honey and sugar. Take equal quantities of :—

Mahásáhá,
Kshudrasáhá,
Madhuka,
Sadanstra.

Two tolás of the mixture are to be infused in a pint of water' which is to be put on the fire until reduced to one quarter, when it is prepared.

Parturifacients.—Medicines for promoting the expulsion of the fœtus from the womb were not known by the Hindu practitioners. In cases of lingering labor, manipulation (mantha) was employed to promote delivery.

Sialogogues. Medicines for increasing the secretion from the mouth when too dry, are often had recourse to for expelling morbid humours from its neighbourhood. They should never be used before the 5th year. The medicines which are considered as belonging to this class are; calomel, (rasavása) and corrosive sublimate, (rasakarpúra). The other medicines of this class are black and long pepper, dry ginger, rock salt, acid fruits, *Vacha* and other hot spices.

External agents stimulating the vital powers. These act either externally or internally.

The external agents are those that produce a determination of blood to the part; 2nd, a secretion of semen; and 3rd the formation of pustules. The following are generally used :—

Chitraka,	Plumbago.
Akhanda,	Asclepias.
Sarshapa,	Mustard.
Pútikíta,	A kind of blistering fly.

Shobhanjana,	Hyperanthera Morunga.
Ardraka,	Fresh ginger.

These substances are made into a paste and applied over the part.

Local and internal stimulants.—Carminatives, or those agents which stimulate the stomach and intestinal tract, and lead to the expulsion of flatulence. This numerous class of medicines have already been enumerated, under the head of Aliments. The medicines (pipaládi) are :—

Pippalí,	Long pepper.
Chavi,	A variety of pepper.
Chitraka,	Plumbago.
Shringavera,	Fresh ginger.
Amlavetasa,	Rumex vesicarius.
Maricha,	Black pepper.
Ashwamodaka,	Common canary seeds.
Valàtaka,	Seed of marking-nu plant.
Hingu,	Assafœtida.
Jíraka,	Cardamum seed.

These medicines are used in powder or decoction with or without other articles.

The astringents are used for curing diarrhœa and dysentery, and another kind of astringent tonics are of use for the cure of ulcers and for stopping hœmorrhage; the principal are :—

Priyanga,	Panicum italicum.
Samagá,	Lycopodium imbricatum.
Dhátakí,	Grislea tomentosa.
Punnága,	Rottlera tinctoria.
Raktachandana,	Red sandlewood.
Matrarasa,	A kind of kino gum.
Rasánjana,	Sulphuret of antimony.
Padmaka,	A kind of fragrant wood.
Rejanavulí,	Menispermum glabrum.

For ulcers and stopping hœmorrhage the following medicines are used :—

Nyagrodha,	Ficus indica.
Udumbara,	Ficus glomerata.
Ashwattha,	Ficus religiosa.
Plaksha,	Ficus infectoria.
Madhuka,	Liquorice root.
Kakubh,	Pentaptera Arjuna.
Amra,	Mangoe tree.
Jambu,	Rose apple.
Madhuka,	Bassia latifolia.
Vanjula,	Dalbergia ougeinensis.

Tinduka, Diospyros glutinosa.
Rodhra, Symplocos racemosa.

The barks of other trees are used in the form of decoctions or powders.

13. *Alteratives* (*Rasáyana*), are medicines which increase strength and remove diseases. These medicines must be varied according as they are to be administered to the young, the adult, and the old. It is only to the two latter that this class of medicine is to be administered; and before giving it, an emetic or a purgative should be administered; as a cloth should first be cleaned before it is dried. There are four kinds of Rasayana. The first promote pleasure; the second cure diseases; the third increase memory and longevity; and the fourth prevent the usual changes of life, such as age, thirst, hunger, and other wants. 1. Cold water, milk, honey, and ghee may be taken internally, together or separately, to restore a proper degree of strength to the body. 2. Another kind of *Rasáyana* increases the memory, and the person's life. Various remedies are recommended for this purpose, as the fruits of Sítá and Avalguja. They are to be powdered and mixed with sugar, kept in a vessel for seven days, and then used with cold water. During this treatment the person should reside in a close room, and continue this medicine for six months. He should only use rice, milk, and sugar for food, and bathe in cold water towards evening. His memory will thus be improved and he may live for a hundred years. This plan of treatment may be adopted in leprosy and dropsy, with the addition of cow's urine instead of water. With this medicine the juice of the *mandúkaparní* is used, after which milk should be taken, and barley, rice, jesimin, and ghee exhibited for three months. 3. Another kind, retains the person young, prevents the hair turning gray, and the teeth from falling out. If a man use cold water, milk, honey, and ghee separately, or together, he will not soon have the marks of old age. For the same purpose other medicines are recommended. 4. There is a medicine called *Soma* which produces longevity, and removes the marks of age. There are many varieties, but none are now known, as sinful persons are often in sight. Numerous other medicines of this class are used for increasing the pleasure of the society of women. These are nutritious diet, such as ghee and animal food. Of this class is considered good food and drink, good news, anointing the body, especially towards the full moon, the presence of young women, love songs, clear nights, betel-nut, wine, flowers, such as garlands round the neck, sweet smells, beautiful gardens, and a fine prospect. The powder of *Vidára* with ghee and honey, and also the powder of Amlaka with sugar, honey and ghee, the flower of barley, &c., with milk and

16

the seeds of Atmagupta increase the person's happiness, and his desires. These desires will be diminished—when they are against the heart, when the inclination is wanting, when much bitter, hot, salt, or sour articles of food are eaten, which diminish the (dhátu) and desire. In like manner desire will be removed by its abuse, certain diseases of the external organs, and the division of the vessels. Some cure their desires through the influence of the mind, as holy fakírs did; and another class of persons are born without such carnal desires.

14. *Oleaginous applications,* (*Sneha,*) such as oil, ghee, fat, &c., may be given by the mouth as a laxative, as an errhine, as an enema, or for anointing the body, or as injections for the ear and urethra, and with food. There are two kinds, vegetable and animal oils. Of the latter cow's ghee is the best—and tel (sesamum seed oil) is the best kind of medicine of the vegetable variety, Some of this class of medicines are digested with difficulty, others with less difficulty, and a third kind easily.

Ghee is good for weak persons who have a bad memory, who are affected with poison, and in diseases of air and bile. Oil is to be used externally, but it may be given internally in cases of worms, and in costiveness. Warm water should be taken after the oleaginous substances.

15. *Agents* acting by depressing the vital powers are *Refrigerants,* such as cold infusions both internally and externally. Fire is also used. *Narcotics.*—Very few narcotics were stated in the ancient works, sidhi (ganja, bháng) obtained from the hemp, was used, as also Dátura.

16. *Chemical Agents.*—These medicines are 1st, Escharotics and caustics. 2nd, *Lithontriptics* or solvents of urinary stones or gravel. The escharotics and caustics will be considered under the next chapter on Surgery.

Lithontriptics are sometimes employed. For this purpose the usual diuretics are exhibited, particularly *Arjuna,* (Pentaptera Arjuna,) and *Ashwavedaka,* (Plectranthus scutellaroides, Roxb.)

When administered by an ignorant person medicine is compared to poison, is like the knife, fire, or lightning; but when administered with the necessary knowledge, medicine is like *Amrita* or the water of immortality. There are said to be two kinds of medicine, one of which gives strength to the body when no disease is present, and another class cures diseases when they are present. In like manner poison may be administered in the proper manner with great advantage in the cure of disease.

—:o:—

CHAPTER IV.

SURGERY, (*Shala.**)

The frequent accidents which must have occurred among a race of people devoted to hunting and agriculture, and the feuds that were so frequent among them, induced the Hindu sages to pay attention to wounds, fractures, and dislocations. In this manner, we explain the importance which the ancient writers of the Hindu system of medicine give to this branch of the healing art, and the attention which they bestowed upon it. These remarks prove that at a very remote period of their History, the Hindu practitioners were accustomed to perform lithotomy, the extraction of the dead fœtus, paracentesis, thoracis and abdominis, &c. This proves the extent of their practical knowledge, and the energy and boldness in executing hazardous operations which distinguished their ancient surgeons. This is the more remarkable as these treatises were supposed to be written by *munis* or divine sages, who would not compromise their character by recording precepts utterly contrary to the ritual of their law, or at variance with the principles and prejudices of their countrymen. Indeed, these precepts are often completely irreconcileable with their present notions, which must be considered as slowly growing out of the altered state of society, and are unsupported by their venerable ancient, and most remarkable civil and moral as well as medical institutions.

According to the Hindu Shastras diseases are cured by the influence of prayers and medicines; and when these are ineffectual it is necessary to have recourse to the knife or other such means. According to the shastras, surgery, therefore, may be defined to be that branch of Medicine which principally effects the cure of diseases by the application of the hand alone, the employment of instruments, or the use of topical applications.

At the great battle of the Asuras and Devatás, Jagya was severely wounded in the neck, and the Aswiní Kumára, or the practitioners of heaven, soon cured the wound. This pleased the devatás so much that they were received among them with much respect, and a share of their honors is still bestowed upon them. Bramhá also declared that the art of cutting, healing ulcers, setting bones, and the use of escharotics, was the first branch of the healing art imparted by the deity to mankind; and as the operations of Surgery are rapidly performed, and afford immediate relief, they impart holiness, riches, and a good name

*To remove rapidly; or the art of removing foreign substances from the body, particularly the arrow.

to the performer, and will ensure his passage to heaven after death.

In the Ayurveda, Surgery is considered as the first of the eight departments of the Medical Science; and Dhanwantari was born to teach this as well as the other departments. He declares, indeed, that surgery cannot be practised with success unless the practitioner is familiar with the practice of medicine of which it is only a branch.

The following remarks on Surgery will be considered, under the heads of :—

1st. The structure of the body, and their natural and relative positions, so as to enable the Surgeon successfully to perform operations.

2nd. The nature of surgical diseases; including inflammation, ulceration, and fistula.

3rd. Description of surgical instruments and bandages.

4th. The means of removing blood from the body, including cupping, leeches, and scarifications.

5th. Styptics.

6th. Caustics, actual and potential.

7th. Burns and scalds.

8th. Directions for performing operations, for removing foreign substances from the body, and for treating wounds.

9th. The means of improving, and of forming new ears and nose.

10th. Of fractures and of their treatment.

11th. Of dislocations and their treatment.

—:o:—

SECTION I.

The importance of having a knowledge of Anatomy in those who exercise this branch of the healing art, is so evident; and has been already noted so fully, that it will be sufficient to refer to the previous chapter of this book.

—:o:—

SECTION II.

Nature of diseases which are to be cured by Surgical means.

Inflammation (Vrana,* shotha, or shopha). Saraswata divides inflammation into two kinds, the one produced by accidents or external injuries; and the other by internal causes. Injuries of

*Vrana differs from shotha by its being accompanied with less inflammation, and by its not suppurating.

the body produce the first kind of inflammation, while derangements of the air, bile, phlegm and blood or their combinations produce the second variety.

Under the class of accidental inflammations, swellings of all kinds will be considered, as they always commence with a certain degree of inflammation.

The essential symptom of inflammation, is pus, and the peculiar symptoms are produced by the humour that is affected: In all cases the inflammation commences in one point, from which it extends on all sides. The varieties of inflammation are produced—

a. By diseased air.
b. By deranged bile.
c. By deranged phlegm.
d. By the derangement of air, bile, and phlegm.
e. By deranged blood, and
f. By external or accidental causes.

a. The variety of inflammation produced by derangements in the air, is characterized by the swelling being irregular and soft, by its red or dark colour, and from its being sometimes large and at other times small. The pain of this variety is sometimes severe, and of various kinds, and it swells and ripens in different ways, the discharge being limpid.

b. The second variety of inflammation, produced by deranged bile, is characterized by the swelling being of a dark red yellowish colour, or the colour of a ripe wild fig. The part feels hot and painful like the application of a hot iron, and it is accompanied with fever. The swelling quickly forms and ripens into a yellow discharge.

c. When the inflammation is produced by diseased phlegm the swelling is elevated with round edges, with a central depression. It is cold and shining, of a pale yellow colour, with itching pain. The swelling slowly forms and ripens. The discharge from the deranged phlegm is white.

d. When the three humours are deranged, the swelling is of different colours and is accompanied with various degrees and kinds of pain, according as the one or other of the humours predominate, and the discharges are of different colours, but generally resembles bile and blood, being red, black and yellow, and of various consistencies. This variety is cured with difficulty; it is large; sometimes forms quickly, in other cases slowly. Sometimes it becomes prominent as it ripens, at other times it remains flat.

e. When blood is deranged, producing inflammation, the swelling resembles that produced by deranged bile, but is of a darker red colour. When large it has a dark yellow colour; and is very hot and painful with much fever.

f. Accidental inflammation, produced by wounds, bruises, &c., resembles the other varieties in the symptoms, and only varies in the treatment, by cold applications being proper in this class, but not in the other. When the blood is deranged in this variety, it resembles bile, but is of a darker red colour. When air, bile and phlegm are much deranged, the swelling will be incurable but will suppurate, as also when the physician does not apply proper medicines. When such a patient does not eat or act in the proper manner the wound will not heal. By the wound of a part the air is deranged producing pain, and the blood of the part becomes mixed with the bile of the part and becomes deranged. In this manner, pain, fever, thirst and heat of the body occurs, followed by the other symptoms of deranged bile.

Inflammation is likewise divided into three stages, the invasion, the acute, and the suppurating stage. In the first there is not much heat nor discoloration, or hardness of the part. The pain and swelling of the part is likewise slight. In this stage the inflammation is said to be, *Ama* (unripe). In the second stage the pain is lancinating, or like the bites of ants, or as if they were running about. In other cases, the person feels as if the part was burnt, torn, pressed or bound; the person becomes restless and uneasy, and the swelling is much increased and discoloured, accompanied with much heat, thirst, loss of appetite, and other symptoms of fever. This stage is called *pachamána* (ripening stage). The third stage is distinguished by the part becoming pale, the swelling diminishing, becoming soft and wrinkled, and the skin becoming rough, scaly and elastic. The pain becomes throbbing, with a feeling of itchiness; the abscess opens, the fever diminishes and the appetite returns. This stage is called *pakwa* or ripe.

This pus is produced by the air, bile, and phlegm, the bile preparing the pus from the blood. In inflammation the air produces the pain, and the bile ripens the swelling.

The inflammation varies with the tissue which is involved in the disease, of which there are eight varieties, according as it affects the skin, flesh, vessels, tendons, bones, joints, abdomen, and sensible parts of the body. When confined to the skin, inflammation is cured quickly; but when it affects the other tissues, it is cured with more difficulty and passes through the different stages.

The air, bile and phlegm when deranged produce inflammation, which will vary in its effects according to the part which is affected. When it affects the abdomen, it produces gulma, &c., with a puffiness of the abdomen, which resembles the white ant's nest. Such inflammation and swelling may also occur at the anus, pelvis, or penis; at the navel or sides, in the groin, mammæ, or spleen, in the liver, pancreas, or the organ of thirst. This internal inflammation varies in the same manner as the external does. When the former occurs in the anus it retains the air in the pelvis, and urine is secreted in small quantities and with pain. When it occurs at the navel there is a hiccough, and a gurgling noise. When the sides are so affected, it is from diseased air; and when the groin is so affected, the loins and back feel very painful. When the breast is so diseased, the person remains doubled up, and respiration is performed with difficulty and pain. When the spleen is diseased, and when the breasts are affected, the whole body is uneasy, and feels painful; and in the latter disease there is a copious secretion of phlegm. When the liver is affected with inflammation, it produces noise in the breathing, with hiccough; and when the pancreas is so diseased, the person is continually wanting to drink.

When the inflammation occurs in sensible parts, whether the disease be recent or ripe, whether it be large or small, it gives great pain. When the internal inflammation is above the navel, the pus will be discharged by the mouth; and when under this, by the lower outlets. In this case the person will live, but in the former he will die.

When the breast, navel, or pelvis is diseased the person will die when it suppurates internally; but he may recover when the abscess bursts externally. The first five varieties of inflammation may be cured; but when produced by air, bile, and phlegm the disease is incurable. In all cases of inflammation when it is accompanied with the symptoms of *Shotha*, such as swelling of the abdomen, discharge of pus or blood, vomiting, hiccough, thirst, painful and sonorous respiration, the fatal result may be expected.

It is of much importance that the surgeon should be able to detect the stage of the inflammation; as if the opening be made before the swelling is ripe, or if it is not opened when ripe, bad consequences will follow in either case. In such cases the surgeon will be known from the quack. This follow by opening the unripe inflammation, cuts into blood vessels, tendons, &c., accompanied with a great discharge of blood, or followed by a great accession of pain: again, if the inflamed swelling is not opened when ripe, the pus buries itself in the neighbouring parts, forming large cavities, or fistulous openings, which are cured with difficulty. In such cases, the pus, like fire, burns the surrounding parts, which like fuel are consumed.

In the generality of cases of inflammation, (Brana, Shotha) the cure will be soon accomplished; but if injudiciously treated it will be tedious. The inflammation is of an unfavourable kind when large, when not prominent but shrivelled, when hard or when very soft, when very prominent or when very dark, when very cold or very hot, when of a black, yellow, red, or white colour, when it has an unhealthy disagreeable appearance. It is also unfavourable when the pus is in large quantities, when the muscles, vessels and tendons are numerous in the part ; when the discharge has a fœtid smell and has fibrous substances mixed up with it, when the swelling is large, or there are numerous small swellings, when bad blood is evacuated and when the patient is very old.

The general indications to be followed in the cure of common inflammation are, the use of sedatives, local bleeding, poultices, opening the abscess, cleaning it, healing the breach of continuity, and lastly restoring the natural colour to the part. Sushruta describes sixty different indications to be employed in the cure of inflammation and ulcers, such as, rubbing and anointing the part with certain medicines that dry it up,* pouring water upon the part, fomentations, frictions with ghee, poultices with maturating substances, with the observance of spare diet, emetics and purgatives, &c. There are eight kinds of incisions which are to be used for the evacuation of the pus and blood ; also means to promote adhesion, as pressure, stopping the bleeding, diminishing the heat, the application of thick poultices and astringents, the application of lints covered with medicinal pastes, the use of oil, the juice of certain plants, the application of certain powders to the ulcers, fumigation, means to depress elevation, and to increase or diminish the hardness of particular parts, and the application of caustic and cauteries. The last consideration is to restore the natural colour to the part, to restore or remove hair, the employment of enemas, of bandages, of certain leaves to the ulcers, the means to destroy worms, the use of tonics, of errhines, of gargles, of fumigations, and of regimen.

A few remarks will now be added on some of the above subjects. For maturing a swelling, the best medicines are several dangerous barks and roots, linseed, carrots, the seeds of (surunga) the morunga tree ; of mustard seed, the flowers of surávíjaz, and the sediment or lees of a kind of beer or spirit. These are all to be combined with heat. When the patient objects to the ripe inflammation being opened with the lancet, the following medicines may be applied, the flower of the marking nut (balá) ; the leaves of the castor poleandrum (danti), the leaves of the lombago

---

* Medicine supposed to pass internally by the roots of the hair and the perspiring pores.

Zeylanica (chitra) or of the Nerium odorum (corbeer). Pigeons or adjutants dung is also recommended, and various escharotic substances.

Old ghee slightly heated is to be applied to the part, and the food should be thin and light with the flesh of wild animals, light boiled vegetables mixed with oil and salt. The drink should consist of boiled water.

The opening of an abscess should be made when the swelling is soft, without pain, is undefined and of the colour of the skin. A lancet should be used, which is immediately to be withdrawn when the pus is seen. In performing such an operation care should be taken to avoid the vital parts, large vessels and tendons. When the abscess is large, the opening should be the length of two fingers breadth. When the abscess is prominent, oblong and large it will soon be cured, and in order that the operation be properly performed the surgeon should possess the following qualities:—boldness, steadiness, presence of mind, quickness, and should possess a good instrument. Should a fistula exist with the inflammation it should be opened. In the following parts of the body the incisions should be oblique, as in the eyebrows, cheeks, temples, forehead, eyelids, lips, gums, axilla, and groins. In the sole of the feet and palms of the hands the incisions should be circular, and in the arms and penis cruciform incisions should be made. It will prevent the wounding of nerves and vessels. After the opening has been made the patients face is to be bathed with cold water, and he should be encouraged by kind language. The abscess is to be evacuated by pressure, and it is to be cleaned with a piece of cloth wet in warm and astringent water. A lint made of a piece of rolled cloth and covered with a paste made of teel seeds, honey and ghee. A pledget of cloth covered with a simple soothing ointment is to be put over the wounded part, with a poultice and bandage. The prescribed prayers are then to be repeated over the patient; and he is then to be removed to a well aired, though sheltered room, and placed in a large bed, with his head turned to the east, the residence of the gods, and is to be surrounded by cheerful friends. Directions are next to be given as to his diet and regimen. Great care is to be taken to keep the patient clean. The wound is to be dressed on the third day, and care is to be taken not to allow the wound to heal too soon. After it has been healed, the patient is to take care not to use indigestible food, he is also to avoid violent exercise, such as running, until the cicatrization is complete. In dangerous cases the abscess will often require to be dressed twice a day, as it in such cases resembles a house on fire that requires prompt assistance.

A person with this disease should avoid new rice, heavy pulse, hot, heavy, bitter salt and sour articles of food, with dried flesh, and vegetables. In all cases the patient should be recommended to avoid spirituous liquids, to eat little and regularly, and sleep at night the usual time.

Ulcers (*Bruno.*)

Ulcers are either produced from exterior or internal causes. There are fifteen varieties, some say sixteen. Each of the humours or a couple of the humours, then the three humours deranged at the same time, or when combined with deranged blood, produce such ulcers. There is another kind called a healthy ulcer (Sudo Bruno) which is characterized by having a smooth and equal surface, being soft, accompanied with little pain and without any discharge.

When the ulcer is produced by deranged air (bayu) it is characterized by its black or red appearance, it is superficial, and discharges a cold, mucilaginous and scanty discharge. The pain is also peculiar, being of a crackling stiff kind. This pain is severe and does not affect the flesh.

When deranged *Bile* produces an ulcer, it is of a yellowish blue colour, and is surrounded by a red colour and yellow eruptions, spreads quickly, and discharges a hot and red matter with a burning pain.

The *Phlegm*; when it produces an ulcer, there is much itchiness, and it is deep seated. The vessels and nerves of the part are affected, and it is hard and white without much pain, and the discharge is white, cold, mucilaginous and thick. The part feels heavy.

When produced by *Blood*; the ulcer becomes red and is surrounded by black vessels. The smell is like that of a horse stable; with much pain, great heat, and it discharges blood and is accompanied with symptoms of bile.

The ulcers which are produced by the combination of the decreased humours partake of the combination of the peculiar symptoms of each.

The ulcers are likewise divided into large extent of ulcer, large deep seated, very hard and soft, much elevated or depressed, very cold or hot, very black, red, yellow or white, or disagreeable looking ulcers, or covered with a slough, with a fœtid discharge, very painful or bloody discharge, or very old; all these are unfavourable cases of ulcer. When the discharge is yellow, thin and has the smell of raw flesh it is superficial. When the ulcer is situated in the flesh, the discharge is thick, only white and mucilaginous. From vessels the discharge is with much blood and it is also watery with much purulent matter. When bones are affected; the discharge is mixed with oily matter and blood, when in the joints they cannot be moved, and the discharge is mucilaginous, frothy and bloody. When any of the viscera are affected; the discharge may be accompanied with urine or feces, or a watery discharge.

Treatment of ulcers. The cure of ulcers is easy when treated by a skilful practitioner, and when the patient follows the proper regimen. When treated by an ignorant person, or if the patient does not follow the proper regimen, the cure will be much more difficult. The person should live in a large airy and clean house, upon a large bed with his head towards the east; he should be encouraged by the presence and attention of friends; he should not sleep during the day, as it will produce much swelling, and a copious discharge with itchiness. He should avoid much walking and the presence of women. He should avoid new wine, different kinds of peas, and fruits, too much salt, pungent articles, jagree, cakes, dry vegetables, and the flesh of fish and amphibious animals, cold water is likewise to be avoided, with curdled milk and indige-table food. He should avoid exposure to wind and dust, smoke, too much eating, and disagreeable sounds or smells. He should avoid watching at night, and eating at unusual hours. He should keep his hair, beard and nails short, wear clean clothes, and perform the usual ceremonies of religion, and his food should be light and nourishing.

The ulcers are to be dressed with a cloth covered with new ointment, and secured by a bandage of silk or cotton. The ulcers are to be cleaned with a watery decoction of cassia fistula and other astringent vegetable medicines. Ghee should be prepared with the sulphate of iron (kaceera), black Hellebore (kotorohunee), turmeric, and the root of the játee. In other cases they add astringent barks or astringents as nimbo, rajbeerka, yellow (Hurrital) and red arsenic (monosillaa), powders prepared with rock salt, the sulphate of iron, and the lees of urine, with boch and turmeric, &c.

Fumigations by means of different rosins, the smoke of which are applied to the ulcers.

Pastes are also applied to the ulcerated surface. They may be made of—

Somongua
Somo
Sorolaa
Somobolko
Chandana'
Kaapola, &c.

When the ulcer is much elevated apply the powders of the following substances, sulphate of iron, (*kasus,*) rock salt, red arsenic, mixed with eggshells and the buds of (jaatee). These may be combined, or one or two of them may be mixed and applied to the ulcerated suface.

Purgatives, emetics, and fasting are to be occasionally used in ulcers, and the other indications which have been already stated under the head of treatment of inflammation.

Should there be much bleeding from the ulcer it is to be stopped by means of styptics; when accompanied with fever and much burning on the part, apply cold applications; when there is little discharge, the ulcer superficial, and the surface irregular, apply poultices made of seeds containing oil, as linseed, with fomentation. When the appearance is very dark and the smell disagreeable apply astringent decoctions. When sloughing and dry looking, apply medicines to clean the part. When the edges of the ulcer are very hard, local bleeding by scarification or by leeches is to be used with fomentations. When the edges are soft and flabby apply astringents. When the edges are elevated and of long standing apply caustics. When the cicatrix is white it will be made black or of the natural colour by the preparations of the marking nut. For restoring hair to a part apply the ashes of ivory with crude antimony. If worms are generated in ulcers, apply the decoctions of ophiorrhiza mungos (*surubaa*) and Symplocos Alstonia.

When the worms are produced by cows urine and the like, caustic solutions are to be applied. These are obtained from the ashes of certain trees. A piece of recent flesh may also be applied over the ulcer so as to attract the worms to it. When the ulcer is very old and the person emaciated and weak, give him nourishing food, and medicine of a tonic nature. When produced by poison they are to be treated as poisonous wounds.

The intelligent practitioner will vary the local and general treatment according to the peculiarity of each case, and the state of the patients constitution.

The fatal symptoms of ulcers; are, fever, diarrhœa, fainting, hiccough, vomiting, dyspepsia, difficulty of breathing, cough and great thirst.

Fistula (*Nulla Bruna*) á fistula is either produced by derangements of the humours, or by external causes. In the latter case the abscess may not be opened when ripe, the pus hurries itself into the neighbouring parts and forms a canal. When derangement of air produces the fistula; the orifice is small, the surface rough, and it is accompanied with much pain. It discharges largely, especially in the night, and the discharge is accompanied with froth. This form is to be treated with poultices.

When the fistula is produced by deranged bile, it is accompanied with thirst, fever, and heat; the discharge is copious particularly during the day. The part is to be carefully rubbed, and when ripe it is to be opened with a knife, it is then to be cleaned, and a hot iron probe is to be introduced into the canal. Several kinds of medicines are to be mixed and thrust into the wound.

When produced by diseased phlegm, the discharge is thick and white, and its edges are hard and shining. It is itchy and slightly painful at night. A mixture of several medicines is made to rub into the part so as to soften it; other medicines are to be employed to wash the fistula with, and a director is to be introduced and the fistula laid open.

When air, bile, and phlegm are deranged, together producing a fistula, it is accompanied with great heat and fever, sonorous breathing and coma. The mouth is dry and the other symptoms peculiar to the diseases produced by the separate humours. In such cases the disease is incurable.

Fistulous openings are usually found in the mammœ of women after abscesses. In such cases the abscess is to be opened and the fistula is to be treated as in Budodu. When the patient is of weak constitution, is emaciated, is fearful, has lost his appetite the cure will be very difficult. When the knife is not allowed to be used; a thread is to be passed through the fistula and is to be strongly tied so as to divide the skin which is contained in it. A lint made of the following medicines will likewise be found very useful. The bark of the *guntafulaa*, rock salt, lac stick, and beetle nut, these are to be mixed with the milk of the euphorbium and introduced into the fistulous opening.

Descriptions of Surgical Instruments and Bandages.

The description of these instruments is neither minute nor precise; and not being illustrated by drawings, or now employed, a few only of each class will be delineated. In general the name of the instrument was derived from the resemblance to certain objects such as certain leaves, &c.

The hand is considered the first, the best, and the most important of all Surgical Instruments, as it is with its assistance that all operations are performed.

There are classes of instruments, one of which are blunt (*jontros*) the second have sharp cutting edges (*sotros*); and the third are named unosustro or substitutes for cutting instruments, such as caustics, fire, horns of animals open at both extremities by which suction is made, and gourds which are used as cupping glasses and are applied before as well as after the scarifications. I shall now add a few remarks on each of those classes.

1st. *Jontros*, or blunt instruments, consist of *Swasteeka*, *Sandansa*, *Talajontros*, *Narujontros*, *Solaakaa* and *Upajontros*.

a. *Swustee ka-juntra* are curved or hooked instruments which are used to extract splinters of bones, or foreign bodies, and including pinchers, nippers and the forceps. They are formed of iron, usually eighteen inches long, having heads or points shaped like the heads of animals, the beaks of birds, &c.

b. *Sandansa-juntra*, or tongs, which are of two kinds, one with, and another without a handle, and are used to remove extraneous substances from the soft parts, as the flesh, skin, veins, &c. They are usually sixteen inches in length.

c. *Tala-juntra* resemble, though smaller than the last named instruments; and were employed for removing foreign substances lodged in the outer canals as the ear, nose, &c.

d. *Naru- juntro* consist of twenty varieties of tabular instruments, of different sizes and shapes, according to their intended use, including canulæ, catheters, syringes, &c. They are used for removing extraneous substances from deep seated canals, as the intestines, urethra, &c.; for examining deep seated parts, for the application of other instruments, for drawing off fluids by suction, &c.

e. *Solaakaa* or *Probes* are rods and sounds. There are twenty eight kinds, varying in size and shape, for extracting foreign matters lodged in parts of difficult access, for clearing internal canals, more particularly the urethra; some have points like a half pea, others like an earth worm or the point of an arrow. Some of them have small cavities at their extremities for applying caustic solutions, &c., to the diseased part. Some of these rods have ends like the rose apple, for applying it heated. There are six varieties of these rods, three resembling the head of a rose apple, and three being hooked. Another instrument, resembles the half of the shell of the plate for eradicating nasal polypi; a frequent and troublesome disease (*nakra*) in many parts of Hindoostan. This disease is alleviated by forcibly extracting the irritating excrescence. Another instrument of this class, has a head like the foot stalk of the *Maleetee* flower. It is used for cleaning the urethra.

f. *Upa-juntros* are accessory instruments, as twine, leather, bark, skin, cloth, loadstone, caustic, fire, finger nails, tongue, teeth, &c.

There are many other instruments which cannot be enumerated, as they are only varieties of the above, modified by experienced surgeons, for particular purposes.

The second class, are cutting instruments (*sotros*), of which there are twenty kinds. These instruments should be formed of good iron, and neither too large, nor too small. They should be well polished, and sufficiently sharp to divide a hair. For this purpose a stone was used. They were in general six inches in length, of which the blade formed a half or a quarter of that length. They should have good handles and firm joints, and be kept quite clean, wrapt in flannel, and kept in a box of sandle wood

The following are the names of twenty forms of the principle Cutting Instruments used in Surgery:—

1. *Mondolúgra,* or round instrument for scarifying
2. *Koropotrá,* or Saw.
3. *Beeteeputrá,* or Lancet.
4. *Nokosustrá,* (eight fingers breadth in length.)
5. *Modreeká,* like the first joint of the index finger.
6. *Utpolopotroká,* like the petal of the blue water lily.
7. *Urdodáro,* or Knife.
8. *Suchee,* or Needles.
9. *Kuchápotra,* like the leaves of the kushograss.
10. *Akemoka,* like the beak of a bird.
11. *Soráreemka* or Scissars, (10 fingers breadth in length.)
12. *Untormuko,* to break down (the internal side cutting) parts.
13. *Tricorcoko* (*trocar*), three cutting surfaces
14. *Kotáreeká,* like a gum lancet or bistoury for tapping.
15. *Breehumoka* or *Trocar,* with a head like a grain of rasi for tapping.
16. *Ará* or *Aul,* a long sharp needle in a handle for tapping.
17. *Bedusopotraka,* long sharp cutting instrument like the leaf of the ratan for tapping.
18. *Booreeso,* or hook.
19. *Dontosunku,* pincers for extracting teeth.
20. *Asunee* or *probes,* eight fingers breadth in length.

Those instruments, the length of which is not marked; are six fingers breadth in length.

Unosustra, are instruments which may be used when cutting instruments are not at hand, or when the patient is too fearful to admit the use of cutting instruments. These are the sharp bark of the bamboos, different kinds of hard stones, or glass, leeches, fire, caustics, nails, rough leaves, such as those of gogee, seefaleeka trees, &c.

Practical Instructions.

After the student has been taught science by books, he is next to be instructed in the practice of the use of the instruments, &c. Without practical skill, theoretical knowledge is of no use. The different surgical operations are to be shown to the student, upon wax spread out upon a board, gourds, cucumbers and other soft fruits. Tapping and puncturing should be practiced on a leather bag of water or soft mud. Scarifications and bleeding may be practiced upon the fresh hides of animals from which the hair has been removed, or upon the dead bodies, and the puncturing or lancing the hollow stalks of water lilies or the vessels of dead animals. The manner of holding and the use of the probe is to be practised upon a piece of hollow bamboo or the like. The removal of substances from cavities, by removing the large seeds of the jack or bel fruit, and the extraction of teeth is to be practiced upon dead bodies and animals. For sowing he should practice on leather and cloth. The application of bandages and ligatures should be practiced upon flexible models of the human body; and the means of making noses, ears, &c., be practised upon dead animals; the application of caustics, and cauteries to be done on animals. The use of injections is to be practised with a water pot having a canal.

There are eight kinds of surgical operations. They are *chedaana* or incision, as in fistula-in-ano.

2. *Bhedno*, opening parts as of large abscesses.

3. *Lhekhno*, or drawing lines, by which the parts are nipped, sacrified or innoculated.

4. *Bhedhno*, or puncturing, as opening veins in hydrocele and dropsy.

5. *Eshyno*, to probe or sound parts as in fistula, to ascertain the presence of foreign substances.

6. *Ahárno*, or the operation of extraction as of the stone; of the teeth, and of the fetus.

7. *Vishravâno*, to remove fluids; as pus, blood, &c., or of bad humours as in Leprous blotches in Elephantiasis, &c.

8. *Seebeeno*, to sow parts together, as in wounds, especially near joints. The substances to be used for sowing are thread, twine, or small ligatures made of the skin of animals, or fibres of vegetable substances, roots, hair, &c. The stitches are to be longer or shorter according to the nature of the wound. Before sowing a wound it should be carefully cleaned, and all extraneous substances, should be removed. The needle should be from two fingers breadth in length, to three or more. They are to be long, three edged for deep fleshy wounds, and a third or curved kind should be used in vital parts and in wounds of the scrotum and abdomen. For fixing a torn off ear ! the parts are to be brought together and sown. For practising these operations; pieces of leather and cloth are to be sewn together. After a wound has been sewn, a mixture of equal parts of the seed of the preunga; *unguno*, (sulphate of antimony,) *justaabo* (liquorice) and *lodro*

(an astringent bark) is to be thickly sprinkled round the wound, which is then to be covered with a piece of lint or silk cloth, and the whole secured with a bandage. The physician is then to give proper directions as to diet, &c.

Besides the above instruments, the surgeon should provide thread, leaves, pledgets, heated metallic plates for erubescents, and a variety of astringent and emollient applications before commencing an operation.

Bandages.

There are fourteen kinds of Bandages:—

1st. *Koosa,* or a hollow cylinder or sheath for the fingers, penis, &c.

2nd. *Dáma,* a large bandage to support parts.

3rd. *Susteeko,* a circular bandage to apply to joints, forehead, chest and under the ears.

4th. *Uneebuluta,* a roller or bandage to encircle the extremities, &c.

5th. *Protobe,* a broad bandage for the neck, and the external organs of generation.

6th. *Mondola,* a circular bandage for the head.

7th. *Stogheeká,* a bandage enclosing a splint to keep the parts firm, as the joints of the fingers, the penis, &c.

8th. *Gomoka,* a double bandage which is applied to ulcers.

9th. *Kotá,* a four tailed bandage for the cheeks, temples, lower jaw, &c.

10th. *Cheena,* a bandage for the angles of the eyes.

11th. *Bebonda,* a bandage for the back, abdomen, and chest. It is a firm circular bandage.

12th. *Beetana,* a large bandage for the head.

13th. *Gopaná,* a concave bandage for the chin, eyes, lips, shoulders, scrotum and pelvis.

14th. *Ponchanghu,* a bandage for the clavicle with four tails.

The surgeon is to decide on the kind of bandage in each particular case. Its application varies with the disease. Sometimes the bandage is to be applied above, below, or upon the wound or ulcer according to the effect required. In general the bandage is to be applied after the application of the necessary ointment spread upon linen. There are three degrees of tightness with which the bandage is to be applied, the first being tight, the second loose, and the third moderately tight. When bile and blood are deranged, or when blows and poisons produce the disease, the bandage should be loosely applied; and when phlegm and air are deranged the tightness may be increased. In other cases bandages may be applied more tightly. To the chest, buttock, belly, loins, axilla, groins, and head, a tight bandage is to be applied. To the extremities, face, ears, throat, penis, scrotum, back, and to the sides of the belly and chest the pressure of the bandage should be moderate. In diseases of the eye and joints loose bandages are to be used. Should the bandage be applied tight, the medicine will not produce the desired effect, and all the symptoms of the disease will be aggravated. This will also be the case when no bandage is applied, by the formation of insects, and by exposure to the influence of heat and cold, which will aggravate the ulcer, and prevent the cure. When accompanied with acute inflammation, and when the part is hot, painful, and sensible, no bandage is to be applied to the part, for the cure of the disease, but to retain the applications to the part. Nor are bandages to be applied when the sore has been produced by fire, or excoriating, when it contains pus; when sloughing, or if it is near the anus; when produced by extravasation of urine from Leprosy, &c. If bones are fractured, or joints dislocated, or if the bone is thrust through the flesh, the bandages will be of much use. This is also the case when the tendons and vessels are divided. In the treatment of ulcers; bandages and all other means that diminish pain will tend towards the cure.

When the ulcer is in the flesh, skin, joints, bone, abdomen: in wounds of vessels and tendons; when deep, and when superficial, they are cured with bandages. The judicious surgeon will in each particular case, decide on the propriety the kind of bandages, which will vary not only with the nature of the disease, but also with the season of the year, &c.

—:o:—

SECTION 4.

Means employed to remove Blood from the body. These operations are venesection, cupping, and the use of leeches.

1st. Venesection.

Before a patient is bled, he should have his body anointed with oil; a warm bath is to be used; and some prepared barley or rice is to be given to eat.

In performing the operation the patient is to be placed either sitting or standing before the Surgeon with his face turned towards the east, with an assistant holding him from behind. The Surgeon is to rub down the blood in the prominent vein which is to be opened, and apply bandage of the bark of a tree, of cloth or of eather, not very tight, above the part to be opened; the instrument used for opening the vein; is the *kutaarekau*, this is to be thrust into the swelled vein while the patient retains his breath; the wound should be the size of a barley corn. The blood should flow in a stream. After the required quantity of blood has been obtained, the bandage is to be removed and the wound is to be cleaned with cold water, a few drops of oil are to be let fall upon the wound, and if the bleeding is not stopped a bandage is to be put round the part. Should this not be sufficient to stop the bleeding; caustics, and even the actual cautery may be used. The quantity of blood which is to be removed, should never be so large as to weaken the person. When the patient is very strong, and the disease very severe, blood to the extent of one seer (Prusto or Hij) may be removed. If much blood is lost, it will produce head-ache, loss of sight, with pain in the eyes; will produce thirst, severe pain, insensibility of one side, and of one member, hiccough, cough, difficulty in breathing, jaundice, and the person may die, or it will produce the diseases of air. After bleeding the body should be anointed with oil, milk, lymph of animals or other remedies which quickly stop the flow of blood. If all the bad blood is not discharged by the first bleeding, another is to be performed on the second or third day after the first. Do not endeavour to remove all the bad blood by the first bleeding, as a little bad blood may be purified by the use of remedies; and thus the danger of bleeding too freely will be avoided. When a swelling requires to be opened; and from the nature of the part, as when near the windpipe; a communicating vein proceeding from the diseased part may be opened. Bleeding should not be performed when the person is below 16 and above 70 years of age, when the female is pregnant or soon after delivery, nor when the body is dry; when in a state of drunkenness or when there are sores upon the body; when the humours (datu) are diminished; when there is copious perspirations; or when there are diseases of air present. Patients should not be bled in very cold, hot, or stormy cloudy days; when there is no disease present, when the person is weak, after watching, or when digestion has not taken place. When afflicted with general dropsy, in jaundice, during free perspiration, piles, in madness, after vomiting or purging, in severe fevers, in tetanus, in palsy, &c. When venesection is to be performed, the air should be clear and warm. If possible it should be avoided during the rains; but always the abstraction is to take place by degrees, at the intervals of one or more days according to the circumstances of the case. In the cold weather venesection should be performed in the middle of the day. The flow of the blood from the wound in the vessel may be retarded when the person is very fearful, faint, and much fatigued; when he is very thirsty, when the bandage is not properly applied, and when he has much bad blood.

When the person is bled for a disease of the spleen, the vein is to the opened at the bend of the left arm, or the vein between the left ring and little finger in asthma and severe cough; in disease of the penis open the vessels near the middle of the penis. In hepatic diseases open the temporal artery. In madness and epilepsy, and in diseases of the tongue or teeth, open the veins under the tongue. In tertian ague open the veins at the juncture of the sacrum with the spine. In epilepsy the veins of the neck may also be opened.

There are twenty ways of improperly performing venesection:—

1st. *Durdeeda*, when the instrument is too small, and the blood does not flow freely, followed by a painful swelling.

2nd. *Oteebeda*, when an ignorant person opens a large vessel, or makes the wound in the vein large by which the blood passes among the cellular substances of the part.

3rd. *Chuncheetá*, resembles the last.

4th. *Pitcheetá*, when the knife is blunt and tares the parts, which swell.

5th. *Kuteeka*, when several attempts have been made to open the vein.

6th. *Oprorsreetá*, when the person is fearful, the weather very cold, and the blood is not discharged.

7th. *Otudeerá*, when the knife is large, sharp, and a large wound is made.

8th. *Obeedá*, when little blood flows.

9th. *Poreesuská*, when little blood flows from deranged air which dries the wound.

10th. *Kunteetá*, when the wound is too small, and little blood flows.

11th. *Bateetà*, when the arm had been improperly bandaged, and when the hands shake, and no blood flows.

12th. *Onuteetobeená*, like the last.

13th. *Shostropota*, when there is a great flow of blood from the large wound in the vessel, which cannot be stopped by the usual applications.

14th. *Tirjokbeedà*, when the wound is not direct, and is not sufficiently large.

15th. *Opobeedà*, when the knife is not a proper one, and several attempts are required to open the vein.

16th. *Obiodeeà*, when blood letting is not proper.

17th. *Bidurdà*, when the patient's body is in an unfit state and diseases are consequently produced.

18th. Denuká, when the part requires to be rubbed much before the vein can be opened, and when the blood only flows at intervals, like the milk of cows.

19th. Punopunorbeedá, when the knife is too small, and several small wounds are made in the vein.

20th. Seersoodee, when nerves, tendons, and vital parts have been wounded, it produces severe pain, restlessness and death. When the operation is thus improperly performed, the wound is to be treated by the application of fomentations, and other remedies, which will be stated in the section treating of wounds.

An able Surgeon is therefore required to bleed, as veins are always changing, and if not properly performed, it produces various troublesome diseases of veins; which are not cured by the usual remedies. It is not enough to know the situation of veins; but he must likewise know the time, and the extent to which the bleeding is to be carried. In some diseases, bleeding is half the treatment; in the same manner as enemas are in many medical diseases. As cutting, fire, &c., give pain; Rajahs, rich people, children or old people, and fearful and weak people, when they require to lose blood, may have leeches in preference to venesection; more especially in the cases of bad blood produced by diseased air, bile and cough. When bad blood has been removed from a vein, the person feels happy, the part light, the pain ceases, and the morbid symptoms diminish.

After bleeding avoid anger, violent exercise, too much sitting, walking, exposure to great heat or cold, or improper food, for a month; especially very heating and cooling articles. The patient should live on good and light articles of nourishing food, until his strength is restored. If this is not attended to, bad blood will be generated.

Bad blood in the body, produces itchiness, swelling and pain like that of fire; with a red appearance of the part which suppurates. When deranged air has produced bad blood; it does not flow from the wound in the vein like water; it is covered with foam, is dark, thin, and draws slowly. When deranged by bile; the blood has a yellow blue colour, has a bad smell, and it dries slowly. When the blood is deranged by phlegm the blood is oleaginous, and smooth; it is cold, of a pale yellowish colour, is in large quantities and flows slowly. When bile and blood are deranged in a part; it has a dark colour. When two or three of the humours are deranged in a part; the blood has the peculiarities of the individual, and deranged blood combined. Should severe pain occur in opening a vein, as if fire had been applied, the part is to be rubbed with warm ghee and *gestemodo* (a plant.)

The blood is in a healthy state when it is of a bright red

colour like that of red jelly, or of the rainbow; when the senses are perfect with a desire to exercise them; and the person is strong and in high spirits.

2nd. Scarifications. By means of a thin and sharp knife; longitudinal or transverse lines at equal distance are to be made neither very deep nor superficial. They should be applied quickly, avoiding vital parts, joints and large vessels.

3rd. Cupping. The local accumulation of bad blood may be removed by means of cupping, which is performed by a horn cut smooth, and even, at the large extremity; with a small opening at the narrow end. The large extremity is applied over the scarified part, the air in the horn is sucked out, and the finger is then dexterously placed over the open upper end. An accumulation of blood in the part included in the horn is discharged from the scarification. The horn is repeatedly applied, and the air exhausted in the same manner, until the necessary quantity of blood has been removed. These horns are made of different sizes, to suit the part which is to be operated on. In other cases a hollow gourd is prepared, with a small smooth hole which is placed on the part; the air is then exhausted by burning something in it, before it is applied over the scarified part. The horn is used when the air of the part is particularly affected; and when the phlegm of the part, is much diseased, the gourd is preferred.

4th. Leeches (*Jaloukà*). Leeches have been employed from time immemorial in Asia, but particularly in Bengal, where they considered as the best means of removing blood from a part. They are particularly used for Rajahs, for women, and timid persons, and for the very young and very old.

There are twelve varieties of leeches; six of which are venemous, and six useful. The venemous leeches are :—

1. *Indráyudhá,* háving longitudinal lines along its back like a rainbow.
2. *Alágarda,* are large with a black head, and hairs on their body.
3. *Krishná,* are large dark leeches with a large head.
4. *Sàmudrikà* have numerous stripes and spots of various colours upon their bodies.
5. *Gochandanà* have a small head and narrow mouth with a large body and bifurcated tail
6. *Karbura,* is long like an eel, and moves irregularly.

These deleterious leeches, when they are employed, produce heat, swelling, pain, and itching of the part; followed by excessive irritation and fever, with spasms, sickness and syncope. These effects will be best treated by applying to the bites a mixture of certain medicines, which are considered as antidotes against the poison, other antidotes are given internally, with errhines ; the bites of the Indráyunda leeches are considered fatal. These kinds of leeches are found near putrid fish or animals, in foul, stagnant, and putrescent water. Such leeches are consequently to be carefully avoided.

There are six varieties of good Leeches :—

1. *Kapilà,* or tawny leeches. These have a brownish breast, with smooth glossy sides.

2. *Pingulà,* have round bodies, are of a pale red colour, and are very active.

3. *Sankumukhì,* have long sharp heads, are of a liver colour, and bite quickly.

4. *Mushíkà,* are of a mouse colour and have a bad smell.

5. *Punduríká-mukhí,* are of a brown hue, and have a mouth like that of a lily.

6. *Shabaríká,* are of a green colour like the leaves of a water lotus, and are ten fingers breadth long. This kind is only proper for removing blood from animals.

These leeches are found in Persia (Yavana), ancient Delhi (*Pandu*), at Mutra (*Pautana*), &c. They are found in small numbers in clear, and deep pools of water, which contain water lilies, and are surrounded with sweet smelling plants. The middle sized leeches are the best.

These leeches are to be caught in a piece of leather or cloth, and placed in a new water-pot, in which some clay and pure water has been put, some grass or leaves of aquatic plants are to be placed on the pot for them to lie upon, and the roots of water lilies and dry flesh are to be given them for food. The water is to be changed every third day and the water pot every seventh day.

When the leeches grow very large and are very vigorous; when they are weak, or emaciated, when they do not bite, or take little blood, or are of the venemous kind they are not to be used.

When the part is not very sensible it is to be rubbed dry, and it is then to be covered with cow-dung and earth to dry the part. The leech is then to be taken from the water-pot and its body is to be anointed with mustard seed paste. It is then to be put into a bason with fresh water for a short time and then removed and surrounded with a piece of cloth, and the mouth is then to be applied to the part affected. If it does not fix quickly, apply a drop or two of milk or blood to the part, or make one or two very slight scarifications, which will induce them to fix themselves more readily. When the leeches are sucking, sprinkle a few drops of cold water upon their bodies. When the leeches have removed the necessary quantity of blood sprinkle a small quantity of salt upon their heads, to make them drop off. Put the gorged leech upon some dry bran, put a little oil and salt upon its mouth and then strip them. Put them next in fresh water, and if they are lively they will live, and may be used again; but if they are languid, they will soon die and they should therefore be at once thrown away.

The part upon which the leeches have been is to be smeared with honey, cold water, and astringent substances. In other cases poultices may be applied.

——:o:——

SECTION V.

STYPTICS.

If all the bad blood is not removed by the bleeding it will leave a swelling, redness, heat, itchiness, and pain in the part. But if too much blood has been removed it produces headache, blindness (*gutta serena*), inflammation of the eye, convulsions, hemiplegia, great thirst, burning sensation of the body, hiccough, difficulty in breathing, jaundice, and death. Avoid abstracting too much blood, particularly when healthy, as it is the root which sustains the body; "for the blood is the life of the body."

There are four ways of arresting hœmorrhages:—

a. By the use of astringents.
b. By the use of ice (*hima.*)
c. By caustics and
d. By the actual cautery; should the other means not prove sufficient.

a. Astringent applications. Different flowers are mixed together, and then powder is to-be sprinkled by degrees over the part, and should the blood not stops; the finger is to be placed over the bleeding vessel. The following is one of these mixtures:—take of the flowers of

Lodhra
Madhuka
Gairika
Sarjarassa

in equal quantities. Or take of the flowers of—

Màsha
Jaba, barley.
Godhúma, wheat.

These are to be mixed and sprinkled on the part, and if it does not stop; the finger is to be applied to the part for the same purpose.

The barks of different trees, as the Banian tree, Catechu, gum resin, are mixed, reduced to powder, and used as styptics.

The ashes of burnt silk, will also be found useful; over which a tight bandage is to be placed. The patient is to be kept in a cool room, and a cool and antiphlogistic diet and regimen is to be enjoined. Afterwards broths, made from the flesh of deer and other wild animals, are to be used, with light and nourishing food.

b. Cold and ice, by drying the blood, has a strong tendency to stop hœmorrhage, and is often used for this purpose.

c. When the above means have not been sufficient to stop the hœmorrhage, escharotics should next be used. These will be considered in the next section.

——:o:——

SECTION VI.

Cauteries.

The cauteries used by the Hindu Surgeons, were the actual and potential.

The actual Cautery.

Fire can sometimes be employed; when neither the knife nor escharotics can be used, as it is the strongest of all the escharotics. It is applied in different ways, sometimes by means of long-pepper, goats dung, the tooth of a cow, an arrow point, long circular or hook shaped iron probes; for superficial purposes; and straight probes for muscles or deep seated parts. There are three varieties of these irons; one being small, another large, and a third of a moderate size. After amputations, &c., boiling fluids were used to stop hœmorrhage, as boiling jagree, oil, honey, &c.

The actual cautery is applied in four different ways, according to the nature of the case; sometimes the application is made in spots; in other cases in circles, or in parallel and concentric lines.

When the application is properly performed, there is a peculiar noise heard and smell felt, at the moment of the application, and the skin is immediately contracted. When the cautery is applied to the muscles, it changes them to a gray colour; the swelling of the part diminishes, and it stops the discharge of blood, pus, &c.

Fire is useful in some diseases of the skin, flesh, vessels, ligaments, joints, and bones; and when there is severe pain or hard swellings of the flesh and insensible parts; which sometimes occur in carbuncle, piles, boils near the anus, in elephantiasis, and in small swellings; and in bites of serpents live charcoal is recommended to be applied; to prevent the dangerous effects of their bites. It is also useful in penetrating wounds and in all cases where it is accompanied with considerable hœmorrhage.

The small sized actual cautery is employed with advantage to the eyebrows, forehead, and temples for headaches and diseases of the head. When applied to the eyelids near the border the eye is to be defended with wet clothes. This is the treatment recommended for intergium. Fire is also applied to remove indurated parts; to the side, in cases of diseased spleen and liver; and to the abdomen for enlargement of the mesenteric glands. It is also applied to the soles of the feet for the cure of colic; and it is said with the best effects, as it seldom fails to cure the disease.

Fire deranges the blood and bile, and produces severe pain and fever. A mixture of ghee and honey should be applied to the part after the cautery.

The actual cautery should not be used in the cold and hot months, as in September and October, and in May and June more particularly in the two last months. It should not be used to persons of bilious or sanguineous temperaments; or in whom the blood is diseased; when diarrhœa is present, and external applications have not removed it; when the person is weak and timid; when there are many ulcers on the body; and when the patient is very young or very old.

The diet of a patient to whom the cautery is applied should be very thin, and of the same kind as that recommended for a woman with a dead fœtus in her abdomen. In the more dangerous forms no food is to be allowed.

When the different cauteries have not proved sufficient to stop the hœmorrhage, the vessel may be opened above the bleeding part in order to diminish the flow of blood from the large wound below; and thus give time for the operation of medicines.

When all these means fail to stop the hœmorrhage the physician is to examine the different circumstances of the case, and act accordingly.

Potential Cauteries (*Kkàra*). These cauteries consist of Potassa more or less pure; it is obtained by burning the bark and branches of the

Muskaka tree,
The Kataja tree,
The Palása,
Asakarna,
Arka,

Sthnuhi,
Apámárga,
Pátala,
Chítraka,

Or the bark and branches of these trees are reduced to ashes, which are thrown into six times their quantity of water or cow's urine. Strain them 21 times, expose them to heat, until they are reduced to the consistence of a mucilage. Again, dissolve them in water, strain, separate, remove the sediment and evaporate to the same consistence as before; some shell lime is then to be mixed with them, and when neither very dry nor moist, they are to be taken off the fire and kept in an iron vessel well closed up.

The Potassa thus prepared, may be used internally or externally. In the first form it is used in solution and is good for removing worms, for curing Leprosy, and as an antidote for certain poisons; when long taken it produces impotency. As an external application, it is used in three degrees of strength, the concentrated, the mild, and the weak.

The concentrated Potassa is used for opening abscesses and for producing superficial ulcers, in which cases emollients are to be put upon the part after the application, so as to reduce the pain. The solution acts strongly in healing ulcers and in stopping bleeding, and when concentrated it disorganizes the parts. It is applied externally to different cutaneous diseases, to bad ulcers, to fistula-in-ano and other fistula, to piles, to certain diseases of the mouth, as to diseased tubercles, &c. The weak solution may be taken internally in dyspepsia, colic, and indigestion; and for urinary calculi, gravel, worms, and gumo.

The use of Potassa is not proper in the sanguineous temperament, in internal hœmorrhage, in fever, for children or old people, for weak persons, or for persons with diseases of the eyes, &c. When caustic is to be applied to a part, the patient is to be taken to a room shut up, a portion of the Caustic is then to be applied to the part by means of a Probe. The Surgeon is then to wait for a space of time that will admit of his counting a hundred. If well applied the part becomes black, and the juices of acid fruits are to be applied. Caustics are not to be applied to vital parts, where there are many nerves, blood ligatures, joints, ligaments, *taphu*, to the eye, throat, &c. When used by an ignorant person caustics are like fire, poison, or thunder to the patient whom it quickly kills.

When properly applied by a skilful Surgeon it cures many diseases.

SECTION VII.

Scalds and Burns.

There are four degrees of burns :—

a. *Plusta,* in which there is severe pain, and change of colour on the part.

b. *Durdogdha,* when accompanied with blisters, with much redness and pain.

c. *Samadogdha,* when it is black, and does not produce much pain.

d. *Atídogdha,* when the part is separated with the destruction of the vessels, &c., with fever, thirst, faintness, and the wound heals slowly.

In *Plusta* hot articles are to be applied; and in *durdogda* apply cold substances, and sometimes hot, with ghee and fomentations. In *Samadogdha* apply a paste made of *Chandana,* sandlewood; *Gairíka,* yellow earth, and the bark of the wild banian tree. These are to be mixed with ghee; or apply to the part, animal flesh, chopped. The flesh of domestic animals may be used for this purpose.

In *Atídogha,* separate the loose parts, and apply cold. Then apply the decoction of the cold bark of the Tinduka tree with ghee. In other cases apply wax, liquorice root, ghee, rasin: make into an ointment, and apply to the part. Cold applications are likewise useful.

When a person is struck with lightening, and is not killed, anoint the body with oil, with frictions.

When choaked with smoke, the patient has difficulty in breathing, which is sonorous, attended with coughs burning of the eyes, and redness. This is succeeded by thirst, fever, difficulty in hearing and smelling: the juice of the sugar-cane, and grapes should be given for drink, with water and sugar. The juices of sweet and acid fruits may also be used with an emetic to clean the stomach.

SECTION VIII.

Directions for performing operations.

When an operation is decided on; a fortunate moment is to be selected, and the Brahmins and the Surgeons are to be propitiated with gifts. A clean and well lighted room is to be chosen in which the operation is to be performed; and cloth, the leaves of trees, thread, honey, ghee, the juices of different kinds of trees;

milk, oil, cold and hot water, and strong and steady persons are to be in readiness to hold him, while care is taken not to frighten the patient. Should the patient be very fearful of the knife, or very young, escharotics, the nail or a sharp piece of the bark of the bamboo may be substituted; and for the mouth or eyelids a kind of grass (*goji*) or other rough leaves may be substituted by rubbing them over the part. The patient is to be placed with his face to the east, and the surgeon before him with his face to the west.

The knife should be wet with water before being used.

The season for operating is when the sky is clear during the rains, and in the hot weather in the evenings and mornings. If possible the operation should be performed near the new moon, as this is the most proper time. Should the person be weak, much diseased, insensible, or when the disease has come on suddenly, the operations should be performed during the evening or morning when the weather is steady and seasonable; a propitious day and hour is to be found out. Curdled milk, corn, &c., are to be offered up to the gods for the success of the operation and Brahmins are to be propitiated.

When a boil is to be opened, or the flesh divided, the part is to have certain escharotics rubbed over it to diminish the pain. When a vessel, joint, or sensible part is to be divided, oil is first to be rubbed over it.

The Surgeon should hold the knife firm in the hand; if thrust into a boil and no pus follows it is to be quickly withdrawn. If there be much pus in the part, it may be opened several times if necessary; boils are not to be considered dangerous if elevated upon a flat surface. Should this not be the case, and the boil does not rise, but extends, the diagnosis is less favourable. The surgeon is a proper person if he be strong and operates quickly; his knife should be good, and he should neither perspire, shake, nor make exclamations. In performing such operations, the sensible parts of the body are to be avoided; as the palms of the hands and soles of the feet, vessels, tendons, joints and bones. When near vital organs the knife should be held so as to cut outwards, and should any such organ be wounded it produces severe pain, and is cured with difficulty.

When the fetus is dead in the uterus, in ascetics, piles, certain excrescences and swellings near the anus, which have existed upwards of a month; the patient is to take his dinner before the operation, and the operation is to be completed while withdrawing the knife. Cold water is then to be applied to the part, the person's spirits are to be kept up, the pus is to be squeezed out, and the part cleaned with tepid water. Lint smeared with honey or ghee is then to be put into the wound to prevent it closing. The wound is to be rubbed with honey or ghee and a bandage is then to be placed round the part

During the operation, care must be taken to keep a fire in the room near the patient, in which sweet scented substances are to be burnt, in order to prevent the entrance of devils by the wound.

After the operation some holy water is to be sprinkled over his body, and proper prayers repeated ; such as the following :— Oh Brahmá! Do thou, as well as other Gods, order the serpents, *Pishacha*, *Gandharba*, *Pitrí* (spirits), *Jakha*, *Rakhyasa*, who are desirous of acting wickedly to desist from their intention, either on earth, in the sky, or in any direction ; and that prophets may cure this wound : Do thou, Oh Brahmá! direct the Planets, and rajah prophets, mountains, seas, and rivers, to retain the soul and *bayu* in this body ; that they remain healthy by the influence of the rajah of the moon, and *devata* of the clouds ; *opana Bayu* by the lightning, *odana-bayu*, by thunder, *saman bayu* by Indra ; strength by Soloh, sense by Booan. Oh *Samudra* (sea), the navel who know every thing retain thy supplicant ; and thou sun retain the eyes and ears healthy. Direct your correct ears, moon retain your pure heat ; stars your body fair ; night your shadow, and water your semen healthy. May medicine retain your heart, while the sky will retain the elements of the body in health, and the earth the body pure. Thy head Oh Brahmá (Parakrama) will retain energy healthy. Iswar the energy of the male. Bramhá spirit ; *Dhruba* eyebrow ; all the Devata will retain the body healthy, and live long, Bramhá and other Devata will cure you. The sun and moon will do the same thing, as also *Narada* ; *parbata* prophets, fire, Bayu, Indra and other Devata. Bramhá composed this prayer, and will increase the age of the repeater ; may it be propitious, and the pain will always disappear.

Bramhá preserve you, and the Devata, and Chandra and Surjya preserve you. May you live long, and be quickly restored to health."

The patient is then to be taken to his own apartment, and the physician is to give the necessary directions regarding his diet ; which should be very light and spare, and the patient must avoid exercise, laughing, expressions of anger, pleasure or grief, &c. On the third day the bandages are to be opened and clean ones substituted. Should the bandages be opened on the second day, the wound will not be sufficiently united, and it will retard the cure, and increase the patient's suffering ; should the pain continue for several days, and be severe, with heat and swelling, the leaves of bitter plants are to be boiled and applied to the part.

When tents are used they should be removed every third day, and they are to be continued as long as pus flows from the part.

Means of removing foreign substances from the body.

There are two kinds of such extraneous substances, one of which is firmly fixed in the body, and the other is loose.

The first is the only kind requiring remarks. They are sometimes removed by drawing out, or by thrusting through the part. If at the time of wounding, the person faints; water is first to be thrown upon his face. After the blood has been discharged, from the wound; heat, oil and ghee, and the like are to be applied to the part. Then apply ghee and honey over the wound, bind up the part; and order diet, &c., as usual. If a vessel or tendon be wounded the instrument is to be removed by pincers. If it has disappeared under the swelling it is to be pressed, so as to force out the iron; or if there be barbs; enlarge the wound and so remove the arrow. If it has penetrated the bone, it is to be removed with force, and if required a string may be tied to the tooth of an elephant or, neck of a horse and thus forcibly removed, or with a bent branch of a tree. If in the throat, the extraneous matter may be discharged by thrusting down a hot iron to dissolve it or soften it and so remove it. In such cases, the hot iron is passed through a metallic tube. A Probang, for removing fish bones, is usual; by drinking fluids and emetics it is also dislodged; this may also be done by beating the person upon the back of the neck.

There are 15 modes of removing extraneous substances:—

1. *Swabhaba.*—When removed by the natural discharges, as by the tears.

2. *Pachana.*—Medicines to promote suppuration, which will be discharged with the pus and blood.

3. *Badhana.*—By a slight incision.

4. *Darana.*—By longer incisions.

5. *Pirana.*—By pressure.

6. *Pramarjana.*—By washing, by warmth, or by a hair cloth or hand.

7. *Bidmapana.*—By blowing, as a substance introduced into the larynx, which produces great irritation and strong efforts of coughing, &c.

8. *Bamana.*—By emetics.

9. *Birachana.*—If the extraneous substances have passed to Pokosio, purgatives are to be given.

10. *Prakhalona.*—If pus or blood be retained in a place, they are removed by warming.

11. *Pramarsa.*—If in the nostrils, errhines are to be used.

12. *Prabahana.*—If air, urine, and dejections are not discharged; or the fetus is retained; and are not removed by the efforts of the person, they are to be discharged by manual means.

13. *Achusana.*—When air is deranged, or water, or poison deranges the blood; or there is bad milk in the mammœ, this milk is to be removed by sucking or cupping, as the poison of erpents are extracted.

14. *Yaskanta.*—A loadstone may be used when the substance is straight, and is not tightly embedded in the flesh.

15. *Harsa.*—When grief is the cause, joy will remove it.

When the foreign substances produce fever, uneasiness, swelling, suppuration and death.

Wounds, Acute Ulcers, (*Sodo Bruno.*)

Wounds are produced by accidents and are of various shapes and forms. There is one kind which is simple, and another is complicated with the presence of a foreign body. Wounds vary with the part wounded, and the instruments by which they are inflicted. When the *skin* is wounded, it changes its colour, swells, and is hard. If in the *flesh* the swelling is greater, the wound gapes, discharges thick matter like ghee, and does not scab.

When a *vessel* is wounded it is accompanied with much pain, blood flows from the wound which swells, and when it suppurates pus is discharged. When *tendons* are wounded they swell and the discharge is like ghee or phlegm from the nose mixed with blood.

When *bone* is fractured various degrees of pain are produced; the marrow disappears, and the colour of the bone changes to that of a cockle shell. Pus and marrow are discharged from such wounds.

The six varieties of wounds are as follows:—

1st. *Chhinna,* or incised wounds, with a large open surface.

2nd. *Bhinna,* or penetrating wounds, as by pointed instruments, as the horn of a cow, &c.; this wound discharges little externally, when it penetrates a cavity it fills it with blood, and the contents of the organ; this is followed by fever, thirst, loss of appetite, difficult breathing, and the stoppage of the secretions, as urine and sweating. When the stomach is wounded it is accompanied with a vomiting of blood, and a swelling of the abdomen with severe pain. When the small intestines are wounded there is much pain, heaviness of the part, cold extremities, &c.

3rd. *Biddha,* or punctured wound, when the sharp pointed and narrow instrument is removed, or is retained in the wound.

4th. *Khata,* this is composed of the two last, being accompanied with destruction of the superficial parts or it is a contused wound.

5th. *Pichita,* when by pressure, or the weight of a heavy substance fracturing the bones, and injuring the soft parts, the wound is filled with marrow and blood.

6th. *Ghrista,* or bruised by coming in contact with a hard body.

Treatment.

In the four first kinds of wounds, there is a large discharge of blood. If there is severe pain apply poultices made of animal flesh and the like, with fomentations, followed by cold applications; an oily glyster is to be administered internally; and ghee prepared with medicines which correct, or diminish the diseased air.

In the two last kinds of wounds, there is a slight discharge of blood; and in such cases if there is not a loss of blood from the part, much inflammation and suppuration will be the consequence. In such cases, cold applications are to be used. This is the general treatment of all wounds.

The following is the treatment to be pursued in particular cases.

When the wound is near the head with a flap of skin, it is to be sowed, and a bandage applied to support the part. If the *ear* is separated it is to be restored to its natural position, and by sutures and a bandage it is to be kept there.

When the windpipe is wounded, and the air passes through it, sow the wound closely, put some ghee of the goat, and over it a circular bandage. The person should be kept on his back, and should take only fluid food. If the extremities are severely wounded with fracture of the bone, retain the parts in their natural position, apply oil, and a roller over them. In wounds of the back part of the body, the person is to be supported lying on his back, taking care that no pressure is made upon the wound. If on the breast, he is to be placed upon his breast in the same way. This direction is given in order to avoid the matter collecting within the wound.

When an extremity is separated, immediately pour boiling oil on the surface. Then apply a cap-formed bandage, and remedies to heal the wound. The following oil is recommended for healing wounds:—Take of a decoction of

Chandana,	(Sirium myrtifolium.)
Podmoka,	(Mentha sativa.)
Ragadhra,	(Amaranthus atropurpureus.)
Utpala,	(Salvinia verticillata.)

Príungu, (Panicum Italicum.)
Hurdira, (Curcuma longa.)
Mudhuka, (Bassia latifolia.)
Porscea, (Galega purpurea.)
mix, boil, and strain for use.

The unfavourable symptoms of wounds, are great fever and heat of the body, a collection of blood in the part, cold extremities, redness of the eyes. stoppage of the evacuations, delirium, giddiness, convulsions, difficulty of breathing, severe pain, with a serous discharge from the wound. The senses become obtuse.

Severe wounds are sometimes accompanied with erysipelas, tetanus, madness, hectic fever, cough, vomiting, diarrhœa, hiccough, shivering, &c

If the eye is divided the sight is lost, but if displaced without injuring the nerves, it is to be carefully returned with the assistance of a water-lily, and apply ghee as an errhine.

Means of improving, and forming new Ears and Noses.

A particular ceremony is performed for boring the ears of children, which it is not necessary to describe. As ornaments are hung from the ears, it is of consequence to remove defects from them. Sushruta gives directions for performing fifteen different operations. However, the experienced Surgeon will vary the operation according to the circumstances of the case, and according to the nature of the defect. Sometimes these are produced by accidents, or by internal causes. If the helix or antihelix are defective the body of the external ear is to be half cut through so as to bind it in the natural position. If there is a deficiency in these parts, a portion of the skin of the same size and figure is to be raised from the cheek, the blood stopped, and a bandage applied so as to keep the parts together of the natural figure and shape. The patient should not sleep during the day, should not eat much, should remain in a cool situation, and avoid fatigue. When the part is properly healed, apply oleaginous ointment, prepared with wax, oil, and fat. When the parts are healed up the lobe may be pierced according to custom.

If not properly performed many bad consequences will follow these operations, as indurated swellings, ulcers, &c.

When the nose is cut off, or destroyed by diseases.—The former is a frequent punishment in our courts. A fresh leaf is first cut of exactly the size of the nose, it is then to be placed upon the cheek, and the necessary quantity of skin and cellular membrane is to be dissected. The nose is then to be scarified, and after dissecting up the flap it is to be placed upon the raw part of the nose to which it will adhere. Sutures and bandages are applied to keep the parts together. After the bandage has been applied, a couple of wooden canulæ are to be introduced into the nostril to allow breathing, and to support the new nose. A piece of linen cloth previously soaked in oil is to be applied over the bandage. An aperient is then to be given to the patient, and his general health is to be attended to. Should any other deficiency of the nose be present it may be supplied in the usual manner. If the nose should be deformed it may be reduced in size by the knife.

Accidents.

Fractures and *dislocations* are produced either by falls, pressure, blows, by sudden and violent extension, and other incidents of violence.

Dislocations either lengthen or shorten the joint, or it is turned inwards or outwards, is tender and painful, which is much increased by the least movement. There are six varieties :—

1. *Utpista* when the dislocated joint is crushed and swelled, both above and below, with much pain, which increases at night.

2. *Bislistia* or separated. In this variety there is less swelling, the pain is continued, and the movements of the joint are totally lost.

3. *Bibartita,* when the joint is twisted.

4. *Tirjokhepta,* when one part of the joint is turned out ward with severe pain.

5. *Otkhepta,* when one of the bones of a joint are dislocated while the other remains in its usual place.

6. *Abakhepta,* when a bone is forced downward with much pain.

There are twelve varieties of *Fractures* :—

1. *Korkotaka,* when the fracture is in the middle of the bone with swelling.

2. *Aswakurna,* in which the bone protrudes like the ear of a horse.

3. *Churnta;* when accompanied with bruises and the bone is crushed.

4. *Pichchita,* when depressed by a heavy weight without swelling.

5. *Astheechulleta,* when a small part of the bone is elevated.

6. *Kandabhagna,* when a larger bone is fractured and disabled.

7. *Majámugoda,* when the broken part of the bone enters the same bone.

8. *Atipatta*, when the fractured bone is separated.
9. *Bokora*, partial fracture.
10. *Cheena*, when only a small part remains undivided.
11. *Pátta*, when comminuted without pain.
12. *Sphutita*, when the bone is swelled with small openings.

A fracture is distinguished from a simple swelling of the part, by the crepitating noise when moved, by the looseness and pain in the part, and by the great uneasiness.

Treatment. – Fractures do not unite quickly in those persons who eat little, and who are intemperate, or when accompanied with severe diseases. Such patients should not use salt, astringent and acid food, also connexion with women, exposure to the weather, fatigue. They should not take dry food, but use rice, animal broths, milk, ghee, and such like nourishing food. For these fractures use a decoction made of the bark of the *Moduká*, *Urumbora*, *Ossoka*, *Polassa*, and then apply splints of bamboo. A bandage is to be renewed every seventh day in the cold weather, in temperate weather every fifth day, and in hot weather every third day, or according to the individual circumstances of the case. The bandage, should neither be too loose, nor too tight. In the first case the apposite of the broken bones is not sufficient, and in the latter case it will produce much pain, swelling and inflammation. Cold astringent decoctions of the barks of different trees are to be applied; such as

Nagrodha,	Citrus aurantium.
Batá,	Millingtonia pinnata.
Aswatha,	Ficus religiosa, &c.

The part should be kept perfectly at rest, and every care should be taken to prevent suppuration.

After a few days warm oil should be applied to the part prepared with different drugs, according as the air, bile, and phlegm are affected.

Compound Fractures.—Apply ghee and honey to the wound, with astringent decoctions; and then follow the same plan of treatment as recommended for simple fractures.

Fractures are easily united in youth, and they require usually one month for the cure; in middle age two months; and in old age three months. In order to reduce a fracture, the bone that overlaps another is to be drawn down.

The following fractures are always dangerous:—

When one or more bones of the head are fractured, when the fracture is comminuted; when the thigh bone or pelvis are fractured; when the fracture extends to joints, when the fracture is produced from a fall from a great height. Fractures are also dangerous when the person is very weak, or very old, has old ulcers, leprosy, and when bad symptoms of deranged bayu are present.

In the Treatment of Dislocations.

First apply fomentations and warm oleaginous applications with frictions so as to soften and relax the parts. The surgeon will then reduce the dislocation by forcing the bone out of its new position, and by pressing and binding the joint in the opposite direction from that in which it has been displaced, so as to allow the bone to slip into its natural position.

When the hip or knee-joint are dislocated, the extension must be made with a kind of pully called *chakra.* The patient should then be placed in a bed and the part kept at rest. When of long standing, fomentations and oily frictions are to be diligently applied before the reduction is to be made.

A dislocated *rib* is to be reduced by pressing with the thumb and second finger, after the soft parts have been well relaxed by being rubbed with ghee. A proper splint and bandage, is then to be applied.

The dislocated *humerus* is to be reduced by pulling the bone strongly downwards, or along the side after a pillow or ball has been put in the axilla; when the bone will slip into its place. The joint is then to be surrounded with a bandage which passes round the axilla and the neck. This bandage is called *Swastiká.*

The dislocated *elbow-joint* is to be reduced by the extension and flection of the fore-arms, while pressure is made by the thumb and fingers upon the displaced head of the bone.

The same means are to be employed in order to reduce the dislocations of the wrist and ancle joints.

When the bones of the neck are dislocated, it is to be reduced by a person placing his thumbs under the angles of the jaw-bone, and fingers upon the side of the neck and drawing the head slowly upwards, while another person retains the body at rest. When the dislocation is reduced, the person is to be kept in an erect position for a week.

The dislocation of the lower jaw is to be reduced by drawing it downwards, when the bone will slip into its place; the part is then to be rubbed with warm ghee, and a four tailled bandage is to be applied over the chin, so that two of the bands are tied behind, and two on the top of the head.

When the bones of the nose are depressed, they are to be raised into their natural position by means of an instrument called *Sháláká*; a hollow wooden tube is kept in the nostrils, so as to retain the bones in their natural position. Ghee is then to be rubbed externally over the part.

After a dislocated bone has been reduced, a plaster is to be applied to the part; consisting of munjista, liquorice, red sandal wood, and rice, and are to be all pounded and mixed together. The plaster is then to be formed by mixing the powder with ghee which has been washed a hundred times in water. This plaster is to be continually applied over the dislocated joint, for a considerable time after it has been reduced. Should there be much pain in the part, a cold infusion of magrodude, pucha, mulie in milk, and chakra oil are to be applied.

Every morning during the treatment some prepared ghee mixed with such medicines as will improve the health, and keep the bowels relaxed, is to be taken.

In sprains and bruises nothing is to be done, except the applications of cold lotions and plasters. In some cases circular bandages wetted with ghee by itself, or mixed with a decoction of *casha* (a kind of grass), is to be applied over the part.

The treatment is said to be proper when no deformity is left in the part, and it has its natural action.

——:o:——

ORIGIN AND HISTORY OF MEDICINE.

In the sacred works of the Hindus it is recorded that the four immortal Védas,* named Rig, Yajur, Sáma, and Atharva were received from Bramhá, one having been produced from each of his four mouths. These works were the original code of divine legislation, and contained all the knowledge required by mankind during the Satya Yuga,† or the first age, during which man remained prosperous, virtuous, happy, and free from disease.

In the second age, or Treta Yuga, a third of mankind were reprobate; and disease appeared, life was curtailed, and memory impaired. In the third age, or Dwápara Yuga, half of the human race were depraved; and during the Káli Yuga, the present age, the corruption of mankind was such as to cause a still farther curtailment of life, and embittered it by numerous diseases.

Bramha, however, had such compassion on man's weakness and suffering, that, he produced a second class of sacred books

*From *Ved*, to know. Besides the four Vedas, the Hindus have other sacred records; as the Shastres, or commentaries upon the Vedas, now the great rule of faith. Eighteen of the most celebrated Puranas were written by Vyasa, the "compiler," as inspired Brahman, one of the seven immortal beings of the regal race of Puru. He was aided by other celebrated Pandits such as Paila, Vaisam Payana, Jaymini, and Sumantu. Besides these, the Hindus have numerous other commentators of their sacred works.

†From *Sátya*, truth and *Yuga*, age.

called Upavédas,* one of which named Ayur-veda, which was intended to teach the proper manner of living in this world, by preventing and curing diseases in the present state; and while the individual thus enjoyed health he may perform the various purposes of this world, and thereby ensure his happiness and prosperity in another state.

Other Shastres say that this Ayur-veda was obtained from Siva. It is the sacred medical record of the Hindus; and is of the highest antiquity, and authority. This work is said to have consisted of one thousand sections, of a hundred stanzas each, or a lack of verses (slokas). Bramha, pitying the weakness and suffering of mankind, and the impossibility of their learning so large a work, abridged it, and divided it into eight parts (tantra). Little of the original work has escaped the destructive ravages of time. Fragments only have been preserved, in the works of commentators; but, as all the information on the science was derived from what was considered the full and true account of every branch of the healing art, we are enabled, through their works, to judge of the arrangement of the great original: these divisions are as follows:—

1st.—Salya, Surgery, included the mode of removing external substances accidently introduced into the body, as grass, wood, stones, iron, earth, bones, hair, and nails. Pus, which has not been evacuated, and also the means of removing the dead child from its mother; of healing wounds inflicted by sharp instruments, as knives; of applying bandages, and using surgical instruments, in the different operations; of applying escharotics and fire; and of the treatment of different kinds of inflammation, abscesses, and other surgical diseases.

2nd.—Sálákya, includes the description and the treatment of external and organic diseases of the eyes, ears, mouth, nose, and other diseases which are situated above the clavicles.

These two divisions constitute the surgical diseases of modern schools.

3rd.—Káyachikitsá. That is describes the diseases which effect the whole body; as fevers, dysentery (atisarâ), hematemisis (raktapitta), consumption (soshá), mania (unmada), epilesy (apasmara), Leprosy (kusta), diabetes, (bahumutra), gonorrhœa (maha), and other diseases of the same kind.

This may be considered as constituting the practice of Physic.

4th.—Bhutavídya, or the means of restoring the deranged

---

* Joined to, or appended to. A kind of supplementary Vida, said to be derived immediately from the Vedas. There are four of these, the first is called Ayur-veda; *Ayus,* signifying the period of living; and *ved,* to know.

faculties of the mind, supposed to be produced by demoniacal possessions; as by the anger of the God's (*Devtas*), devils (*asurs*), or another kind of devils (*gandarba*), demigods or devils (*Jaksha*), giants resembling devils (*rakshas*), spirits of dead men (*petrigriha*), and other kinds of devils (*pihochas*).

These various demigods, when enraged, were supposed to enter into the person, and produce the various diseases of the mind; which could only be removed by prayers, medicines, ablutions, and offerings to the offended deity.

5th. Kaumárabhritya, comprised the treatment of infants, the effects of bad milk and improper diet; the nature of infant diseases, including those produced by the displeasure of certain demigods (*Graha*)*. In this division also was included the treatment of wet-nurses when their milk was bad.

6th.—Agadatantra. In this division the administration of antidotes for poisons was considered; as for preventing the effects and diseases produced by mineral, vegetable, and animal poisons; as the bites of dangerous serpents, insects, &c.

7th.—Rasáyanatantra treated of those medicines which cure diseases in general, and restore youth, beauty, and happiness. This division embraced chemistry, or more properly alchemy; as the chief end of the chemical combinations described in it are mostly metallurgic, and the intention was to discover the universal medicine, the panacea that would render health permanent and life perpetual. Such a medicine was supposed to preserve the energies of youth, strengthen memory, lengthen life, and prevent as well as cure diseases.

8th.—Vájíkarana-tantra. This division made known the best means of increasing the human race, by pointing out the mode by which tone was given to the weakened organs of generation, when the sensibility of these parts became diminished or deranged.

These remarks, on the division of this most ancient work, as given in Susruta, &c., are the only parts which have come down to us. They afford the most incontestable evidence of the Hindu Medical writings having been the result of observation and experience; although the authors assigned a divine origin to them, in order to increase the respect paid to the books, and to themselves. They thus seem to have arranged the diseases according to the frequency of the assistance required from the art, and in the order in which the knowledge of medicine naturally advanced.

---

*Many of the diseases of children are still supposed to be produced by the entrance of devils, into the child's body; which are expelled by particular prayers offered up to *Panchanana* (Siva.)

The sacred *Ayur-Veda* contained also a description of the structure of the human body obtained from dissection; an account of the causes and diseases to which it is subject, reduce to a systematic form; the enumeration of many useful remedies; and the precepts for preserving health, and curing diseases.

In some of the shastras (Charaka, Susruta) it is stated that Bramha first instructed *Dakhsa* the *Prajapati,* the father of *Durga,* in the *Ayur-Veda,* as he was an ocean of wisdom. He wrote a book named the *Chikitsa-Darshan,* and by him it was communicated to the two *Ashwins,* or offspring of the Sun (Surja). Others say that Bramha gave the *Ayurveda* to *Surja,* who like the Phœbus of the Greeks, was supposed to be the fountain of medical knowledge among the Hindus. The Ashwins became the medical attendants of the gods, wrote works on medicine named *Chikitsharatnatantra,* and the *Bramhagya.* By their remarkable cures, the *Ashwins* became very celebrated. When the fifth head of Bramha was cut off by *Bayraba,* it was joined again by them, so great was their knowledge of Surgery. They also cured immediately the wounds in the battle between the gods (*devtas*), and giants (*asura*). Indra had another opportunity of judging of their knowledge by their curing his paralytic arm. Many other remarkable cures mere accomplished by the two Ashwins. On witnessing these effects Indra became desirous of examining the *Ayurveda,* and he was taught by the Ashwins.

Some time after this, mankind, in consequence of their wickedness, became divided into sects, ignorant, restless, unhappy, and afflicted with numerous painful, and dangerous diseases; and as health is the origin of desire, virtue, holiness, riches, and external happiness, so disease diminishes strength, energy, faith, knowledge, holiness, and length of life. It also debilitates the senses, and defiles and destroys the soul.

The sacred Sages (Munis) were grieved at a spectacle so melancholy, and, in order to search for a remedy, *Bharadwaja, Atreya,* with numerous sages, met in the Himalaya mountains.

According to Charaka their names were as follows:—

Angira, Jamadagni, Vasishta, Kásyapo, Bhrigu, Atreya, Gautama, Sánkhya, Pulastya, Nārada, Osita, Agasta, Bamadeva, Markandeya, Aswanáyan, Parikshi, Bhikshuratreya, Bharadwaja, Kapinjala, Viswamitra, Aswaranya, Bhargaba, Chyabana, Obhijit, Gargya, Sandilya, Kaundilya, Abarkshi, Devala, Galavo, Sankritya, Vaijavapi, Kusika, Vadarayana, Barisa, Saraloma, Kapya, Katyayana, Kankayana, Kaikasacy, Dhauma, Marichi, Casyapo, Sarkarakshyo, Hiranyakshyo, Lokakshya, Paingi, Saunaka, Sakuneya, Maitreyao, Gautamayani and others.

These holy sages were distressed at the sight of the weakness

21

and sufferings of mankind, which had increased to such a degree, that they saw, with the eyes of their understandings, that the only method of removing such calamities was by the assistance of Indra.

These prophets resolved to send one of their number to the thousand eyed Indra in Heaven, to make known to him the condition of mankind. *Bharadwaja* agreed to go to Indra to acquire a knowledge of medicine. He went, and beheld him resplendant like fire, and by the following prayer propitiated his favor : Oh ! king of the Gods ! created for the salvation of mankind, I have been sent by the sages of the earth, to ask your assistance. Take pity on the weakness and infirmities of man, and teach us the *Ayurveda*. Indra was pleased to grant the prayer of the petitioner, and enlightened him in the precepts of the science of medicine ; as, from his acquirements, these alone were required to be imparted. These precepts embraced an enumeration of the causes, symptoms, and the properties of medicines for those in health, as well as in sickness.

With this knowledge of *Ayarveda*, the sage returned, and related to the *Rishis* the principles which he had thus acquired. These consisted of :—

1. General character of every thing (Sámana.)
2. Classification (Visesa.)
3. Elements (Drabya.)
4. Qualities (Guna.)
5. Actions (Karma.)
6. Combinations (Sanjoga.)

By means of such a knowledge, the Rishis remained healthy, and happy. Among these *Atreya* imparted the knowledge which he had thus acquired to his pupils, for the good of mankind ; among these, the chief were *Agnibesa, Bhela, Jatukarna, Parasaro, Harita, and Kshyarapani.*

The understandings of these sages being opened, by the instruction they received, and they distinguished the peculiarities of diseases, the qualities of medicines, and gained much distinction by the cures they performed. They are said to have lived in health to a very old age. These sages wrote works called by their own names, as *Agnibesatantra, Bhelatantra, Jatukarnasanhita, Purasárasanhita, Haritasanhìta* and *Kshyarapanitantra.*

These works were read before the assembly of the sages (*Rishis*), who were so much pleased with their arrangement, and tbe instruction conveyed, that with a noise which reached to Heaven they resounded the praises of the authors. *Agnibesa* was declared to have produced the best practical work, and after it was corrected by *Charaka* it received his name. He therefore became the instructor of practitioners upon earth, as the *Prajapati* were in heaven; and this is the most ancient and the most celebrated Hindu Medical work.

As it is arranged in the form of dialogues between the master and his pupils, the plan is desultory; for although it follows the division into eight parts of the Ayurveda, the subjects discussed seem naturally to have arisen at the conferences, between the master and students. Thus, the first division contains the Materia Medica, the arrangement, and the uses of Medicines, the rank of practitioners, the origin of medicine, &c.

The following may be offered as an example of the manner in which philosophical subjects are treated in one of the chapters of Charaka. They are the questions asked by the pupil *Agnibesa*, which were answered by *Atreya* their teacher. "What is the soul? How is it produced? What is the cause of the formation of the body? Is the soul ignorant or wise? Is it eternal or destructable? What are the temperaments? What are the diseases? What are the proofs of the existance of the soul? Why do some pundits say that the soul is inert, independent, represses the passions (bhassi), omnipresent, and omnipotent? Why do they call the soul *ketragan*, or emanation of the deity? Why is it called witness of the actions of the body (*Sáki*)? If inert, why do we see its actions? If independent, why does it enter the body? When a represser of the passions (*bhassi*), why is it always desirous of enjoying the passions, and greaving over our misfortunes? If the soul is omnipresent, why does it not feel the pains of others? If omniscient why do we not see it in mountains, and hills, and other things? Does the soul exist before or after the formation of the body? If the soul is the science or witness, has it any other judge? How does it support the pains of disease? Do practitioners employ means to prevent disease, to cure them when present, and what is the treatment? What is the cause of pain in disease, and where is it situated? How many kinds of pains are there? How are the pains removed?"

The work of Charaka is of the highest rank; but from the author's want of exact anatomical and pathological knowledge, his manner of treating the subject, and arrangement of diseases it is often obscure, although his descriptions may be accurate. In this work simple medicines are described, as well as their combinations. These remedies increased in number, and became more extravagant in their combinations, in the theraputical department of more modern works.

In other works of authority, it is stated that when the Vedas were lost in the deluge they were recovered by the great serpent

Ananta * upon the thousand head of which the world rests. At the churning of the ocean by the gods (*Devtas*), and demons (*Asuras*), the water of the ocean was converted into milk, and then into butter, from which precious gifts (*ratnas*) were derived. Among these was Dhanwantari, the physician, or holy sage, the possessor of the water of life (Amrita†) drank by the immortals.

Dhanwantari was instructed in the *Ayurveda* by Indra, and practised medicine with great success in Heaven, and became celebrated there: But witnessing the ignorance and misery of mankind, and the frequency and fatality of the diseases which afflicted them, he descended upon earth to cure their maladies, and to instruct them in the means of preventing, as well as of curing diseases. He became king of *Kasì*, or Benares, and acquired much celebrity by the cures which he performed. The divine sages, aware of his great knowledge, and witnessing the misery of mankind in consequence of their ignorance, resolved to petition Dhanwantari to assist them.

With this intention *Oupudhnuba*, *Baiturana*, *Aurabhra*, *Poushkalabata*, *Karabirja*, *Goupuraa*, *Rukeeta*, *Sushruta*, were selected to visit *Devadasa* or *Dhanwantari*, king of Kasi, formerly the practitioner of Heaven. On their arrival at Benares, they found that Dhanwantari had retired to the Jungles. They followed him to his retirement, and as they approached him, after mutual salutations, they delivered the following address:—"Deign Sovereign Ruler, to bestow upon us the power of preventing and curing the many diseases under which mankind is suffering,—affecting their bodies (*Sarira*), tormenting their minds (*Manah*), and which, with the numerous accidental (*Aguntaka*) and natural diseases (*swabhabika*), distress them so much that they seem to be without friends. Their seeming destitution grieves as much, and we pray that you will bestow upon us a work to instruct us in the cause, the nature, and the cure of diseases; for retaining health, and for promoting the welfare of the soul in another world. Like scholars, we come to receive this information from you." Dhanwantari answered, "your wishes shall be granted." The sages then informed their preceptor that as they were all of the same sect; one of them should ask the questions, and write down the answers required, and the others observe the answers.

Sushruta, son of *Visámitra*, a contemporary of Rama, was chosen to be the person to be instructed in Medicine. Dhanwantari said that Aurveda is for the cure of diseases, and for the

* A *Devta* also *Vishnu*; which is to say the end, endless, eternal, boundless.

† *Amrita*, that which gives life.

preservation of health. But it is too voluminous to be recollected by the present degenerate race of mankind; he therefore recommended Sushruta to abridge it, and to arrange it into parts, so as to be easily understood by every one who perused it with attention.

The work which Sushruta prepared is still preserved, and after Charaka, it is the oldest book in medicine which the Hindus possess, and is still of high authority. The manner in which it was produced is as follows:—

Dhanwantari asked his pupils, on what shall I first lecture? They answered, on Surgery; because formerly there were no diseases among the gods, and wounds were the first injuries which required treatment. Besides the practice of surgery is more respected, as affording immediate relief, and is connected with the practice of medicine; although the latter has no connexion with surgery. This was agreed to; and we find the explanation of the eight parts of Ayurveda, in six Books of Sushruta, as follows:—

1st.—Surgery (Sútra Stháṇa), in which is considered the origin of medicine; the rules for teaching, the duty of practitioners, the selection and uses of instruments and medicines, the influence of the weather on health, and the practice to be followed after surgical operations. Then follows the description of the diseases of the humours and surgical diseases; the restoration of defective ears and noses; and the removal of extraneous substances which have entered the body; the different stages of inflammation with their treatment, different forms of wounds and ulcers, and the regimen of patients labouring under surgical diseases. The description of good and bad diet; of prognosis; the kind of messengers to be employed by the sick; and of diseases, produced by the deranged actions of the senses, and of incurable diseases. Then follows the preparations required for accompanying a Rajah in war, the duty of the practitioners, the difference of climates, the different classes of medicines according to their sensible qualities, a description of the fluids, and of the different preparations, and articles of food. These subjects are treated of in forty-six chapters.

2nd.—Nosology (Nidána Sthána) the description and Diagnosis of diseases produced by vitiated humours, or derangements of blood, bile, wind, and phlegm. The symptoms and causes of Rheumatic diseases of piles, stone, fistula-in-ano, leprosy, diabetes, gonorrhœa, and scitis; the symptoms of unnatural presentations in midwifery, large internal abscesses, erysipelas, scrofula, hydrocele, venereal diseases, and diseases of the mouth. These subjects are considered in sixteen chapters.

3rd.—Anatomy (Saríra Sthána), or structure of the body.

The description of the soul, and the elementary parts of the body; of puberty; of conception; of the growth of the different parts of the body; of bleeding; of the treatment of pregnancy, and of infants. This division has ten chapters.

4th.—Therapia (Chikitsa Sthána), in which the exhibition of medicines, the history of inflammations, the treatment of fractures, rheumatic diseases, piles, stone, fistula-in-ano, leprosy, diabetes, and dropsy are given: the manner of extracting the child in unusual positions, the remedies for restoring health and strength, and for prolonging life; the means of preventing diseases; the use of clysters; and of errhines, and the use of the smoke of different substances. These are considered in forty different chapters.

5th.—Toxocology (Kalpa Sthána). The means of distinguishing poisoned food, and descriptions of different mineral, vegetable, and animal poisons, with their antidotes is given under this head. This division is treated of in eight chapters.

6th.—The supplementary section (Locales Uttara Sthána) includes various local diseases; as those of the eye, nose, ears, and head, with their treatment; the symptoms and treatment of fever, and its varieties; dysentery; consumption; *gulma;* diseases of the heart; jaundice; discharges of blood, and fainting. This is followed by the treatment of intoxication, of cough, hiccough, asthma, hoarseness of voice, worms, sterterous vomiting. cholera, dyspepsia, and disuria. It also treats of madness, epilepsy, apoplexy, the different tastes of substances with their effects; the means of retaining health, and the different opinions of practitioners regarding the humours. These subjects are treated in sixty-six chapters.

It thus appears that the ancient commentators on the Ayurveda did not allow the prejudices that now exist against touching the dead body, to interfere with that important and necessary branch of knowledge, which can alone be acquired by dissection.

The Charaka and Sushruta are the ground work of the more recent medical systems; in which their authors have uniformly adhered to the classification, and general details of the originals. But these imitators being ignorant of anatomy, and the usual causes of diseases, are still more defective in their descriptions particularly when they did not follow the more ancient writers.

It was by means of the works of Charaka and Sushruta that all the sages (Munis) are alleged to have been instructed in medicine; and the variety of opinion to be found in the treatises they afterwards wrote, was in consequence of the shortness of their compilations, their poetical form, and the great extent and difficulty of the subject. These sages are said to have practised medicine as a means of accomplishing much good to mankind; and they became famous by the number of lives which they saved. Those who were taught by Charaka, became Physicians; and the followers of Sushruta, Surgeons.

Charaka is superior to Sushruta in the accuracy of his descriptions, in the classification of diseases, and in the plan of treatment which he recommends. While Sushruta is principally celebrated for his anatomical descriptions, and judicious principles of surgery which his work contains.

The two following medical works deserve to be mentioned here. *Babhata* compiled a treatise called *Ostongo-reedoya.* This was principally taken from Charaka and Sushruta. The manner of treating the subject, and the arrangements are much the same. It is written in a clear style, and the author explains passages which were not before understood, in the original works.

About three hundred years ago, a compilation was made from all the most celebrated medical works, and called *Bhabaprakasha.* The author collected all that was most precious from the works left by other sages, and named the work after himself. By its clearness, and excellent arrangement this work explains the difficulties of the more ancient medical shastres, forgotten, and corrupted. This work was compiled for the use of practitioners, and is prefered by them, as it gives an admirable account of all the practical parts of the Hindu medical science.

—:o:—

CHAPTER II.

Rank of Practitioners, and Duties of Teachers.

In the Purânas it is stated that a young woman of the *Vaisya* caste, called *Ambá,* was serving as a menial to *Galaba,* the Muni. He was much pleased with her, and while blessing her, informed her, that she would have a beautiful and respected son. She told this to her parents, who asked the sage how that could be, as she was not married; and that the birth of a child would bring disgrace upon the whole family. The sage told them that it would be so; that the child should be called *Virabhadra* (very fortunate), that he would be much respected, and his profession would be that of medicine. This child was the first of the Vaidya, * or Medical caste.

His thirteen sons were taught by the sacred sages the works they had written, and they became most learned pundits, and skilful physicians. It is from their descendants that the Hindu

* Or one who understands *vidyá* (*i.e.*) the Ayurved, or Medical Shastra.

physicians are derived, and now form the caste of Vaidhyas. These physicians have free access to various shastres, or commentaries on the sacred writings. Brahmins learn the medical shastres for their advantage; Khetriyas for the benefit of their health, and Vaidyas for their subsistence. The two first castes are not allowed to receive any pecuniary recompense for their assistance to the sick.

Other castes may learn the medical works when they are honest, learned, and men of good descent. Even those of the degraded Sudra caste may be taught the Ayurveda, under such circumstances.

Teacher. "The feet of the Teacher is the origin of all happiness, and, like a light in a dark room, he will illuminate the contracted, and dark mind of the pupil; or, as quicksilver, properly mixed with other metals and exposed to heat, will be changed to gold, so will the words that come out of his mouth be pure and valuable".

In the ancient works it is stated that the teachers of the medical profession were Rishis, or Ascetic sages. They conveyed their instruction in the form of lectures, which were delivered in open public places, at which many students attended. These sages travelled about with their pupils, curing diseases, so as to afford them the means of witnessing the effects of different manners nnd customs, and different medicines, climates, and forms of diseases. The pupils kept notes of these lectures, and many of these compilations are still in existence.

At present the Teacher instructs three or four pupils, in many cases his relations, who are maintained at their own houses. In other cases the Teacher supports them. They continue five or six years reading the shastres, seeing the preparation of medicines, and their employment, for the cure of the sick. The teacher in many cases receives no emolument from his pupils, being content with the honor aud merit of bestowing knowledge. This merit is considered to be of the very first order; procuring for him renown in this world, and the highest benefits in a future state. In most cases however, an allowance is made to such Teachers by their rich neighbours

"A good teacher is like rain falling upon the germinating seed, and should possess the following qualifications:—A perfect knowledge of the shastres, joined to extensive practical knowledge and skill. He should be kind and humble to every one; he should have no defects of body, and should always be ready to expose the good, rather than the bad qualities of others; he should be clean and neat in his person, and possess and exhibit to his pupils all kinds of medicines and instruments. He should always be increasing his knowledge of books, and should neither be angry by the improprieties of others, nor fatigued by their importunities. He should be kind and considerate to his pupils and be able to explain the most complicated statements, in the simplest, and most perspicuous language. Such a person as this, who instructs a pupil, when of good parentage, is like the seasonable cloud and rain upon the corn field, which quickly matures its valuable produce."

"Such a man is not therefore aged, though his hair is gray. The Gods considered as aged, the person who, though young in years, has read, and understands the vedas. As an elephant made of wood, or an antelope made of earth, such is an unlearned Brahman: who has nothing but the name." (Menu, P. 44. and 156 157.)

Should a Teacher give improper instructions to his pupil, or peruse with him bad books, he will bear the weight of the sin of his pupil, and the seeds which he sows will not produce good fruits.

These vaidya teachers are often more learned, and have less pride than the Brahmans.

——:o:——

CHAPTER III.

Character and duties of Pupils.

Brahmans should teach the sons of Brahmans, of Khetriyas, and of Vaidyas, who belong to the third order of Hindu castes. The last are the professed, though not the exclusive medical class among the Hindus. Other shastres state that a Khetriya should teach the son of a Khetriya, and Vaidyas a Vaidya, &c.

"In all cases the Medical student should be the son of a respectable and ancient family, who is either the son of a practitioner, or of one who respects the medical profession. He should be inquisitive and observant, not covetous, zealous, or lazy; he should be a philanthropist, possess a generous heart, and his disposition should be amiable, and happy. The indications of such qualifications are, an agreeable voice, a small tongue, eyes, and nose straight, with thin lips, short teeth, which do not expose the gums, and thick hair which retains its vigour."

"With such qualifications even the son of the Sudra may be taught the shastres, with the exception of certain prayers (mantras). The teachers faith in God will thus remain, and be conveyed to such a pupil; and the teacher will afford glory to the scholar, even should he be a Rajah, and after death the Teacher will go to the heaven of Indra (Indraloka).

The successful student should be active in his duties, and not fatigued by his studies, he should possess gravity, a good memory, acute senses, and considerable acquirements.

Without such qualifications and indications the youth should be rejected.

These students of medicine enter their names as the pupils of some celebrated Brahman or Vaidya, who teach the science of medicine. When the student has learned one branch of the medical art, or that followed by his Father, he is not allowed to change it for another branch, although he can change his profession at any time.

A fortunate day is to be selected for the pupil to commence reading the shastres. On that occasion he is to be clean in his person, and the place in which he is to study should be purified. A raised part of the room, a cubit square, is to be cleaned with cow's dung and strewed with Kusa grass, after which fire is to be placed upon it, with several kinds of sacred wood, upon which ghee is to be poured, while prayers (mantras) are repeated. The pupil while being initiated should stand near the fire with his face towards the east.

The master (Guru) and other Brahmans are then to pray over some dried rice, and the Guru should sprinkle water over the assembly. He is then to place a Brahman on his right hand, over which he prays as he throws a mixture of curdled milk, honey, and ghee over the sacred fire. The scholar does the same, and his lesson begins. The Guru declares that he must henceforth discard lust, anger, covetousness, ignorance, laziness, vanity, pride, envy, revenge, cruelty, lying, and evil actions. He must always be engaged in the search after truth, and in the performance of good actions; he must be clean in his person, wear a humble and peculiar kind of coloured clothes; and his beard and nails should not be cut during the period of his study.

He must always respect his teacher and parents; put the dust of their feet upon his head, and obey them in every thing. He is thus addressed by the Guru:—

"When I say you may eat, drink, sleep, and rise from bed, you must immediately obey. If the scholar does not perform all this he sins, his understanding will diminish, and his glory will be quenched."

"Whatever I say you must believe, and carefully follow my instructions. You must be careful to act so as to please me, and if I do not acknowledge your good actions, I shall sin and my knowledge will be barren."

"In the treatment of the diseases of Brahmans, Gurus, and the poor and helpless or people who come from a distance, you must be as careful as you would be of your own relations, by which you will make more friends, acquire virtue, wealth, and a good name. You must not be displeased at my treating you as a son, a servant, or a beggar, you must harbour no bad thoughts, you must be moderate in the indulgence of your appetites, and you must be contented with a small recompence. By night and by day your anxious desire should always be to consider how you are to cure the sick under your care. You will avoid bad company, and neither give medicines to a culprit who has been condemned by a Rajah, to a woman whose husband and guardians are absent, nor receive any thing but food from a wife, without the consent of the husband. You must avoid entering a house, as a medical man, without an invitation, you must walk slowly, without gazing, and observe deliberately, but you must only observe the patient, and the symptoms of his disease; and you must not express the period of a fatal disease. You must not vaunt your own knowledge, for although the learned may be pleased, the ignorant will be angry at the exhibition of learning in such a situation. After visiting the sick, should the disease be complicated, you must detail the symptoms, and consult other physicians as to their nature and treatment."

"As the shastres contain the precepts of numerous prophets and great physicians with their descriptions of diseases reduced to a proper order, you must study them with care; by which the stupid and illiterate pupil will be instructed in his duties, and the intelligent and industrious in the manner in which that knowledge is to be improved and extended."

"The shastres are not to be read on unlucky (astami) days, or when the sun is obscured by cloud; on the two first days of a new moon; when it thunders; at unseasonable times; at the morning dawn, or evening twilight. The student must not study on holidays, or the day on which he meets a corpse, on which the Governor of the province is sick, when fighting occurs, or when war approaches."

The Brahmans were first called Brahmanha, and when they have received the string they are called Dwíja, or twice born; in like manner, the Physicians are called Ambashta, and Vaidya from Veda when they have acquired the ayurveda, or medical shastres. Besides the Ayurveda, the physician requires to know different other sciences. But if a Vaidya does not know or does not follow the precepts of the shastres, he will be like a thief, and such a person exercising medicine, will commit as great a sin, as beating a Brahman.

The preceptor, during the time he teaches his pupil, should wear two pieces of cloth, his mind should be calm, and he should be regular in his attendance.

In teaching, the progress of the student must be at first slow, commencing with the nomenclature of the profession, and then acquiring single subjects, and lastly the whole system. He must first read slowly and distinctly, without much effort, and avoid a monotonous intonation, or acquiring a dislike to the subject. The instruction should be given without pain to the instructed; and sweet gentle speech must be used by a Preceptor who cherishes virtue. When at his lesson, care must be taken not to allow any one to pass between the pupil and Teacher, as it will interrupt the supposed passage of good qualities from the latter to the former.

If the Student seek for long life, he should eat with his face to the east; if for exalted fame, to the south; if for prosperity, to the west; if for truth and its reward, to the north. (Menu P. 28 ch 2 52)

When a student has studied medicine, and has understood, examined, and remembered the symptoms of disease with the actions of medicines and has acted for himself, he is to receive the authority of the Rajah to practice medicine.

——:o:——

CHAPTER IV.

Duties of the Physician, of his attendants, and of the Patient.

There are four circumstances required in the cure of a disease, —a physician; a disease that is known; a reasonable patient; and medicines, instruments, and attendants. Each of these subjects will be considered in this order.

Duties of a Physician. The duty of a Physician relates to his person, character, acquirements, and observances.

Person. The Physician should possess a healthy body; he should keep his nails and beard short; his body pure, his clothes clean, and wear shoes, and a small turban. He should carry an umbrella, and stick in his hand.

Should the Practitioner not know his duty, the cure of the disease will be tedious and imperfect; it will also be so when the pulse cannot be felt at the root of the neck, and when the senses are affected. In such cases the Practitioner should always inform the relations and friends of the sick person of the state in which he is in, before prescribing.

Character. The successful student, after leaving his preceptor, should be cleanly in his person, love and obey his Teacher, and should be active and studious to find out the proper meaning of the difficult passages he had learned by heart. Should these passages not be understood, or should the student know the shastres, and not practice the profession, he will be like an ass carrying a heavy load of fragrant wood without discovering, and enjoying the fragrance of his burthen.

The Physician should possess a good memory, and be always amiable, cheerful, and collected. His language should be mild, candid and encouraging, rather like that of a friend than an acquaintance, and he should be always ready to assist the sick. His heart should be pure and charitable, and he should carefully follow the instructions of his Guru, and of his predecessors. Such a physician should possess a character for strict veracity, of calm temper, and of the greatest sobriety, and chastity. He should be a man of sense and benevolence, and his constant study should be how he is to do good. As a person may be afraid of his father and mother, friends, and guru, but not of his Physician; so the physician should be more kind and considerate to the sick than a father, a mother, a friend, or a guru. To these qualities should be added, that of affection for learned friends, the constant habit of visiting the sick, and seeing them treated by experienced persons. Without such a combination of qualities, knowledge will retard rather than advance his progress. He should know the causes and varieties of disease, and the means of preventing and curing them, and have the reputation of accomplishing cures quickly. He should study to remove curable diseases, but must avoid treating healthy persons. A good physician will continue to visit his patients diligently, examine them carefully, and be not fearful, but give medicines always when the patient can live: But if a physician attempts to treat an incurable disease, it will diminish his reputation, friends, and riches.

Acquirements. A good Physician should be acquainted with his profession, but so various are the qualifications that the combination is rarely to be found, even in heaven. He should be acquainted,—

1st.—With the introductory remarks of ***Sutrusthána,*** which considers the relation of customs and habits, and the knowledge of those duties which the shastres regulate, with reference to disease.

2nd.—*Sárira,* or structure of the body.

3rd.—*Nidán,* which includes the invasion (***Purbura***); and symptoms (***Rupa***) of diseases.

4th.—*Chikitsa* and *upasáya* concerning the regimen and the Medicines which cure diseases.

5th.—*Upadraba,* including all unusual symptoms which

develope themselves in the course of disease; as delirium, thirst, &c.

6th.—*Kolpa,* concerning poisons.

To such acquirements, the physician must have practised his profession as well as studied the shastres, which were compassionately revealed by the Gods. Without such a knowledge of books he will be confused, like a soldier afraid in the time of action, will be a great sinner, and should be capitally punished by the Rajah. On the other hand, a want of practical knowledge will impede his advancement, and his senses will be bewildered, when called on to treat acute diseases. Such a physician will not be esteemed by the great, as he cannot practice with success when only instructed in half his duty. Such a person is the murderer of his species, and the medicine prescribed by him may be compared to poison, or lightning—such ignorance prevents all the good effects of remedies. As the two wheels of a chariot, or the two wings of a bird, assist in their progress, so will the knowledge of the shastres, and of practice, lead the physician to proceed with safety and success in the treatment of the diseased; but, should the physician want either of these essential qualifications, his progress will be impeded, as one wing or one wheel will impede the progress of the bird, or the chariot. It is the combination of both these qualifications which is required; when medicine becomes like the water of immortality (*Amrita*). Such a physician, if he is to acquire celebrity, must still daily endeavour to improve his mind by an attentive perusal of scientific books. If such a physician does not gain money after he has been taught the shastres it is his own fault.

When such a *Vydya* is spoken to by a patient in a peevish or hasty manner, he will remain calm, mild, and courageous; and cherish a cheerful hope of being able to save the sufferer's life. The practitioner should avoid frivolous or improper language, particularly with females; he should not sit down upon the same bed, and the only presents he should receive from them is food. He should be frank, communicative, impartial, and liberal, yet ever rigid in exacting an adherence to whatever regimen or rules he may think it necessary to enjoin. Should death occur under the care of such an earthly saint, it can only be considered as his inevitable fate, and not the consequence of presumptuous ignorance.

The presence of a physician for the cure of a disease is most important; indeed, as indispensable as a pilot is to a boat, as a coachman in guiding a chariot, or as a general to an army. If a physician is not consulted when a person is ill, he will soon die, as a lamp exposed to wind is continually liable to be extinguished.

Some severe diseases are cured immediately, by a good

physician; but simple diseases are increased much by the want of early assistance. At the commencement, like a young plant, it is readily rooted up, but as it expands and grows in strength the difficulties are much increased. Even for a slight disease the assistance of a practitioner will be of much use; for as a large man at the bottom of a pit may get out by long continued exertion, his extrication will be much facilitated by the assistance of a friendly hand. As in war, a sword may defend many, so in the hand of an enemy it will destroy. In like manner the shastres and water may become the cause of destruction instead of benefit to mankind.

Some practitioners have many instruments and medicine which they do not know how to use, such are calculated to deceive; and by their arrogant manners, and being without a knowledge of the shastres, are enemies to mankind, and are called *Chhadmachara.* Those who possess the favourable qualities of Physicians, without the necessary knowledge, are called *Pratirúpaka*; and those who know the medical shastres, and are well acquainted with the causes, symptoms, and means of curing disease, and their prevention, will be fit to be the physician to a Rajah. Such persons are called *Sidhi Sádhaka.*

The first two are sometimes allowed to practice by the neglect of the Rajah, and they may be known by their vanity, and ill will towards the good physician. Such persons flatter the patients friends, are diligent, take reduced fees, are hesitating and doubtful in performing difficult operations, and pretend that their bad success is caused by the bad attendants, &c.; such persons avoid the society of learned persons as they would a jungle.

Still some patients will be saved when under the care of such a physician, as a worm in destroying one of the sacred shastres will sometimes leave in its depredations the rude representations of some of the sacred letters. A bad physician may cure one patient, by which he endeavours to establish his fame, without considering the thousands he has killed; such a person is like a boat in a storm without a pilot, or a blind man in the performance of any work, and is to be looked upon as the angel of death. If such a fellow has his fancy inflamed, he is like a deadly serpent, and should be avoided.

The Practitioner who knows the value of quicksilver, &c.; is like a god; one who knows the qualities of herbs and roots is like a man; one who knows the use of the knife and of fire resembles a demon (Asur); and those who know the proper prayers to be offered up in the time of sickness is like a prophet.

The following characters will never be respected as Physicians :—When the person is born in, and inhabits a village which has a bad name, or visits the sick without being called. A bad Physician does not pay respect to the Brahmans, spiritual Teachers, or superiors; he leaves the duties due to the memory of his father unfulfilled; wears bad clothes, speaks on improper subjects, and in an improper manner, or neither speaks nor gives medicines. Such a person does not pay respect to astrologers, to the seasons and times, to the influence of the planets, to the opinion of friends, or acknowledges the power of holy men. Such a physician will never be respected; and the great physician, *Dhanwantari* himself, possessed of such qualities, would not be liked or esteemed.

Should a proud physician reject the shastres, and the advice of his Guru, all sorts of evils will follow him; and if he cannot repeat the usual prayers, is ignorant of the nature of disease, and takes money, he should be punished by the Rajah, as a thief. Should a physician speak disrespectfully of the shastres, or incorrectly of the *Ayurveda,* or of astrology, the same punishment shall be inflicted, on him as that for killing a Brahman.

From these observations, it appears that the duties of a physician requires the exercise of sound judgement, unimpeachable integrity, profound learning, embracing an intimate acquaintance with many shastres, and a constant and extensive practice of his profession. To these qualities must be joined unremitting attention, a good heart and disposition, a knowledge of the appearance and varieties of disease, and the manner of preparing, and exhibiting the proper remedies.

A physician should not visit the enemy of a Rajah; as he should always speak the truth, avoid speaking disrespectfully of ancestors, and of other good, exalted, and pious persons. He is not to walk with the wicked, foolish, or low-born persons, or with the patients enemy. He must avoid riding on wicked horses, elephants, or the like, living in empty houses, or in places where bodies are burnt; in very retired places, containing wild beasts or reptiles, where people are quarrelling, especially with cutting instruments in their hands, or animals armed with horns. He is carefully to avoid walking behind biers containing dead bodies, moving in the shadow of the images of the Gods, of cows, Brahmans, or in the smoke of burning bodies, diseased persons, or great sinners. The physician as well as other persons should neither look at the rising nor setting sun. He should neither inform a person that a cow is eating what belongs to him, nor speak ill of a Rajah. He should not walk upon the tops of rocks, beat the water or earth with his hands or feet, prevent or resist any inclination of the body, to discharge any thing. He should avoid drinking or eating out of a broken vessel, or out of the hand; and should not sleep with his face to the north. Ganesah had his head chopped off for so doing by Sunni, and the head of an elephant substituted, as it was found sleeping with its head in the same direction.

Observances. When called upon to attend a patient, the physician is to mark the following circumstances:—He is to observe the manner, speech, and dress of the messenger; the state of the planets, and the time of the day; and the good or bad omens. He should note the occurrence of accidents, in walking, or in seeing impure, weak, imperfect, or divided objects: In such cases the person will die of the disease. This will be rendered more inevitable, should neither presents nor respect be shewn to the practitioner.

Before a physician visits a patient, he should first remark the position he is in when the messenger arrives to consult with him; and, by the persons countenance and conversation, endeavour to ascertain, whether or not the patient will survive. As he proceeds to visit the sick person, he must carefully note any good or bad omens that may occur regarding the messenger, the flight of birds, the relative position of animals, &c. Seeing cows, or Brahmans on the right hand side are favourable, as also corpses, jackals, vessels of water, &c., when seen on the left side. It is unfavourable when lizards are heard when leaving the house, when vultures, or bad characters are seen, or when the Physician is called by another person, or is hit by any thing behind, or when a person sneezes.

If the physician meets a person carrying out a vessel of water, earth, seeds, fruit, ghee, sees a bull, Brahman, or scorpion, when coming out of the sick person's house; or the figure of a geni, a fire vessel, or a bow for arrows, the person will die. Seeing animals in unclean situations, on the right and left hand, bad sinners, very old and blind persons, or an enemy, are bad omens.

If the Physician arrives at the same time at the patients house with milk, the omen is favourable.

The physician should avoid visiting a sick person during the night. When he gets up in the morning, and has performed the necessary purifications, he is to visit the patient residing in a clean place.

The physician should avoid visiting a patient in a place where there is hair, bones, spikes, stones, chaff, ashes, broken stone vessels, charcoal, or in impure situations.

If the first object seen in the morning is a holy man, the

person's money will increase; and if a bad man it will diminish. Should the person be at enmity with a soothsayer, he will become poor; with a physician, he will soon die; and with a Brahman toil will be the only recompence he will get for his exertions, and he will soon lose his life.

Should the air at the time be cool, and pleasantly scented it is favourable; but if with a strong wind blowing with a disagreeable smell, the prognosis of the disease should be more guarded. These and various other indications are explained in the Medical works, and seem to be founded on the Hindu belief in fatalism; a system, though sufficiently plausable with the ignorant, is fraught with many and great evils.

Useful indications are supposed to be derived from the dreams of the physician, as well as from those of the sick person; and a long list of the good and bad subjects of dreams are given. In general, favourable dreams consist in seeing brahmans, cows, rajahs, clean water, splendid houses, &c.; and the reverse in seeing the person cleaning himself, riding on an unclean animal, low caste persons, dead acquaintances, killing or fighting, unclean animals, falling down a precipice, loss of eye-sight, and other impure objects or defects, &c. The good and bad dreams in different diseases is likewise given, which seem to be good or bad according to the greater or less importance of the changes of the symptoms which they indicate.

The physician should first ask questions at the attendant regarding the disease; what things he has eaten, and what he has done to produce, or to influence the disease. The physician should then mark the signs of longivity in his patient. These are long arms and fingers; large eyes, forehead, trunk, teeth, mouth, and hands, feet, and shoulders. Persons will live to an old age who have long respirations, and a large space between the mamilæ, the fore-legs short and fleshy, the neck short, and speak and act sensibly. A person with a large body and good voice, deep navel, vessels and joints well formed, much hair on the body, the external ears long, the body strong, more particularly the head, quickly dries when wet with oil or water, from above downwards, and the senses are good: such a person will live long, and should be treated by the physician. The want of such signs will indicate a short life, not exceeding 50 years; and when moderate in their manner of living, and rich, they will not exceed the age of 70 years. When such a person has not been diseased from his birth, has grown fat gradually, as well as in his knowledge ot the shastres, he will live long. The person will live a moderate period when the lines on the palms of his hands, and long longitudinal lines on the back are well formed, but with large external ears, and the end of the nose prominent, the person may live 70 years. When the bones of the fingers and forearm are short, testicles pendulous, breast and back contracted, ears short, nose prominent, and gums are seen on laughing, and eyes are not steady, such a person will live 50 years. Then follows the proper proportions of both the large and small members, and the proportions of the size of each part of the body for indicating the length of the persons life.

It is necessary to recollect that a good Brahman, and a Rajah, will be cured of a disease with difficulty, as they will not always take the proper remedies, and the physician is afraid to urge his instructions strongly. The same is the case with women, children, and old people, who do not observe the proper directions. In like manner, those who do not explain their complaints, who are weak in intellect, are poor, and avaritious; who will not spend their money, or have bad tempers or dispositions, are dissipated, and are without friends, will be cured of their diseases with difficulty, as they will not strictly follow the directions of the physicians. In such cases the disease may be rendered incurable.

2nd.—The Nature of the Disease. The physician (chikitsáka) should next mark the nature of the disease, the seasons of the year, and enquire from what country the patient comes. He is to mark which of the humours (*dhátu*) are diseased, and how they can be cured.

There are three kinds of these duties :—

1st.—To cure the diseases of wind (vayu), bile (pitta), and phlegm (kaph) which occur without causing other diseases. These derangements are the usual cause of disease, and produce the change of disposition, and the peculiar feelings of the sick; besides one disease may produce another, which sometimes diminishes the symptoms of the first.

2nd.—When a disease is present, how it is to be cured? and

3rd.—When a primary and secondary disease are present, and require to be cured?

The physician is to observe the general appearance of the sick person, his age, and the condition of his body, his temperament and strength, the state of the mind, and the food which he has been used to. He should examine the symptoms of the disease with his eyes; consider the probable result of the disease by his judgment, and its similarity with other diseases; as there is a good and a bad form of every disease. The symptoms enumerated in the shastres, should be observed, more especially the state of the pulse, of the tongue as to moisture and dryness, the condition of the bowels, urine, and sleep; his general feeling, more especially the state of the nose, head, hands, feet and abdomen. The state of the patient's appetite and internal fire; the part of the body attacked, and the state of the various vessels (*serà*), and the abdomen (kastha); particularly where the stomach presses upon the food to digest it (pokasia); where the undigested portion is situated (ámasia); where digestion takes place (*pakasaya*); and where the dejections are retained (*molàsaya*) next the bladder and pelvis. The seat of the blood (Jokerit, &c.) the heart (hit) and the lungs (phuspus) are to be considered; and the period when the disease increases, and intermissions occur. The kind of caste, temper, and disposition; the degree of fear; the state of the dejections; and, in females, the state of the catamimia, &c. If the patient cannot speak, those about him should be asked the usual questions about the disease.

The disease is next to be examined by the five active senses, and by speech. By the touch is distinguished the feverish heat or coldness of the surface, the dryness or moisture, the softness or hardness, the size of the vessels, and the irregularities of the skin. By the hearing, the passage of air in deep seated abscesses, wounds; and in the intestines, by coughing, &c.

By the signs of longivity and strength of the body, and the changes in the colour of the skin, &c.; as leprosy, and various forms of cutaneous diseases; by the state of the tongue and of the urine; the quantity of which is to be noted, and the quality, which is known by ants being fond of it, by the sight, and by the smell. In like manner the other secretions and discharges, as from ulcers, &c., are to be examined.

By speech, the Practitioner learns the time of invasion and progress of the disease, the sex and habit of body; the nature and degree of pain; and the state of the appetite, the strength, and the evacuations. Unless the disease is well explained, seen, and known the practitioner will not understand it, and will be made foolish by his ignorance; whereas the knowledge, and judgment of the physician, like a lamp which illuminates a room, enables him to understand the nature of the diseases of the body.

The physician has special duties to perform to a Rajah as they differ from other men; not in the formation of the body, but by their nature, which is to command and to pardon. These qualities are received from God; and, as an exalted being, he is distinguished by the superiority of his voice and manner, by the pureness of his heart, and by the justness of his actions. The physician should be careful in the time of war, to point out the road he is to travel; of his water, food, and shelter; and of the food of his horses and elephants. The physician is to live near the person of the Rajah, and be like his shadow, or his standard. Medicines and instruments should always be at hand; and he should be allowed to have free intercourse with the sick. But the care of the physician should not end here. It should extend to the water, and the food of the army, as well as of the beasts of burthen which the enemy may endeavour to destroy by poison. The good physician will detect this, and may be the means of saving the army.

3rd.—Medicines and Instruments. When called to a patient, the practitioner is first to remark if there is still life, and strength, in the sick person; his age, temperament, and country, and this knowledge will modify the kind and quantity of medicine to be given. As long as life remains in the root of the throat, and the senses remain perfect, the physician may give medicines, as the person, under such circumstances, may be cured. Even old, inveterate, and incurable diseases, may be alleviated by a judicious line of treatment. If, therefore, a practitioner, after the necessary examination, knows the disease, and that it may be cured even with difficulty, his duty is to endeavour to alleviate the sufferings of his patient. Should the alloted period of his life upon earth have expired, he will die notwithstanding the best directed means for his recovery. It is proper, however, that much caution be used in the employment of medicine in fatal diseases, as a physician may alleviate pain, but cannot give life; and by administering medicines in such cases, without previously stating the danger the patient is in to his relations, he will only bring discredit on himself, and on his profession. Taking such precautions, the practitioner may give medicine even when the patient is senseless, without any pulse, and only breathes.

The medicines proper for the individual case, and the manner in which it will be most proper to administer them, must be carefully observed; care must also be taken that the medicines be obtained from a good soil and neighbourhood. Those from Hímálaya Mountains are the best. The physician should, however, not only know the names but likewise the various qualities of these medicines. For this purpose he should penetrate forests, and climb mountains, to examine them in their natural situations; and should not despise the information obtained from hunters and shepherds, who may have had opportunities of witnessing their effects.

The medicines should be collected on a fortunate day, and at a lucky hour. They should be gathered by the physician himself, with suitable prayers. Should a person of another caste touch or prepare the medicines, and not the physician who prescribes, they will be rendered inert, even should a Brahman have prepared them. When the proper medicine has been gathered and prepared in the prescribed manner, and administered at the proper time, the effect will be as if Vishnu had administered, and entered into the body of the sick person; but the medicine will be of no use to the sick unless administered by a physician, as it will otherwise be like the lump of prepared clay, without the aid of the potter to fashion it. A physician should, therefore, be his own apothecary, preparing and prescribing those medicines which are peculiarly appropriate to each particular case, and being unknown to others, constitutes one of his peculiar excellencies

The qualities of medicines, depend on their colour, smell, and kind of juice. The active power of medicine should be great, but the quantity should be small. These quantities should be carefully observed, and the medicines given at the proper season, and stage of the disease.

The person's disease is then to be examined, the state of the humours and blood; the seven essential parts (dhátu), and lastly the evacuations. He is next to decide on the nature of the disease, administer the proper medicines, and give directions regarding diet and regimen.

It is of much importance that the disease be treated at the proper time; and the patient be of the proper degree of strength to admit of the disease being cured. Active treatment should not be employed in a slight disease, nor a mild treatment in an acute disease. Should the treatment employed be doing no good, it should be changed; but when the symptoms are yielding, under a particular plan of treatment, it should be continued.

That kind of treatment will be successful which diminishes the disease, by equalizing all the humours; and that is bad treatment, which increases one, as it diminishes another humour. The treatment should be commenced from the first appearance, of the disease; as it is like fire, poison, or the enemy, and a small portion deranges health.

Should a physician exhibit medicines the first day he has seen the patient, without properly ascertaining the nature of the disease, he will be like the angel of death (Yama). Such medicines as cure vital air, bile, and phlegm when diseased, are not disagreeable to the person; do not produce any bad effects; and, given at the proper time, are the remedies to be employed. A Vaidhya should prepare the medicines; although this is stated in other shastres to be the province of Brahmans. The Sushruta shastre says that any competent person may administer medicine, but the Vaidya declares whoever does not take medicine from this caste will go to hell. Even Brahmans are declared to have no authority in the practice of physic. Any other caste preparing or touching medicine, but the physician who orders its preparation, will render it inert.

4th.—Messenger and attendants. The person who is sent for the physician should not be of low caste, a fool, one of questionable veracity, or a great sinner; he should not appear before the physician distressed from fatigue, by a rapid journey, or appear to be fearful of the result of the sick persons ailment. The messenger who has his hair knotted, clothes old or wet, or is scantily or slovenly dressed, carries a cutting instrument, &c., as a sword or stick, holds ashes in his hands, will be as the angel of death. If he be a Dandí or Fakír, or is deformed, or defective in a member, or rides upon an ass, camel, or buffaloe; or wears a band of red flowers round his neck, the prognosis is unfavourable. If the messenger has his body anointed with oil, or if covered with the deposit of a river, or blood be flowing from his body; or if he be of a bad temper or disposition, so as to speak hastily or indiscretely it will be unfavourable. If he rubs his shoulders, back, head, or hair with his hand while speaking, it will be like a decree of *Yama,* the angel of death. Should the messenger arrive so as to meet the physician on the south, and the physician not wishing to visit the sick; or if the messenger stands on one foot, sneezes, or stumbles at the patient or physician's house, these signs are unfavourable. Should he find the practitioner with his face turned towards the south; with cutting instruments near him; in an unclean situation; naked, bathing, eating, sleeping, or making holes in any thing; these signs are unfavourable. It is also a bad omen when the messenger finds the physician preparing a body for the funeral pile, killing birds or the like, or boiling or preparing medicines with fire. Should the messenger arrive at the house of the physician at twelve at night, or at noon, or when certain stars are in the ascendant the prognosis is unfavourable.

The messenger should always present a present to the physician. He should be of the same caste as the sick person, and should be dressed in clean white clothes, have a good appearance, and be strong and intelligent; of a mild disposition, and know the lucky seasons, and the shastres.

The medicines should be given by a healthy dependant, possessed of an amiable character, so as to prevent the machinations of the patients enemies.

The friend who relates the progress of the disease must be exact in his descriptions, and be careful that the patient takes the medicines regularly.

5th.—Duty of the Patient. A person rejecting a Vaidya or physician, will be punished in Hell; whereas when a Vaidya is employed the patient will go to heaven, even should he not be able to see the sacred Ganges in his dying moments.*

The diseased person will carefully recollect the directions of the physician, must follow them with exactness, and must not be afraid of the effects of the medicines which have been ordered.

Should the disease commence at an unfavourable time, or if the physician visits the patient at night, or during an unlucky hour, or should he have been borne at an unfavourable moment, the person will die of the disease. A patient with a good disposition, with his body of the natural colour, and with the signs of longivity; who is patient, has a strong mind, senses perfect, with no fatal symptoms, and has confidence in his physician, is easily treated, and will have the best chance of being cured. Should the patient be strong, the disease curable, and he has riches to defray the necessary expence, and follow the usual customs and directions of the physician; and his mind is favourably influenced by the shastres, and has faith in his physician, he will recover. The prognosis will be unfavourable when the sick person is impatient, angry, and disobedient; wanting in courage, is ungrateful, and desponds; also, with those who have no confidence in the practitioner, fatal symptoms will quickly follow. Persons at enmity with the physician, and endeavour to deceive him, are cured with difficulty, and are to be avoided as much as possible. The patient will die who lives in the house of a person who despises the physician. The different appearances observed on the physician's approaching and leaving his patient will vary his prognosis.

The patient is to expect to be visited in the morning, after the customary prayers and ablutions, is to prepare the medicine as ordered, and is to sit in a clean, convenient part of the house for both the sick person, and the physician.

—:o:—

CHAPTER V.

Recompence of the Physician.

When a physician has cured a disease he is entitled to the usual gifts for the performance of a good action. These will vary with the rank and condition of the patient. Money will be the recompence bestowed by the rich; friendship, reputation, increase of virtue, prayers, and gratitude will be that of the poor. When a Guru, a Brahman, or a Dandí, a relative, a humble and good friend, or one without relations consults a physician, he must not

*Many respectable Hindus will only receive medicines from a Vaidya.

accept of any pecuniary recompence: His reward in such cases will be an increase of knowledge, and the gratification of his desires in having an opportunity of performing a good action. His cures will ensure the admiration, and the esteem of all men; he will be honoured and respected as a master, and after death he will go to heaven. Should the patient prove ungrateful after being cured, his holyness and good fortune will pass to the physician. But the physician must avoid administering remedies, to hunters or great sinners. Such people do not deserve his assistance.

—:o:—

BOOK IV.

PRACTICE OF PHYSIC.

THIS EXTENSIVE SUBJECT WILL BE CONSIDERED UNDER SOME GENERAL REMARKS ON DISEASE; AND THE DESCRIPTION AND TREATMENT OF PARTICULAR DISEASES.

——:o:——

CHAPTER I.

General Remarks on Disease.

In this chapter I shall consider the nature, classification, causes, and description of disease, with a few remarks on Pathology as explained in the shastres.

Nature of Disease.

Disease is distinguished in the shastres by the causes, peculiar signs, and effects of certain substances in diminishing or increasing particular sets of symptoms, and lastly by Pathology or more properly morbid anatomy.

The nature of disease was explained by the Hindus on the same principles as their physiology. Nature, which exhibited the highest degree of order in her operations, is liable to occasional irregularities; from the impurities, and the imperfect manner in which the elements, and qualities, are mixed together. In like manner the harmony of the humours of the body are liable to derangement. At one time the disease is owing to an increase of one of the principal humours, at another to its diminution, with regard to the other humours. They thus explained the occurrence, and varieties of disease:—The soul (*jivita*) of the body, like the great soul of the world, tended to retard these derangements, or restore such irregularities. When disorder has been introduced; the soul, (vix medicatrix naturæ) tends to reduce the humours that are increased, and to augment those which are diminished. In like manner certain medicines have peculiar effects in producing these changes, and thus assist the soul in her salutary influences.

As long as the humours remain in due proportion, the individual remains in health, as perfect harmony reigns in the universe while the elements retain their just proportions; but, as soon as the harmony is lost, by the assimilation being imperfectly performed, derangements of the system are the consequence, and the body becomes the prey to disease. Hence, these irregularities in the quantity and quality of the humours, are the proximate cause of diseases. This is rendered more frequent by the body continually undergoing changes by the waste that is going on; which is made up by the supply of aliment

Disease is therefore the pain (*duhkha*) of the soul, caused by the derangement of the humours.

Classification of Diseases.

The ancient Hindu Medical writers arranged diseases according to their prominent symptoms, and not according to the peculiarity of the symptoms and their combinations, which were influenced by the structure and uses of the part. Thus they gave the name of *shúl*, to diseases accompanied with much pain; when accompanied with local swelling it is considered as *gulma*, while more general swellings were considered under the head of *udara*. They thus lost an important principle in the grouping, and inculcated dangerous principles in the treatment of diseases: for some diseases will assume the peculiarities of the three diseases. Others pass from the one to the other, while the nature of each of the diseases, and the tissue affected, are quite different; and require to be treated by methods quite opposite to each other.

In the Ayurveda medicine is divided into eight chapters, which require, it is added, to be carefully studied before a person can be successful as a practitioner. But so extensive is the range of the subject, that one person cannot successfully exercise all, and he requires to confine his attention to one department. The classification in Ayurveda is as follows:—

1st. Injuries, and phlegmoid tumours.
2nd. Diseases of the senses, and head.
3rd. Diseases of the whole body, as fever, leprosy, &c.
4th. Derangement of the faculties, from demoniacal possessions.
5th. Diseases of infants, and of nurses.
6th. Antidotes.
7th. ? Alchemistry; and
8th. The means of increasing the human race. A modification of this division is usually followed in the Hindu Medical works.

Diseases are likewise divided into three kinds, one of which is curable, another is cured with difficulty, being of a chronic nature, and the third class is incurable. Each of these diseases is again divided into primitive, and consecutive; external, or internal; local, or general. These again are divided into three varieties :—The first is, when one disease has occurred and another follows, which is increased by the first, the medicine for which must cure both diseases, but particularly the chief. A second variety is when a disease has been present without any other; and a third is when the precursory symptoms are only present. In such cases medicines are to be given, so as to remove the diseased cause.

Another classification is founded on the origin of diseases, into hereditary, and acquired. These, however, are not divided into sporadic, epidemic, and endemic classes; although this is so natural a division. The contagious, and non-contagious nature of diseases, and their being communicated from one person to another by mediate, and immediate contact, was well known to the Hindu physicians.

In Charaka, and other works of great authority, diseases are considered under four classes :—The first is called *Agantuka*, or accidental diseases, and are produced by external causes, such as accidents and poisons. There are two varieties of these diseases, the first being corporeal, and the second mental. Medicine will cure the one, and management the other.

2nd. Nija (Saurira), bodily diseases, form the three other classes. They are caused by eating and drinking improper articles of food; which derange air, bile, and phlegm; or blood locally, or generally. Both *Agantuka* and *Nija*, may affect the mind as well as the body.

3rd. Mánasa (mental diseases), produced by derangements of the mind; caused by passion, grief, joy, anger, malice, envy, pride, lust, covetousness, delusion, low spirits, &c.

4th. Swábhábika (natural diseases), which act on both mind and body in the same manner; as appetite, thirst, decrepitude, sleep, death, &c.

These four classes of diseases thus act eventually on the soul, as well as the body; and may be cured by evacuating superfluous humours, and increasing those that are deficient, by diet, and management (*Sushruta*).

Diseases have likewise been divided into two classes :—

I. *Shastrasádhya*, or those cured by manual treatment.

II. *Snehádi Kriyásádhya*, or those cured by medicine (*Sushruta*).

The most usual classification of disease is into the following seven classes :—

1st. Adíbala prabritta or hereditary diseases. This is explained by the mother's blood, and seminal secretions of the father being affected with certain diseases, which are conveyed to their children; these diseases are hemorrhoides, phthisis, dyspepsia, epilepsy, leprosy, and elephantiases. (Menu, p. 60. chap. 3. s. 7.)

By care and attention these hereditary taints may be retarded in their appearance, and even prevented from developing themselves. In other cases such taints produce other diseases.

2nd. Janmabalprabritta (disease of the embryo). When the mother does not take care of her food, exercise, &c., this class of disease is produced. From these causes the infant may be born blind, deaf, dumb, dwarfish in size, &c.

3rd. Doshabalprabritta (diseases of the humours) caused by intemperance. Some are produced from the stomach, some from the intestines, some affect the whole body, others only the mind.

4th. Sanghátabalprabritta, or accidental, as when caused by wounds, poison, &c.

5th. Kalabalprabritta, diseases caused by cold, heat, rain, storms, &c.

6th. Daibabalprabritta. When improper actions are performed, a class of disease of the most loathsome appearance, and incurable nature are supposed to be produced; such as by the abuse of the Deities, or Brahmans, the contempt of spiritual preceptors, and other heinous offences. Such can only be cured by a course of severe and long continued penance, by mysterious performances, and liberality to the sacred Brahmans. In the present day these causes sometimes are so aggravated that the sacrifice of the person's life is not sufficient for its purification, as is leprosy. Among the ignorant the only means of preventing this is supposed to be by sacrificing themselves in the sacred Ganges, and it not unfrequently happens that, instigated by friends, these miserable and deluded persons drown themselves in the sacred stream, as an expiation for their supposed sins.

Another division of this class of disease is produced by contact, by breathing the same air, eating together, sitting upon the same seat, wearing the same clothes, or ornaments, of a person labouring under the disease. In this manner Leprosy may be propagated.

7th. Swabhabābalaprabritta, or natural diseases, give pain to the soul; such as thirst, appetite, age, sleep, and death. This class is again divided into the timely and untimely.

When the principal humours (*dhátu*) are deranged, the disease is called by the name of the humour affected; such as *rasaja* (chyle diseases), among which are dyspepsia, pain of the body, &c.; *raktaja*, or diseases of the blood, such as leprosy, erysipelas, &c.; *mángsaja*, or diseases of the flesh, such as fleshy tumours, &c.

Causes of Disease.

Charaka, as we have seen, divides disease into three classes, mental, bodily, and accidental; which he supposed were situated in the semen, chyle, or blood. The general causes of diseases are also three, proceeding from matter or objects of sense (*ortoh*), such as vision, smell, sound, taste, and touch; the second from improper exercise, and the third from the seasons. Thus diseases are caused by improper exposure to too much, or too little light; to too severe, or too little exercise; to a season of too great heat, or too much or too little rain, cold, &c. These are the three general causes of disease. They act in this manner; when a person is too much exposed to light, as by looking at the sun, blindness will be the result. Dyspepsia will be produced by being exposed to bad odours. As an example of improper exercise, that of carrying heavy weights produces Hemoptysis; and by irregularities of the seasons. Cholera, Fever, Dysentery, &c., are produced.

There are also three sorts of medicines: one sort that cleans the body when taken internally, as emetics, purgatives, &c., another sort purifies the external body when applied externally, as oil, diaphoretics, bathing; and the third kind is the use of knives, or instruments; fire, and escharotics.

Charaka states also that there are three objects of enquiry in this world, the first and chief enquiry being the means of preserving life; the second, the means of acquiring wealth; and lastly the means of obtaining beatitude in the next world.

There are three means of preserving life, proper food, sleep, and proper government of the senses and passions. The means of acquiring wealth are such as are not at variance with virtue and religion, such as mercantile transactions, the service of government, and husbandry. We should not envy the wealth of others, but strive to follow their example. The acquisition of happiness for another world will be obtained by study, by a virtuous marriage, by performing the sacrifices pointed out in the shastres, governing the passions, avoiding envy, evil thoughts, by speaking the truth, by hospitality to strangers, by the society of the learned and the good, and by prayers to God.

The particular causes of disease are those which affect the air, bile, phlegm, and blood.

Another form of disease is produced by sin, which is to be suspected, when a disease is not cured by the means pointed out by the shastres. These diseases are called *karmaja*, and are to be cured by good actions, by prayers, by certain forms of penance, &c. "If the disease is incurable, let the patient advance in a straight path, towards the invisible north-eastern point, feeding on water and air, till his mortal frame totally decay, and his soul become united with the Supreme Being." (Menu, p. 175, ch. vi. s. 31.)

The exciting causes of the diseases of air, are fighting with strong men, too much exercise, venery, much study, especially at night, severe cold and rainy seasons, &c. The exciting causes of the diseases of bile, are anger, grief, fear, fasting, indigestible food, acid, and pungent food, &c. The exciting causes of phlegm diseases are sleeping in the day time, want of exercise, sweet and salt food, drinking too much fluids, eating too much, &c. The causes of the disease of the blood are the same as those producing bilious diseases, also sleeping during the day, exposure to heat, too much exercise, indigestible food, improper mixtures of food, &c.

Another cause of disease is when they proceed from other diseases. In this case the original disease disappears leaving the new one to follow its usual course. The original disease in other cases remains, and may produce a second disease. Thus from enlarged spleen, fever and dropsy are produced; from piles, dyspepsia, and *gulma*.

Description of diseases.

The descriptions of disease in the Hindu writers are generally distinct and satisfactory, though often at variance with some of English theoretical notions; sometimes, however, from the imperfect list of symptoms given, it is difficult to distinguish the disease intended to be described, especially as it sometimes appears that the Physicians mistook an accidental combination of a few symptoms, for a distinct disease; and in other cases, placed under varieties, distinct diseases.

The description of a disease is usually commenced with an enumeration of the supposed causes, situation, and humours deranged, as indicated by the symptoms, and the varieties produced by the humours affected.

Before considering the description of particular diseases, it will be necessary to consider the indications of the morbid changes of the humours, which enter into all the diseases. By these indications, the physician is able to know the increase or diminution of any of the humours, which will regulate the particular treatment which he is to follow.

The seven essential parts of the body (*dhátu*) produce various diseases by a preternatural increase, or diminution of their quantity:—

1st. When chyle (*rasa*) is increased, it produces want of appetite, heaviness of the body, as if too much had been eaten, weakness of digestion, large secretion of saliva and phlegm, languor and lassitude, stretching, giddiness, nausia, vomiting, and fever. When chyle is diminished the person is subject to diseases of the breast, his skin is pale, his body becomes light, weak, the eyes become diseased, &c. In such cases the chyle is thin; the person has a depraved taste, is restless, and grey hairs appear early in life.

2nd. When the blood is increased the body feels heavy; the body and the eyes have a red colour, with a burning sensation, eruptions appear over the body; and the person feels giddy, has no appetite, and his urine is red. He is subject to piles, bloody discharges, and baldness. Females in such cases are subject to menorrhagia Such a state predisposes the person to attacks of inflammation of different viscera, and, the formation of large abscesses; to leprosy, rheumatism, erysipelas (*bisarpa*), &c. When the blood is diminished preternaturally, the skin appears dry; the person feels a desire for sour things, and the vessels appear empty.

3rd. When the *flesh* is morbidly increased, the body feels heavy, the muscular parts increase in size, the abdomen enlarges, and the person is subject to coughs, asthma, &c. When diminished; the loins, cheeks, lips, penis, thighs, breast, axillas, hips, abdomen and neck, become thin, the whole body dries up, with pains; and the large vessels diminish in size.

4th. When the *fat* is increased, the surface of the body has a shining appearance, it produces languor and fatigue after slight exertion, thirst, perspiration of a disagreeable smell, bronchocele, diseases of the lips, gonorrhœa, cough and asthma, and an increase in the size of the belly, buttocks, neck, and breast.

When diminished the part becomes flabby, and the joints lax, the body dries up, and soft food is desired.

As a disease fatness is produced by smearing the body with oil, by eating frequently, by want of exercise, by sleeping during the day; by sweet, or oily urine; and by increased phlegm. Such a state produces difficulty of breathing, thirst, appetite, a desire to sleep, perspiration, and a bad smell of the body, which becomes unwieldy. The person cannot speak distinctly, nor work; there is a diminished desire for women, as the vessels are filled, and the circulation is imperfectly performed. The other essential parts which are produced from the fat are imperfectly formed, and the strength is diminished.

Such a person is liable to attacks of diabetes and gonorrhœa, eruptions, terminating in large abscesses, fistula-in-ano, &c. In such a person, disease is always more dangerous according as the accumulated fat fills the vessels.

The causes of *thinness*, are what increases the air of the body, such as much work, frequent connexion with women, study, fear, grief, sorrow, want of sleep, thirst, and not eating and drinking enough to satisfy the appetite. This state of the body is likewise produced by whatever diminishes the essential parts of the body, and dries up the chyle.

This state of the body produces appetite and thirst, and the person is easily affected with cold, heat, wind, and rain. Such a person is weak, breathes with difficulty, is subject to diseases of air, to attacks of spleen, and dyspepsia, from the diminution of internal heat. In this state of the body, every disease is aggravated, and the causes increasing this state should be avoided. Various vegetable infusions, with nourishing and sweet food, are used to increase the size of the body. In like manner milk, curdled milk, ghee, flesh, sleeping during the day, a happy disposition, and certain laxatives have the same effect.

Both great fatness and leanness should be avoided; and the middle state should be considered the most favourable state of the body.

5th. When *bone* is increased in the system, it produces additions on old bones, and the teeth become large. When it diminishes the body dries up, the patient complains of pain in the bones, and the teeth and nails become irregular.

6th. When the *marrow* is increased, the body and eyes feel heavy, the person has an increase of semen, and by drying it causes a difficulty in passing the urine, which is increased with pain and swelling of the bladder. When the marrow is diminished the semen diminishes, and there is pain in the bones, which feel empty.

7th. When the *semen* is increased, there is an increased discharge, and calculi form. Its diminution is accompanied with pain in the penis and testicles, and the person has no inclination for women.

The state of the excretions produce morbid symptoms, and diseases:—

1st. When the *fæces* are increased there is a noise in the belly with pain; and when diminished there is pain in the breast and side, and the air makes a noise in the upper part of the abdomen.

2nd. When *urine* is increased it produces pain in the bladder, there is a frequent desire to perform mictirition, and the evacuation is copious. When diminished there is pain in the bladder, and the urine is scanty. Whatever increases the dejections, removes these symptoms.

3rd. When the *perspiration* is increased, it has a bad smell, and a small eruption appears over the body, which is itchy. When it is diminished the roots of the hair become rough, the skin dries, and the touch is defective, and depraved. Rubbing the skin with oil, and substances which increase perspiration will remove these symptoms.

4th. *Menses.* When morbidly increased, this discharge has a bad smell, and is accompanied with pain, fulness of the breasts, and a copious discharge, with weakness. When diminished, the discharge is scanty, and does not take place at the usual period, and there is pain in the uterus. Those medicines which have the qualities of the sun are to be used, to remedy such deficiencies.

5th. When the *Milk* is increased in quantity, the mammæ are large, with pain, and there is a frequent discharge of milk. When preternaturally diminished, the mammæ are small, with little milk. Such medicines should be used as increase the phlegm.

Diseases of Life (*bala* and *oja*, the place or orgon of *bala*) is of an oily appearance like ghee, of a white colour, and cool, while it remains in its own organ (*oja*), and is different from the essential parts of the body, which retain and support life. Life is situated in the breast of the male, and in the abdomen of the female. This is supposed to explain their want of strength and activity, with the softness of the body, their happy disposition, their quickness and vanity, and the fairness of their bodies. Life is the last formed of the humours, and is the chief; for as long as it remains, the muscles continue to perform their offices, and the person's voice, and the colour of his body continues good, and the ten senses continue in a healthy state. When diminished, the body dries, and without it the person dies. Life may be diminished by injuries, by a diminution of the seven dhatu, by anger, grief, fatigue, low spirits, and fasting. Sometimes life is increased, and at other times it is prostrated. When life changes its usual situation it produces a relaxation of the joints; the person cannot move or work, and air, bile, and phlegm, are diminished. In these diseased states of the body it cannot move, it is heavy, swelled, and the person is languid, depressed, and sleepy. The colour of the body changes, syncopy occurs, the flesh diminishes, the person feels weak, followed by death.

In these cases of diseased life, such articles are to be used, as strengthen and retain it in health. Thus bitter, cold, dry, and constipating articles of food are to be avoided; as also frequent connexion with women, &c. In such cases the body is to be rubbed with ghee, oil, and turmeric, with bathing, &c. The food should consist of very light articles.

From the above remarks it appears that a state of health is that in which the air, bile, and phlegm is in just proportion, in which the abdominal fire is sufficient, the seven essential parts, and the dejections are natural, the semen and mind correct, and the life (soul) happy. It is this equilibrium of all these parts that constitutes health; but it is impossible to distinguish the proper proportion of each of these parts, as they vary in different individuals.

It is therefore by the effects of such derangements that we judge of their presence. When the senses are not in a perfect state, we know that the equilibrium of the parts is destroyed. They also act on each other. Thus when the air, bile, and phlegm are diminished, they derange the essential parts of the body, as heat diminishes the water in a vessel put over it.

These theoretical opinions led the Hindu Physicians, in their description of diseases, to follow the natural order, and to confound the accidental, with the pathognomonic symptoms. Hence they arranged diseases in unnatural groups, from a fancied connection between them. Thus fever was considered as a type of a group of diseases, in which dysentery, diarrhœa, indigestion, &c., were arranged, as these diseases are accompanied, in some cases, with fever.

—:o:—

SECTION II.

Diagnosis.

The nail* of *Vishnu*, like a sun, enlightened *Rishis*, who prepared the shastres. By a knowledge of these, the nature of disease is distinguished by examination, assisted by analogy, thought, and a knowledge of the shastres. By these means the Physician first finds out the nature of the disease his patient is labouring under, the medicines ordered by the shastres, and the regimen to be followed.

The nature of the disease is to be ascertained :—

1st. By the appearance, as the countenance, tongue, &c.

2nd. By the feeling, as the pulse, temperature of the body, &c.

3rd. By questions, embracing the country, temperament, and history of the disease.

Other authors state that the disease is known by means of the five senses, and asking questions. Thus:

1st. By *hearing* he will distinguish the state of the lungs, by the peculiar noise of the breathing.

2nd. By the *touch* he will mark the state of the body, as to cold and heat; and the state of the skin as to the hardness and softness, roughness and smoothness.

3rd. By the *sight*, the physician will know the largeness and smallness of the body, with its colour, &c.

* That is, so great is Vishnu, that the most insignificant part of him sheds lustre upon the most learned of mankind.

4th. By *taste*, as in distinguishing diabetic urine, &c.

5th. By the *smell*, as of the different discharges from the body.

Lastly. By questions, the physician will find out the country, and temperament of the sick person, his sex, manner of life, and the history of the disease. The pain felt by the patient, the degree of his strength, and appetite, and the state of his evacuations.

These observations are all most necessary in order to arrive at a true diagnosis; and without knowing the disease, the physician will be unable to employ the proper means for its cure.

——:o:——

SECTION III.

Prognostics.

As a flower prognosticates the future fruit, smoke the severity of fire, and the clouds the near approach, and the severity of the coming shower, so certain symptoms prognosticate the favourable, or fatal result of a disease. These signs, however, are often but slightly apparent to the general eye, and can only be detected by the eye of an experienced physician. In other cases the death of the patient having fatal symptoms may be everted by the intercessions of holy Brahmans, or by the use of medicines which produce longivity. An accomplished physician should study prognostics, and make allowance for the cure of certain cases. He may otherwise boast that he will cure complicated, or incurable cases; by which he will lose his credit.

The prognostics of disease are either favourable, or fatal. These depend on various circumstances in each particular case; which are obtained from the messenger sent, and collateral circumstances, and lastly from the symptoms of each disease. A few remarks on each of these will next be given.

1st. The appearance of the messenger, his dress, and his manner of speaking will influence the prognosis. In like manner his actions, the time of the day he reaches the physician, and other circumstances should influence the physician's prognosis. On calling the physicians, the following signs, or omens, are considered unfavourable. When there are many men or women collected, or following each other, to call the physician. When the messenger sees a man arrive riding on an ass, camel, or in a carriage; or if he has a stick, or string, or a sharp instrument, ripe fruit, &c., in his hand. When he is dressed in red, or black, or in wet clothes. When the messenger is very sorry, and expresses his fear. When the messenger is defective in a member, is deformed, or has a disgusting appearance. When the person sent speaks in unfavourable language of the sick person, when he is anointed with oil, &c. When the person, who calls the physician, has a shoe or skin in his hand, or is scratching his feet or other parts of his body with his nails, or is crying: All these occurrences are unfavourably, as to the event of the disease.

It is also considered bad when the physician is called at noonday, at midnight, early in the morning and evening, when he has his face turned to the south, or when he is eating or naked; anointing himself, is asleep, or is in an unclean place. Also when doing any thing with fire, is fatigued, is performing the funeral services of his relations, &c.

The kind of disease varies its prognostic; when the patient is affected with a bilious disease, or when he has arrived in a very hot state, and finds the physician near the fire, it is unfavourable. It will be favourable when the person is affected with phlegm, or cold diseases. When the messenger is dressed in white clothes, is a handsome and fair person, is of the same caste as the patient, comes in a carriage with a cow, and is not impatient, are favourable signs.

When the messenger finds the physician sitting in a clean place, with his face towards the east, and the messenger has in his hands a water-pot full of water with an umbrella, they are favourable signs.

Should the physician on passing to the patient see a woman with her son, or a cow with her calf; or a virgin well dressed and adorned with jewels, or sees fish, or unripe fruit, butter-milk or flowers; or meets a Rájá, sees a strong fire, or a horse running, or a goose walking, or sees and hears peacocks, these prognosticate a favourable result to the patient's disease.

If the physician sitting by the side of his patient, the patient rubs one hand against another, scratches his back, answers questions with his face upwards, draws the bed-clothes, or shakes his hand, or constantly moves his head or puts the physician's hand to his breast or head. These are unfavourable signs.

The prognostics will depend upon the complication and kind of disease which affects the patient, and the peculiar violence of particular symptoms.

The severity and nature of the disease will depend on the nature of the essential parts of the body affected. While the skin, flesh, and blood are affected, the phlegm and air are the humours diseased. When the three humours are not affected, and marrow alone vitiated, the disease admits of relief, if not of cure. When the fat, marrow, or bone is affected, and two or three of the humours are vitiated, one of them being the bile, the disease is incurable. This forms the complicated form of disease, which is always more difficult to cure than when a single humour, or the presence of a single disease exists. The eight most severe forms of disease are, nervous disease, as tetanus, paralysis, &c., gonorrhœa (*prameha*), leprosy (*kushtha*), piles (*arshah*), fistula-in-ano (*bhagandara*), stone (*ashmarí*), unnatural presentations of the fœtus, and dropsical swellings of the abdomen (*udara*). These eight are the most severe diseases, and are cured with great difficulty.

In general the prognosis is to be favourable when the patient's voice remains unaltered, when he awakes from sleep without agitation, when eating rather cools than heats the body, and when the sick person does not forget his God, but prostrates himself daily in prayer with humility and resignation. The unfavourable symptoms are the opposite of the above, with indigestion, irregular and obstructed excretions, head-ache, redness of the eyes, loss of voice, generation of worms in wounds and ulcers: from which bloody, and fœtid discharges proceed.

If in any disease the patient is very thin and weak, with difficulty of breathing, thirst, dryness of the body, vomiting and fever, these are bad symptoms. If fainting, diarrhœa, hiccough, occur in the course of the disease they will not be cured. If swelling of the body occurs in the course of nervous disease without feeling in the skin, with shaking, swelling of the abdomen, with wind accompanied with pain, or other such symptoms, the disease will destroy the person.

If the white part of the body suddenly becomes black, without any previous cause, and the blood changes its colour. When the other internal parts do not remain in the usual condition, whether that be rest or motion; if any large organ diminishes in size, or becomes large; what is long becomes short, or short long; if bodies that should be discharged remain, and if those that should remain are discharged; or if the members naturally hot become cold, shining become dull, moist become dry, they are dangerous signs. When members cannot move, or have an unnatural smell, or cannot perform their office, or are removed from their natural position, if they open, or are discharged outwardly, or inwardly, are heavy, or light, the person will soon die.

If in the morning perspiration occurs on the forehead; or tears always fall without any disease of the eyes; if the dandriff in the hair is of the colour of the powder of the cow's litter: if a pigeon, &c. perches on the head of the person; if, without eating, there is a great discharge of dejections; or when there are no dejections, and the person eats freely it is deadly. If the chest or mamillæ swell; if the trunk swells, and extremities become thin, or the contrary; or half of the body swells; or half become paralized; if the person cannot speak, or it is diminished, or changed, these are signs of danger. The same is the case if the nails, teeth, mouth, or body, has the smell of putrid flowers; if the sputa, dejections, or semen sink in water; if the person sees objects multiplied, or imperfectly; if the body and hair have a shining appearance, as if covered with oil; if the person is very weak, without appetite, or with Dysentery with cough, with much appetite and thirst, or if weak with vomiting, especially if the sputa be mixed with blood, and the patient has no appetite. Should the feet, hands, and lips be swelled, with weakness, and want of appetite, while the buttocks, hands, feet and shoulders are diminished in size, and the person is weak with fever and cough; if they vomit their breakfast in the evening are dejected; have gnawing pain, fever and cough, if the person falls, producing a sound like that of a goat, has no strength or feeling in the testicles; and if the head falls on the shoulder, the danger is great. If the chest dries first after bathing, and the person is always biting his under lip or the tongue; is pulling his ears or hair, or considers the gods, brahmins, and his master, friend, and Physician as his enemies, they are fatal signs. If the aspect of the planets are unfavourable; if the stars fall, thunder occurs on the day of the ascent of the star under which the person was born, it is unfavourable.

If the physician has examined properly the person, and finds the disease increasing, and the person feeble, he will not recover. In the course of gonorrhœa (*Prameha*), if any considerable morbid discharge from the *urethra* takes place with fever, and a great flow of urine, it will be fatal.

The dangerous symptoms of leprosy (*kushtha*) are, when the body is covered with sores, from which pus, blood, &c., are discharged; the members drop off, and the eyes are of a red colour, with hoarseness of the voice. When such patients are not able to bear the five forms of treatment, as purgatives, emetics, diaphoretics, injections, and blood-letting, the disease will be fatal.

If in the course of piles (*arsha*) the patient has dyspepsia, pain of the abdomen, with much hemorrhage, dysentery, and swelling of the extremities, the disease will be fatal.

If in the course of fistula-in-ano (*bhagandara*) air, urine, dejections, worms or semen are discharged from the fistula, the patient will die of the disease.

The fatal symptoms of stone in the bladder (*osmarica*) are swelling of the umbiliacus, and of the scrotum, with great pain in passing the urine, which is mixed with gravel.

The fatal signs of complex labour (*múragarbha*) are tumours, or polipi in the vagina, which prevents the passage of the child; unnatural contraction of the vagina, &c.

The fatal symptoms of a dropsical swelling of the abdomen (*udora*) are as follows:—having no feeling in the sides, loss of appetite, and the body swelling, with dysentery. If after purgatives the abdomen again swells, the person should be considered as incurable.

If a person with *Fever* does not see, is insensible, sleeps without any movement, is internally hot, with an external feeling of cold, he will die. When the hairs become prominent upon the body, the eyes red, the breast very painful, and the breathing by the mouth, such a fever will be fatal. If there be hiccough, much thirst, insensibility, eyes fixed, or move involuntary, difficult and noisy breathing, with weakness, the fever will be fatal. If the eyes become muddy, and the person cannot see; sleeps much, with great weakness, and loss of strength and flesh, the fever will be fatal.

When there is with dysentery, difficulty of breathing, great pain, thirst, weakness and fever, the person will die, particularly when old.

Phthisis (*yakhmá*), with cough and bloody expectoration, the eyes white, no appetite, and difficulty of drawing in the breath, diarrhœa, and a copious flow of urine with pain, will be fatal.

When *gulma*, or colicky pains, from a collection of wind in the abdomen, which feels like a moving ball, and is accompanied with difficulty in breathing, thirst, no appetite, and weakness, the disease will be fatal.

Internal abscesses of the abdomen (*bidradhi*) if accompanied with swelling, without any discharge, and if the person vomits, has hiccough, thirst, pain, and difficulty in breathing, he will die.

Jaundice (*pandu*). If the teeth, nails, and eyes are yellow, and every thing seems so, in such case the disease will be fatal.

In hemorrhagea (*raktapitta*). When the person vomits blood, has his eyes red, and every thing appears so, the disease will be fatal.

Madness (*unmáda*). If such a patient always either stoops or keeps his head raised, is thin, weak, gets no sleep, has no fear, he will die.

Epilepsy (*apasmara, mrigi*). If the fits occur frequently with weakness, the eyelids always move about, and the eyes become unnatural, the disease will be fatal.

The signs of death are as follows:—

Sight. When the person imagines he sees red, black, or yellow colours before his eyes, when he has lost all shame, strength, memory, and his natural appearance. It is also a fatal sign when the eyes become small, sunk, and unequal; and when they are of a red colour, and cannot move; under such circumstances a flow of tears is also a fatal sign.

Mouth. When there is a falling of the under, and rising of the upper lip; when they are crooked, and are of a dark blue colour, the person will die. When the teeth become reddish or dark coloured, or fall out, or are of a grayish colour, the person will soon die.

Tongue. When the tongue is of a black colour, and extraneous matter appears upon it, or it cannot be moved, or is dirty and swollen, or its papulæ are very prominent, with fetor of the breath, the patient will soon die.

Nose. When it becomes pale, dry, and shining, and is turned to one side; the nostrils extended, dry, and dirty, and the passage of the air produces a noise; or when the point of the nose retracts, and is flattened, with weakness and depression, the person will soon die.

When therefore the eyes, by which we see; the ears, by which we hear; the tongue, by which we taste; and the skin, by which the sense of heat, and cold is performed are defective, or differ from the state of health, the patient should be considered in a dangerous state.

Hair. If it falls naturally in a line on each side (as in women), and the eyebrows become contracted and repressed, and the patient pulls his eyelashes, the person will soon die. If such a person have no disease, he will die within six, and if diseased within three days.

If the person cannot swallow, if he cannot move his head, and remains at rest, and is insensible, he will soon die. Whether strong or weak, should he faint on being raised up, the person will die.

If a person diseased sleeps with his face turned upwards, and he is cotinually stretching, and bending his legs, he will soon die.

When the feet and hands are cold, and the person breathes quickly and irregularly, or retains his mouth open, like a crow in hot weather; such a person is not to be treated by the physician, as he will die. If a person always sleeps, or he is always watching and cannot speak, the physician is not to give medicine.

When the tongue is always moving along the upper lip, with continual hiccough; or if a person speaks incoherently to another person previously dead, he will not live. If blood flows from the pores of the hair, and the natural openings of the body, without poison, the person will soon die. When the hysterical ball (*astila*) from air, occurs in the breast, and prevents the swallowing of food, and the pain extends, and there is no appetite, the person will die. If an unusual swelling in the feet occur in the course of a disease in a man, or in the face of a female, it will destroy the person.

If in consumption, dysentery, asthma, fever, hiccough, vomiting, and swelling of the external urinary organs occur, the person will die. If such a sick person has much burning over the body, or much perspiration, hiccough, difficulty in breathing, even a strong person will die. If with the yellow or black tongue, the left eye be sunk, with bad breath, the person will die. If the mouth be filled with tears, the hands and feet perspire, and the eyes lose their shining appearance, and become dull, it is a sign of death. If the person swells or becomes thin very quickly, he will die. If the smell of the body resembles clay, fish, fat, oil, or other unnatural scents; or when lice leave the hair, and come to the forehead, or animals will not eat the food the patient has left; or when the patient is very restless he will die. When fever, dysentery and swelling of feet, or hands, occur alternately, it is unfavourable; should the person lose his strength suddenly, he will not live. When the patient has no appetite, has frequent stools, with severe pain in the head, and thirst, the person will die, when combined with other bad symptoms.

It is also a bad sign when the patient is very weak, with thirst and hunger, which is not appeased by the usual quantity of food or drink; and should a practitioner cure any patients with the above indications, he deserves to be Physician to a king.

—:o:—

SECTION IV.

General Treatment of Diseases.

As the generality of diseases are supposed to be produced by derangements in the humors. One or more of which are morbidly increased or changed in quantity, the indications of treatment are to promote the just balance of the elements and humors, by a judicious choice of aliment, and by such means as assist the vital principle in the completion of the assimilation. The management of diet was supposed to be the great means of accomplishing this end; and was regulated in point of quality, quantity, and time of administering it, by the nature of the disease. Should the judicious selection of food not succeed in curing the disease, or when severe, the person was directed to observe an entire abstinence of food, for a certain time, and if this failed, the corrupted humors were ejected from the body. This was accomplished either by emetics, purgatives, or blood-letting. In like manner, when the disease was subdued, it was supposed to be necessary to expel all the vitiated humors; which, if allowed to remain, accumulate, and a relapse of the disease will be the consequence. To prevent this, strong drastic purgatives, which produced from five to eight evacuations, were repeated daily, until the physician was satisfied that the whole corrupted humors were expelled. To prevent such a recurrence of disease, the same evacuating means were employed. But these humors are not to be dislodged indiscriminately, but at certain seasons, and diurnal periods of the disease. Health was thus supposed to be promoted by the exhibition of an emetic once a fortnight, a drastic purgative once a month, and blood-letting twice a year, at the change of the seasons. The vital principle was supposed to give warning when the corrupted humors were ripe for being evacuated; and the physician was directed to observe carefully, so as to be able to assist, and not disturb the spontaneous efforts of nature. The seasons in which she exhibited these beneficial influences, were supposed to be determined by the known cause of the disease, which led to the belief of the definite course, and the mystical powers of numbers; by which nature may be invariably observed to arrive at certain determinate results, which were supposed to be regulated by an arithmetical progression. This led to the belief of the maturation of the diseased humors, and of the existence of a period, in which the perfect state of mixture takes place. These were called critical days, which have long held a place in the pathological belief of physicians. These days were recognised by the Egyptian priests, as related by Pythagoras and others, and denoted the time at which the due admixture of the elements had taken place. The same term was employed by Hippocratus and adopted in Europe, when the humoral phathology was the fashion. So plausible were the opinions of the humoral pathology, that they seem to have been at one time believed, and the most pernicious preventive means followed, over a great part of the globe; and among nations so separated from each other, as to preclude the possibility of their having derived them from each other. Among the Hindus the humoral pathology appears to have originated without any assistance from other nations, and became as generally believed, and carried to the same consequences as it was in Europe.

Another equally plausible opinion was, that all diseases divide themselves into two great classes, of sthenic or asthenic disease. The one being an increase, and the other a diminution of excitement; between the extremities of which health was supposed to be placed This appears to have been an early opinion among the Hindus, is now generally believed over all the Asiatic nations; and has led them to the division of remedies into stimulating, and cooling, which were employed according to the nature of the disease. For the hot or sthenic diseases cooling remedies were used; while hot medicines were exhibited to remove cold, or asthenic diseases. To the class of stimulants belonged pepper, bitters, purgatives, &c.; and to the cooling remedies cold, pawn mixed with lime, bathing, with several excellent stomachics; as *chiraitá*, &c.

—:o:—

CHAPTER II.

Description and Treatment of Particular Diseases.

—:o:—

CLASS I.

Diseases of the Humors.

The apparent actions and changes of the fluids, or humors of the human body, attracted the attention of the Bráhmans at an early period, and upon these changes they founded their theoretical speculations regarding the nature, and production of disease. These opinions seemed to be confirmed by the occurrences of hemorrhage from wounds, the appearance of certain eruptions, and the discharge from abscesses and ulcers; while the solids in these cases seemed passive, with no indications of change beyond what the fluids seemed to produce upon them. Hence the general principles of Pathology were based, by the Brahmans, on alterations of the fluids only, and they supposed that while their elements and qualities remained in due proportion health was sustained; while disease was produced by an undue proportion of these humors.

The diseases of air, bile and phlegm may proceed from the semen of the father, from the menstrual blood of the mother, from the state of the mother's body during utero-gestation, from certain food acting in the same way, from the habits of exercise, from the state of the parts in which the fetus is retained in the abdomen, and from the state of the menses at the time of conception. These causes derange the humors and produce the individual's habit of body, and the kind of disease to which they are subject.

The derangement of these humors are the root of all diseases, and require to be carefully examined by the physician.

All diseases are considered as being produced: 1st, by the derangements of the humors of the part, and 2ndly, by the peculiar diseases of the part.

The different seasons predispose to different diseases: the air of the body is liable to be deranged in the two rainy and two hot months; in the two months before the cold weather bile is liable to be deranged; and during the cold months, the bile remains in health, while the diseases of phlegm are common, and increase in spring.

The diseases of the humours may be arranged according as they affect the air, bile, and phlegm, and their combinations. There are eighty diseases produced by derangements of the air (*báyu*); forty of bile (*pitta*); twenty of phlegm (*kapha*); and sixteen by the combination of the derangements of these humors.

In the embryo state, the humors are in such a state that they do not interfere with the action of each other, as the serpents poison does not injure the animal itself. But in the course of life various causes interrupt this harmony; and various changes regulate and determine, at all times and seasons, the health, and morbid condition of the human body.

Air (*báyu*). The causes which derange air are fighting, abstinence in eating and drinking; the use of dry food, falls, watching when the body is wounded, great discharges, as of blood, semen, &c. The same effects are produced by constipation of air, urine, and dejections; or when they are not evacuated at the proper time. Bathing, great grief, fear, and exposure to cold, produce this class of diseases. The air is also increased when the food is digested, and in the evening.

The indications of derangement of the air, are a swelling of the abdomen, with stiffness of the body; the surface of which is dry, rough, and cracked. The person feels pain in different parts of the body, more especially of the arms, testicles, fat, &c.; is low-spirited, languid, and fatigued, has shivering fits and spasms; the hair drops off, and the person's head is always bowing backwards and forwards, with other irregular movements of the body. The voice becomes altered, and the person speaks much, and dreams in his sleep. When awake he speaks often without thought, he feels a singing in has ears, loses the power of vision, has no memory, with paralysis of one or more of the members. There is a dryness of the mouth with thirst; the body becomes of a red or green colour, and he complains of an astringent taste in the mouth.

Sometimes the person has severe cutting pains in the stomach (*sul*) and over the body. Parts of the body feel hard, with noise in the ears, dimness of sight, obtuseness of the senses, thirst, dozing, irregular movements of the body, watching, and uncomfortable dreams, with a feeling of doing impossibilities, yawning, and roughness of the skin.

Diseases of Air will vary according to its situation and use. The vital air for the mouth (*práná*), which assists in swallowing, produces when disordered, hiccough, vomiting, &c. The air we breathe (*udáná*) produces asthma, consumption, &c. when diseased. The (*sámáná*) or vital air in the stomach produces vomiting, anxiety, fainting, thirst, and pain in the chest and side. In the *intestines* it produces noise along their course, pain in the navel, with costiveness, scanty urine, and flatulence, &c.; in the *ear* it produces deafness; in the *integuments*, a discoloration, roughness, and sometimes there is a diminished sensation, and eruption over the skin. When deranged in the *blood*, it produces different painful eruptions, and tumors. When deranged with *fat* it produces tumors, without pain. In *vessels*, it produces a contraction of their size, with pain and fullness. In *tendons*, it produces paralysis, with shaking pain and spasm. In *joints*, it produces stiffness, pain, swelling, and emaciation; in the *bones* it produces pain and emaciation; in the *marrow* it causes acute pain; in the *semen* it produces a morbid discharge, or a diminution of the secretion; and when deranged over the body it produces a bluntness of sense, paralysis, spasm, swelling, and pain in many parts of the body. Besides these it produces various other classes of symptoms, according to the parts of the body which are principally affected.

The principal diseases produced by deranged air are fainting, *batarakta*, *pitta rakta*, and *kapha rakta*, and leprosy. This last disease commences in the limbs, with dark blotches, and insensibility of the part. It produces rigidity of parts (*apotanoka*) by which the body is drawn to a side, or backwards and forwards; and there is another form of the disease called *dhumus stamb* (Tetanus, Trismus.) It affects particularly the lower jaw, and face, by drawing the neighbouring parts to one side or another. *Choria* (kalaia khunj) is according to the *Nidana* and *Sushruta* produced by derangements of air. This disease is characterized by the person first feeling a trembling or shivering over the body, with dimness of sight, and pain in the neck, jaw, and teeth, or any other part about to be affected. These symptoms are followed by convulsive twitchings of the head, neck, and face; and of one side of the body, particularly of one leg. These parts are pulled to the side affected, and shake involuntary. These movements extend to all the voluntary muscles of progression, producing a dancing motion. The muscles of the upper or lower extremities may thus be affected, of one or both sides, and when it has extended over the body and continued long, it is considered incurable. It is supposed to be produced by irregularity of the bowels, from having eaten indigestible food, which produces costiveness and indigestion. Much talking and laughing, carrying heavy loads, and other causes deranging air, are supposed to produce this disease.

When the *air* is superabundant it will be diminished by cold, and articles of food having this property; by strengthening food, which, on being digested remains long in the vessels, such as ghee, the flesh of goats, &c., mascalai, salt, or sweet or sour food, shampooing, anointing the body with oil, or taking it internally, by drinking sherbuts, by bathing, by medicines which increase the secretion of semen, alvine secretions, urine, and perspiration; which remove thirst and appetite, and render the body more active.

When air is diminished the person cannot work, he speaks little, is unhappy, and his judgment is impaired.

The best means of curing these derangements of *air* is by exhibiting oleaginous, salt, sweet, and acid food, by bathing, by the use of wine, by shampooing, by exhibiting enemas, &c.

Bile (*pitta*) is increased by sour, hot, salt, or bitter articles of food, by eating the shoots of young bamboos, and other such indigestible articles of food. When the appetite is not satisfied with the quantity eaten, or by eating before the food previously eaten has not been digested; when old curries are used; curdled milk, wine, or conjee are drunk; when exposed to anger, to hot weather, especially during the months of September and October, and the middle of the day, or middle watch of the night the bile is increased.

When bile is in unusual quantity it produces a disagreeable breath, hot and sour eructations, with boils over the body. The person is subject to fits of anger, his bowels are open, the skin distended, and he staggers as if drunk; his body is hot, the perspiration copious, and although he eats he has no appetite, is thirsty, and has no memory, but is otherwise intelligent. He does not see distinctly, has a dislike to particular kinds of food, which become sour, bitter, and sweet, in the stomach. The colour of the body is unnatural, being pale, with pain over the body.

Bile is diminished by eating sweet, and bitter articles of food; by remaining in cool shaded places, by night air, and moon light; by sitting upon the ground, in water, or exposed to mists. It is also diminished by the use of ghee, and milk; by those medicines which increase the discharge from the mouth, nose and eyes; by blood-letting, and whatever diminishes thirst and appetite. When so diminished the internal heat is weakened, and the body has an unhealthy appearance. The twitchings produced by increased bile in a part are best removed by rubbing it with milk, and exhibiting cooling articles of food.

When air is deranged with bile it produces inflammation and fainting; with phlegm coldness and swelling of the affected part; with blood it produces a degree of pain like the penetration of a needle, sometimes deprivation of healthy sensation, and other symptoms of deranged bile. When the *prăn-báyu* is deranged with bile, it produces vomiting, a burning heat of the body; with cough, weakness, idleness, drowsiness, and discoloration of the skin. When the *udána báyu* is deranged with bile, fainting, a burning heat of the body, want of memory, cough, want of perspiration, anxiety, indigestion, and shivering are produced. Deranged *apána báyu* with bile produces perspiration, heat, and inflammation; with cough, mucous stools, urine of a pale colour, with shivering. *Samána-báyu* deranged with bile produces inflammation and heat of the body, and in the female a retention of the menses, cough, and heaviness of the lower part of the abdomen. *Biána-báyu* deranged with bile produces a burning heat and restlessness of the body, with cough, heaviness of the body, and pain, so that the person cannot move as he wishes.

Phlegm (*kapha*), is deranged by indigestible articles of food, and sweet, or very cool things; such as milk, sugar-cane, liquid food, curdled milk, sleeping during the day; or by the cakes made of rice, coconuts, ghee, &c. These derangements are more liable to occur in the dewy, cold, and spring months, during the first third of the day, and after eating.

The derangements of phlegm produce a fulness of the abdomen, and the food the person eats is not properly digested; he has no appetite, and his body is pale, heavy, cold, and hard. He has frequent dejections; his skin is smooth, oily, and itchy. There is a discharge of mucus from the nose, eyes, and mouth. Such a person is very languid, is always dozing, and sleeps much; the part where the phlegm is deranged swells, and his mouth has a pungent and sweet taste.

The cure of these derangements is accompanied by the use of dry food, alkalies (salts), astringents, exercise, and the use of bitter, and pungent articles of food; by the exhibition of emetics, by connexion with women, long pedestrian journies, gymnastic exercises, watching at night, smoking, and the use of cathartics, and diaphoretics.

Should two or three of these humors be deranged at the same time, the particular symptoms of each will be present; and the degree of derangement of the one compared with that of the other will be observed, by the prominence of the particular class of symptoms. Their treatment must likewise be varied according to the violence of the symptoms present.

When the body is weak the most peculiar symptoms of the deranged humor do not appear, and the person seems in health.

The diseases of air, bile and phlegm, are also produced by sin, which leads the person to perform wicked actions from ignorance. Such diseases of the humors produce not only diseases of the body, but also those of the mind, and heart; as melancholy, pride, foolishness, &c. These were the diseases in which internal evacuant medicines were used, after which the treatment was to be regulated by the part affected: thus when the skin was affected, external applications were used, as ointments, plasters, &c. While the diseases of the body are cured by medicines, which diminish the humors that are too abundant; those of the mind are cured by perusing the Shasters, by abstinence, by leading a religious life, and by various mortifications of the body.

The blood is supposed to be more generally affected with the deranged humors, than with any other of the essential parts of the body. When so diseased its local, or general abstraction is recommended, and numerous medicines are administered, to purify it.

It is consequently the duty of the practitioner to find out the nature of the disease; to decide on the best remedies; to diminish the air, bile, or phlegm, the seven essential parts of the body, and the dejections (*mala*) which may be preternaturally increased, and if any of them are diminished he should endeavour to increase them so as to restore, and retain the parts, in that state of equanimity, which constitutes health. These effects may be produced by the frequent exhibition of purgatives, emetics, and food which has these peculiar effects.

When a disease is produced by the sins committed in a former state of existence; by the derangements of air, bile, and phlegm at birth, or by any cause producing very dangerous diseases, especially in very old people; it will be cured by medicines and penances. Diseases of the poor will generally be incurable, as they are not able to pay for their medicines.

